Chairman Mao and the Chinese Communist Party

Chairman Mao and the Chinese Communist Party

Andres D. Onate

Nelson-Hall **nh** Chicago

Library of Congress Cataloging in Publication Data

Onate, Andres D   1940-
  Chairman Mao and the Chinese Communist Party.
  Bibliography: p.
  Includes index.
  1. Chung-kuo kung ch'an tang—History. 2. Communism
—China—History. 3. Mao, Tsê-tung, 1893-1976.
I. Title.
JQ1519.A5052   329.9'51   78-11049
ISBN 0-88229-250-1 (cloth)
ISBN 0-88229-646-9 (paper)

Manufactured in the United States of America

10   9   8   7   6   5   4   3   2   1

22929

Contents

Part One:
The Past Is Prologue

Introduction

Young China, Old China

China is a young country with an old memory. For those conditioned to think of a China whose history dates back nearly 3,000 years, the idea of a China as a young country may well seem like professorial double-think. But, China as a *nation-state,* as Chapters 4 and 5 point out, dates only from the late 1890s and early 1920s when such individuals as K'ang Yu-wei, Liang Ch'i-ch'ao, Sun Yat-sen, Sung Chiao-jen, Ch'en Tu-hsiu, Li Ta-chao, Chiang K'ai-shek, Mao Tse-tung, Chang Kuo-t'ao, Chou En-lai, Tung Pi-wu, and Chu Teh—all key figures in the pages herein—agonized over the loss of China's dignity and national self-respect in the midnineteenth century. In 1936, Mao told Edgar Snow:

> I [remember reading] a pamphlet [at the age of thirteen] telling of the dismemberment of China [in 1898]. I remember even now that this pamphlet opened with the sentence: "Alas, China will be subjugated!" It told of Japan's occupation of Korea and Formosa, of the loss of suzerainty in Indo-China, Burma, and elsewhere. After I read this I felt depressed about the future of my country and began to realize that it was the duty of all the people to help save it.[1]

During the "dismemberment of China" in the midnineteenth century by the West (a geographical term which ironically includes Japan), there began the painfully slow process of shedding China's tarnished image of a "sheet of loose sand," as Sun Yat-sen characterized it, and remaking it into something more than a "mere geographical expression," as Professor John K. Fairbank puts it.[2] The one thing that the reformers of the 1890s (K'ang Yu-wei and Liang Ch'i-ch'ao) had in common with the revolutionaries of the early 1900s (Sun Yat-sen, Mao, Chiang K'ai-shek) was that they all could agree why China had lost its national self-respect, but they could not agree on how to accomplish the long hard climb back to national respectability.

The reformers and revolutionaries did not have far to look for inspiration: a great source of pride and patriotism was at hand in the majestic cultural achievements of the "Middle Kingdom," China by its only name. Even Mao was inspired by China's past:

> What I enjoyed [reading as a young man] were the romances of Old China, and especially stories of rebellions such as *Water Margin, Romance of the Three Kingdoms* and *Monkey,* among others. . . . I was fascinated by accounts of the rulers of ancient China: Yao, Shun, Ch'in Shih Huang-ti, and Han Wu-ti, and read many books about them.[3]

The revolutionaries' sources of national pride, however, ran headlong into such demonstrably superior sources of Western pride as scientific technology, gunboats, industrialization, and urbanization, and such provocative ideas as democracy and the emancipation of the individual. It would not be understating the case to say that in the clash of cultures that ensued in the twentieth century, traditional Chinese beliefs and institutions were no match for Western beliefs and institutions. Among the first casualties of the Chinese revolution was China's greatest source of pride, Confucius.

About all that Americans know about Confucius is what they read in fortune cookies or hear in bad jokes. Mao, however, found nothing humorous about Confucius, whose ghost had come back to haunt him in the past few years. To hear the Chinese talk one would think that China is one big haunted house. The Mass Criticism Group of Peking and Tsinghua Universities might well have said it for Mao: "Confucius was a stubborn, fierce but very weak man; he was sinister, cunning and rotten to the core."[4]

In early 1974, Mao decided that despite the outward destruction of the Confucian state and ideology by the early Chinese revolution, too much of Confucius had inwardly survived, especially among such party leaders as Lin Piao, the only one ever specifically named as Mao's successor in 1969:

Lin Piao's preaching Confucius' benevolence, righteousness, and virtue was an important content of his counter-revolutionary revisionist line of "restraining oneself and returning to the rites." A penetrating criticism of Lin Piao's fallacies in this respect, showing how he applied Confucius' reactionary and decadent ideas to serve his intrigues to usurp Party leadership and seize state power, can help us deepen our understanding of the ultra-Rightist nature of Lin Piao's revisionist line.[5]

Lin Piao was also accused of plotting to assassinate Chairman Mao shortly after Lin had been named Mao's successor by the Ninth Party Congress of 1969. When the plot "to usurp party leadership and seize state power" was discovered Lin apparently attempted to escape to the Soviet Union but his airplane, full of other conspiring generals, was brought down by Chinese missiles somewhere in Outer Mongolia.

Besides contaminating party leaders, Confucius has also been accused of various crimes against the revolution including his support for the slave system of feudal China, his emphasis on "benevolence, righteousness, and virtue," his doctrine of social harmony, and his relegating women to second-class citizenship.

This, to be sure, is not the Confucius of the fortune cookies. Confucius was the humanist's humanist:

Chi-lu (one of Confucius' disciples) asked about serving the spiritual beings. Confucius said, "If we are not yet able to serve man, how can we serve spiritual beings?" I venture to ask about death. Confucius said, "If we do not yet know about life, how can we know about death."[6]

As a humanist educator and petty government official living during one of the most violent periods in Chinese history in which no less than fifteen major feudal states were engaged in a civil war, Confucius as well as scores of other philosophers, most unemployed, dedicated themselves to answering the question: "How does one bring peace to the times?" The conservative Taoists suggested that the government that governed least governed best while the ultrarightists, the Legalists, suggested a government based on law, rewards and punishments, and fear. Confucius, the middle-

of-the-roader, suggested a government based on the confidence of
the people.

> Tzu-kung asked about government. Confucius said, "Suffi-
> cient food, sufficient armament, and sufficient confidence of
> the people." Tzu-kung said, "Forced to give up one of these,
> which would you abandon first?" Confucius said, "I would
> abandon the armament." Tzu-kung said, "Forced to give up
> one of the remaining two, which would you abandon first?"
> Confucius said, "I would abandon food. There have been
> deaths from time immemorial, but no state can exist without
> the confidence of the people."[7]

The key figure in his government was the monarch (ruler,
prince, king), whom Confucius shrouded in a carefully constructed
myth of virtue.

> Confucius said: "When a prince's personal conduct is cor-
> rect, his government is effective without issuing of orders. If
> his personal conduct is not correct, he may issue orders, but
> they will not be followed."[8]

A highly centralized bureaucracy oversaw the administration
of the myth by its control of the educational apparatus and the
civil service examination, the theoretical, but sometimes real, traditional avenues of power and status in imperial China. Virtue,
then, was a magical force which could be acquired through a moral
education. In this, Confucius believed in the educability, and therefore perfectability, of man, and in this notion, he introduced a radical, if not revolutionary idea for his times: education was not
class bound. Confucius said: "In education there should be no
class distinction."[9]

The educated, in turn, were quickly coopted by the government, so very early in Chinese history, education and government
service, one of the highest forms of public service, were inextric-
ably linked. This system of recruiting bureaucrats and other petty
officials was to last until 1905, which was just about as long as the
Middle Kingdom itself lasted.

The masses, on the other hand, survived the Middle Kingdom, but between Confucius and Mencius, a great Confucian

scholar and philosopher on his own right, the masses did not stand a chance of having anything to say about how the country should be run nor where it should be headed. Mencius (371–289 B.C.) saw to it that the peasant's labor and taxes supported the elite.

> Some labor with their minds and some labor with their strength. Those who labor with their minds govern others; those who labor with their strength are governed by others. Those who are governed by others support them; those who govern them are supported by them. This is a universal principle.[10]

The "universal principle" insured that China's elite would ride to fame and fortune on the peasant's back. The emperor, the court, the bureaucracy, the gentry, and the scholar accounted for 10 to 15 percent of China's population, but controlled over 75 percent of its wealth. This small elite group also accounted for China's great cultural self-consciousness, and because of them, the political power of imperial China was carefully clothed in a myth of virtue and morality, and not in the barrel of the gun.

Virtue, it seems, was its own reward.

Mao, as may be expected, had something to say about China's great cultural achievements. While investigating the peasants' movement in his native Hunan in 1927, Mao wrote:

> In China culture has always been the exclusive possession of the landlords, and the peasants had no access to it. But the culture of the landlords is created by the peasants, for its source is nothing else than the peasant's sweat and blood. In China, 90 percent of the people have no culture or education, and of those the majority are peasants.[11]

Where Mencius established the different functions of the elite and the masses, Confucius fixed the peasants politically. At the national level the government was a highly centralized structure headed by the emperor, the court, and the bureaucracy. The government was organized to reach down to the provincial and county levels of government, but this is as far as it went—formally. The elitist nature of Confucian education, despite its Horatio Alger mythology, provided the bureaucracy with less than 50,000 officials to govern the country's 1 million villages and the 80 percent of the country's population which was rural.

The social cement which kept the system together was the local gentry, landholders who had a stake in the system and who might have been partially or wholly indoctrinated somewhere along the examination route. Some simply purchased the degree and, thus, respectability. The gentry degree-holder's value system, nonetheless, was that of the central government's. Because their values were translocal, they became the ideal liaison to the government. Their immediate official contacts were the district magistrates, the lowest level of officialdom in the government, who numbered less than two thousand.

Rural China learned about Confucius from the gentry. Oral tradition took it from there.

Under the circumstances government functioned by default, both at the national and local levels. Since the government could not reach directly into village China, it was content to promote those activities which were translocal in nature, such as maintaining the irrigation canals, roads, and defense. The function of government by Confucian standards was to make no policy nor promote any change which might affect the social structure at the village level. The people on the other hand did not interfere with the government's activities at the national level, so rural China was living proof, Taoism notwithstanding, that the government which governed least at least governed. Confucius legitimized the separation of the state from its citizens:

> Confucius said: "A person not in a particular government position does not discuss its policies."[12]

Americans take political participation for granted.

Despite frequent rebellions and occasional dissent from individuals, the spirit of the political contract was to last until the 1890s when disgruntled Confucian intellectuals led by K'ang Yu-wei and Liang Ch'i-ch'ao dared to question the government's lack of response to the foreign encroachments started after the Opium War. Chapter 2 tells some of this story, focusing as it must in this early period mainly on the alienation of the Confucian intellectuals.

The real story, Confucius notwithstanding, was developing in the countryside. Foreign encroachments, failure of the government to reform itself, poverty in the countryside, prosperity in the coastal cities, corruption, treason, high taxes, inflation, Western scientific technology, missionaries, marines, and domestic politics —all brought to the countryside courtesy of the Communists by design and the Nationalists by default—converged to arouse a politically passive peasantry, conditioned by Confucianism to mind its own rural business, into a force in the revolution. The destruction of the traditional Confucian social structure, which was a barrier to Nationalism, and the reconstruction of a new one was what the revolution *had to be* all about. Mao claims to have discovered the peasants' revolutionary potential around 1925, while Chiang K'ai-shek apparently never did or never tried. Chapters 6, 7, and 8 tell something about this story which many China scholars believe is the real story of the Chinese revolution. So does Mao. In this story, Mao rewrote the Confucian political contract, but instead of excluding the masses from political participation, he made political participation a moral imperative and a national ethos. He called his political contract, the "mass line," or, "from the masses, to the masses."

Chinese Communism is not totally free of its own mythology either.[13]

Another issue in the Criticize Confucius campaign is the impact of Confucian thinking on the development or nondevelopment of science in the mainstream of Chinese society. To understand this issue it is necessary to discuss Confucius' views on the relationship between man (humanism) and nature (science).

Confucianism is basically a system of ethics, based on the farmer's firm respect for nature (but not, as we have seen, on the firm respect for the farmer). Confucius believed that the world was really a part of an ordered universe of which man was an intrinsic part. Nature, however, was organized while man was not. Nature could provide the model man needed to organize himself. In this respect, Confucianism was essentially a mechanistic view of the universe, and for the times, it explained why China was in a state of anarchy: man had not organized himself as nature had. Since both man and nature were interrelated, it followed that one could affect the other. In this cause-effect relationship, man carried the burden of maintaining social harmony. The harmonious society, Confucius believed, could exist if things were allowed to operate naturally but mechanically.

> Tzu-lu said: "The ruler [of the state] of Wei is waiting for you to serve in his administration. What will be your first measure?" Confucius said: "It will concern the rectification of names." Tzu-lu said, "Is that so? You are wide of the mark. Why should there be such a rectification?" Confucius said, "Yu! How uncultivated you are! With regard to what he does not know, the superior man should maintain an attitude of reserve. If names are not rectified, then language will not be in accord with truth. If language is not in accord with truth, then things cannot be accomplished. . . . Therefore the superior man will give only names that can be described in speech and say only what can be carried out in practice."[14]

Judging from the writings of his disciples (Confucius, like Socrates, apparently did not write down his own thoughts), Confucius clearly gave humanism so much attention that he unwittingly discouraged the investigation of nature and thus science. "Confucius taught four things: culture, conduct, loyalty, and faithfulness."[15] And again! "Confucius never discussed strange phenomena, physical exploits, disorder, or spiritual beings."[16]

Joseph Needham writes:

> What true sciences could a Confucian scholar legitimately study during the early Middle Ages? Mathematics was essential, up to a certain point, for the planning and control of the hydraulic engineering works, but those professing it were likely to remain inferior officials. With astronomy a man might hope to rise higher. The practice of medicine was possible and agricultural studies were always respectable. But alchemy was severely frowned upon, and familiarity with the crafts of smiths, millwrights, or other artisans, was considered unbecoming to a Confucian. . . . [Confucianism] simply turned away its face, in accordance with the attitude of its founding fathers, from Nature and the investigation of Nature, to concentrate a millennial interest on human society and human society alone.[17]

From his earlier writings as a student at the Hunan First Normal Teacher's College in 1913, a young Mao, too, was studying ethics, but ethics with a twist. In his mentor and future father-in-law, Professor Yang Ch'ang-chi, Mao was strongly influenced by a person who "believed in his ethics very strongly and tried to imbue his students with the desire to become just, moral, virtuous men, useful in society."[18] So far, classical Confucianism. Professor Yang, however, was himself influenced by Friedrich Paulsen, whom Jerome Ch'en notes "was a disciplinarian, placing great emphasis on self-control and will power."[19]

In 1914–15, Mao read Paulsen's *A System of Ethics* and then wrote an essay entitled, "The Power of the Mind," for which Professor Yang awarded him a perfect mark. Mao wrote the essay as if he were debating Confucius on the relationship between man and nature.

> Although we are determined by nature, we are also a part of nature. Hence, if nature has the power to determine us, we also have the power to determine nature; although our power is slight one could not say that it is without influence on nature.[20]

Young Mao was in the habit of writing prodigious notes in the margins of his books, and in another of Paulsen's books, *Virtues and Vices,* it is apparent that Mao's views on self-control, will power, and man's influence on nature had all begun to converge in a nascent radicalism:

> In the past I worried over the coming destruction of our country, but now I know that fear was unnecessary. I have no doubt that the political system, the characteristics of our people, and the society will change; what I am not yet clear on are the ways in which the change can be successfully brought about. I incline [sic] to believe that a [complete] reconstruction is needed. Let destruction play the role of a mother in giving birth to a new country. The great revolutions of other countries in the past centuries swept away the old and brought forth the new. They were the great changes which resurrected the dead and reconstructed the decayed.[21]

Mao was on the threshold of discovering Lenin's doctrine of continuous revolution which when juxtaposed to Confucius' doctrine of social harmony made it clear that China was not big enough for both. One had to go.

Substantively, Mao believes that man's influence over nature is not only slight, but only slightly necessary for China's salvation. A recent article in *Peking Review*, written by a study group in the Criticize Confucius campaign, might have been speaking for Mao and a whole generation of revolutionaries who could remember what the superior scientific technology of the West did to China in the late nineteenth and early twentieth centuries:

> The Confucianists hated all new things and opposed all progressive scientific thinking. . . . Historical facts prove that the Confucianists stubbornly took the idealist stand and consistently opposed the explanation of nature in terms of its own motion. . . . The imperial examination system the reactionary feudal ruling class established was a rope by which Confucian thinking was used to bind and strangle science.[22]

Mao too is interested in human society—Chinese society—and he too believes in the educability and therefore perfectability of man. Unlike Confucius, however, he believes that good people —good Communist people—will not allow the investigation of nature to tear down society. Like Confucius he distrusts scientists and intellectuals, and he has allowed that distrust to become national policy. Once in a while, as in 1957, he will shake things up, but all in all, science has been accommodated in the mainstream of human society, so that just in case anyone gets any notions of dismembering China again, man *and* nature will be ready. To get a young nation-state into the modern world has not been easy, for he, as well as other revolutionaries, have had to carry with them the excessive baggage of Confucius' China. To understand Mao's will power, self-control, and sheer cantankerousness, one must understand that he is, to paraphrase Fairbank, as much a product of China's past as he is of Marx and Lenin.[23]

The past *is* prologue.

America's China Bicentennial

In the past three decades, America has been involved in three major wars on the Asian mainland, and narrowly escaped a fourth (Cambodia). In all four cases, China figured prominently, either as friend or foe. Since the Korean War, however, we have been involved in a de facto war of nerves with the People's Republic of China (PRC), and this in turn, has given Americans a national headache. The recent trips to the PRC by Presidents Richard M. Nixon and Gerald R. Ford have helped to reduce the pain, but the nervous tension remains.

America's involvement in Asia in general and China in particular spans more than a mere three decades. Indeed, Americans might be mildly surprised to learn that another bicentennial celebration is in the making: 200 years of American-Chinese relations. In preparation for that bicentennial, we should know, however cursory, something of our involvement in China for the past 200 years.

In 1784, the American clipper ship *Empress of China* made the first American commercial contact with China, and by 1789, when Washington was being sworn in as this country's first president, there were at least fourteen American clipper ships anchored outside Canton. In this early period,

> American contacts with China developed haphazardly under the spur of three main motivations—to turn a profit, to further our national interests, and, as some saw it, to rescue the Godless millions of China from misery and damnation. Almost from the beginning the American involvement was charged with emotion and sentiment.[24]

America's sentiment changed into disillusionment when the Chinese empire flatly proclaimed to the world that China wanted neither foreign goods nor its "Godless millions rescued from misery and damnation." The Ch'ien-lung Emperor made that clear to King George III of England in 1793:

> You, O King, are so inclined toward our civilization that you have sent a special envoy across the seas to bring to our

> Court your memorial of congratulations on the occasion of
> my birthday and to present your native products as an ex-
> pression of your thoughtfulness. . . . As to the request made
> in your memorial, O King, to send one of your nationals to
> stay at the Celestial Court to take care of your country's
> trade with China, this is not in harmony with the state sys-
> tem of our dynasty and will definitely not be permitted. . . .
> There is nothing we lack, as your principal envoy and others
> have themselves observed. We have never set much store on
> strange or ingenious objects, nor do we need any more of
> your country's manufactures.[25]

Chinese assumptions of moral superiority were to be China's
undoing.

Traditionally, China's conception of international relations
was based on the same inferior-superior relations which characterized Chinese society at large. The so-called "tributary system of
international relations" was simply the global extension of domestic politics. The system was made up of the following assumptions:
(1) China's unquestioned leadership in Asia (and as far as the
Chinese were concerned, that meant the world), (2) the prestige
which went with being the biggest and most culturally advanced
country at that time, (3) the ability to conduct a foreign policy on
its own terms (thus, China dictated to foreigners, including the
West, in the manner of the Ch'ien-lung Emperor, from 1511 to
1839, when the Opium War ended the tributary system), and (4)
the possession of a military to insure foreign and domestic tranquility (or so the Chinese thought).

In 1839, Britain declared war on the Chinese empire in the
name of the right to trade in general and the right to push opium
in particular. Chapter 2 discusses the extent of opium trade in
China. Because of the Ch'ien-lung Emperor's myopia, China was
to know no peace from foreign aggression for the next 100 years.

Americans, for their part, were smug at their reluctance, as
decent God-fearing folk, to wage war on China. What we did not
do in the battlefield, however, we did in the field of diplomacy,
which in the end was to prove more lethal than the British men-
of-war. In 1844 the United States signed its first treaty of "Peace,
Amity, and Commerce" with China, which was another way of
saying that we, too, could among other things, enter into the drug

and soul trade. In the treaty we inserted a clever legal device called the most-favored-nation clause. By this clause, any trading right or privilege which the Chinese granted to another country, gained peacefully or otherwise (usually it was otherwise), automatically accrued to the United States, as well as every other country trading in China. This bit of "me-too imperialism," to use Owen Lattimore's phrase,[26] was to last until 1943, when the United States and Britain were among the last to finally renounce all trading rights and privileges started nearly a century before. Chapter 2 tells something about the fortunes invested in China during this century of economic rape.

In 1849 the scene shifted from China to the United States as Chinese coolies (*coolie* means "bitter labor," from the Chinese word "k'u-li") arrived in California during the Gold Rush. It took the Chinese less than thirty years to lose their most favored, cheap labor status in America. By 1882, Chinese exclusion laws were being passed, and from this point on, the Chinese in America were to know no peace either.

> In the San Francisco area, in 1877–78, lawless elements committed arson, robbery, and murder against the Chinese; in Truckee, in November, 1878, the entire Chinese population of about a thousand was driven out of town. Until the early 1890s, frequent anti-Chinese riots occurred in other states and territories. In Rock Springs, Wyoming, in 1885, 28 Chinese were killed in one day. At Snake River, in Oregon, in 1887, 10 Chinese gold miners were robbed and murdered by men masquerading as cowboys. The incidents reflect the strain in an unstable frontier society; and they are among the darkest stains on the history of liberty in the United States.[27]

Picking on defenseless Chinese was one thing, but when we began picking on the Japanese, that was another thing. Japan, one of the great powers in the first half of the twentieth century, would make the exclusion laws and racial discrimination a major international issue at the Paris peace talks in 1919, and would, in the process, embarrass America for its racial sins. Chapter 4 tells something of this story.

In 1898, the United States acquired the Philippines from

Spain as part of the settlement of the Spanish-American War, and in that instance, America became a Pacific power. Within a year, America was behaving like a Pacific power—with good but misplaced intentions. This was to be our life's story in Asia.

Viewing the "dismemberment of China" rather apprehensively in 1898, Secretary of State John Hay circulated the open door notes which among other things requested that China's treaty ports be kept open to world trade, and in that same powerful breath, declared that America's policy was committed to preserve China as a "territorial and administrative entity." Between 1900, when America made the open door notes official policy, and 1937, when Japan invaded China, America had four golden opportunities to make good on its word, and in each instance, its word was not even worth the paper it was written on. In all four cases, the culprit was Japan, who spoke loudly *and* carried a big stick: in 1915, it presented China with demands backed by the naval fleet for more commercial rights in China; in 1919 it took over Germany's possession in Shantung Province, a move approved by the allies, including a reluctant United States; in 1931 it invaded Manchuria and turned it into its puppet-state of Manchukuo; and in 1937, Japan decided that all of China was preferable to only parts of it.

Most of these topics are covered in this book, and most of it is not pretty reading, but then aggression seldom is pretty reading.

After World War II in Asia our policy toward China waxed hot and cold, vacillating between the paternalism of the early 1900s and our desire to see China lift itself to a position of national respectability in the 1940s. Behind this altruism was our desire to see China fight its own war in Asia. During the war years, nonetheless, American public opinion was solidly behind China's plight. Washington began its romantic interlude with Chiang K'ai-shek's government at this time. "The climax of the Sino-American honeymoon," wrote A. T. Steele, "was reached early in 1943 in the triumphal American tour of Madame Chiang K'ai-shek... when she received a tremendous ovation in her appearance before Congress, and later when 17,000 enthusiastic Americans jammed Madison Square Garden to hear and applaud her."[28] She visited this country for two reasons, to insure that America would aid China in its fight against Japanese aggression and to be assured that America would not aid the Communists, who had by now become a major force in Chinese domestic and foreign politics.

There were, however, some anxious moments during the honeymoon, highlighted by the Stilwell-Chiang feud and China's reluctance to take the offensive against the Japanese. In the eight-year Asian war, Chiang did not take a single *major* offensive against the Japanese. Neither did the Communists. Both said they did. One myth served two.

Americans have a history of fighting other people's wars for them, and the China war was no exception, and the Flying Tigers notwithstanding, most of the fighting was done by diplomats rather than soldiers. By 1946, 50 percent of Americans interviewed thought that we should stay out of the impending civil war in China, and despite some frantic diplomacy by Washington to avert the civil war, the years of mutual distrust and hatred between the nationalists of Chiang K'ai-shek and the Communists of Mao Tse-tung made the result inevitable. It also made clear why neither fought the Japanese.

In the Chinese civil war America poured over $2 billion in economic and military aid to Chiang K'ai-shek's government. It was for naught. It was perhaps also symbolic of the Communist victory that Mao Tse-tung led the victory parade into Peking in a captured American Buick.

The defeat of the Nationalists ushered in a brief period of contemplated disengagement from Chinese affairs. In January 1950, President Harry Truman declared that the United States would not provide any more military aid to Chiang's government, now exiled in Taiwan. Shortly thereafter, Secretary of State Dean Acheson excluded Taiwan from the United State's defensive perimeter in the Pacific. We had had enough of being a Pacific power.

There was also the possibility that President Truman was prepared to recognize the PRC, but we will never know it: domestic politics prevented any rational discussion of it. China had become a major political issue in a divided congress eager to absolve

America from any blame for the Communist victory. In time, Congress was involved in a Communist witch-hunt which reached into the state department. "The Chinese war," declared Senator H. Styles Bridges, Republican from New Hampshire, "was lost in Washington, not in China."[29] Senator John Butler, Republican from Maryland singled out Dean Acheson: "I watch his smart-aleck manner and his British clothes and that New Dealism . . . and I want to shout, Get out, Get out. You stand for everything that has been wrong with the United States for years."[30] Senator Joseph McCarthy, who entered the fray in February 1950, narrowed the betrayal of America and Chiang K'ai-shek to "205" individuals who were "loyal to the ideals and designs of Communism rather than those of the free, God-fearing half of the world. . . . I refer to the Far Eastern division of the state department and the Voice of America."[31]

Recalling this dark chapter in America's diplomatic history and domestic politics during hearings on China just one week before President Nixon's historic trip to the PRC in 1972, Senator J. William Fulbright, chairman of the Senate Foreign Relations Committee, remarked:

> For too many years Americans have found it difficult, if not impossible, to engage in rational, dispassionate discussion of China. . . . We considered ourselves uniquely qualified to play the role of China's savior. . . . These Foreign Service officers in China served their country well, but their country did not always serve them well. . . . They were transferred from China and were denied deserved promotions. Their loyalty was questioned; some were hounded from the Foreign Service. As a result, it was recognized as unwise and unsafe to write about the "real" China whether one was in or out of the Government. . . . Much that has been written about China since the late 1940s was thus an exercise in demonology.[32]

The Communists, for their part, did not help the bad press they were receiving either. Shortly before the PRC was officially established, they imprisoned the staff of the U.S. consulate general in Manchuria, and kept it incommunicado for nearly a year. The Chinese also confiscated American property in China without offering the usual compensation. The Chinese probably figured that Americans had been handsomely compensated during the past 100 years. After June 1950, however, domestic politics did not need Chinese hostility nor the foreign service officers for a scapegoat. Korea took care of that.

Korea confirmed the worst beliefs about international Communism in general and the PRC in particular. America's policy toward the PRC changed proportionally to the number of American deaths and Chinese volunteers in Korea. From the Korean War until 1969, America's policy toward the PRC was double-pronged: military containment and diplomatic isolation. The policy was based on the assumption that if a constant threat of military pressure was kept on the newly established PRC, its leadership might crack, causing an internal breakdown. It was also expected that by denying Peking a voice in the United Nations, it would officially cease to exist. While denying the PRC any voice in international councils, the United Nations (read, United States) recognized the PRC's existence long enough to officially brand it the aggressor in the Korean War.

The basis for American-Chinese conflict was set for the next two decades. Between 1951 and 1972, the policy was continued by Presidents Truman, Eisenhower, Kennedy, Johnson, and Nixon. The five administrations would not touch the China question with a ten-foot pole, and if by some chance a policy review of U.S. commitments abroad was undertaken, by the time China came up, it was usually to the tune of "Bring on the Bloody Marys," as President John F. Kennedy once remarked.[33] In the time span of twenty-five years, China was such a devastatingly sensitive issue in domestic politics that it consumed all who came into contact with it. John F. Kennedy might have been speaking for a generation of American presidential politicians:

> It really doesn't make any sense—the idea that Taiwan represents China. But, if we lost this fight, if Red China comes into the U.N. during our first year in town, your first year [speaking to U.S. Ambassador to the United Nations Adlai Stevenson] and mine, they'll run us both out. We have to lick them [the PRC] this year. We'll take our chances next year. It will be an election year; but we can delay the admission of Red China till after the election.[34]

In the interim, the PRC did not, as usual, help matters. In 1954 and 1958 its shelling of the offshore islands of Quemoy and Matsu nearly involved it in a military confrontation with the United States; in 1959, the suppression of a revolt in Tibet, and the subsequent reintegration of Tibet administratively reconfirmed the PRC's image of an aggressor and, in 1960 and 1962, overt hostilities on the Indian border made aggression its middle name. In those days there were no two sides to the story. The PRC was involved, and that was good enough.

The first alteration of the containment and isolation policy came in the 1968 presidential campaign, when with the help of some professorial sloganeering, it was suggested that the policy be changed to "containment *without* isolation." Presidential candidate Richard M. Nixon, who made his reputation as a staunch anti-Communist, was perhaps giving hints of a softening attitude when he asked Americans to "reach out Westward to the East," and called for recognizing the "reality" of a PRC in Asia.[35] His conciliatory attitude came at a time when the PRC had just come out of the devastation of the cultural revolution, but more importantly, at a time when the Soviet Union had invaded Czechoslovakia and the Sino-Soviet border dispute was beginning to flare.

Peking, under the circumstances, was also in a conciliatory mood. No sooner were the election results official in 1968 that Peking proposed to resume the negotiations in Warsaw. President-elect Nixon favored the resumption of talks. The talks were not held, but the ice was broken.

By mid-July 1969, the Nixon administration took two symbolic steps to relax tensions. First, the administration announced that Americans traveling abroad would be permitted to bring home up to $100 worth of goods produced in mainland China. Up to that point such purchases were prohibited as a part of the nineteen-year trade embargo instituted by the United Nations at the urging of the United States. Second, restrictions against travel to the mainland imposed since 1950 were also lifted for scholars, students, scientists, and the news media. Both steps were unilateral.

Perhaps even more telling was the use of the word "Peking" by the Nixon administration to refer to mainland China instead of the officially approved "Peiping." Peking means "Northern Capital" and is the name used traditionally by the Chinese to denote that the capital was located in the north (as opposed to, say, Nanking, which means "Southern Capital"). "Peiping" means "Northern Peace," and this was the name of Peking when the city was not the location of the capital. Taiwan Chinese to this day *always* refer to Peking as "Peiping," refusing to even symbolically end the civil war. Between 1950 and 1969, Washington officially referred to the capital on the mainland as "Peiping." Washington too refused to accept the "reality" of a PRC on the mainland.

President Gerald R. Ford continued the "normalization" of relations with the PRC begun by former president Nixon. In 1976, President Ford called for the "complete" normalization of relations, a move most observers believe will lead to the establishment of formal diplomatic relations with the PRC. If the dizzy nature of our relations with the PRC teaches us anything it is that the only predictable thing is the unpredictable happening.

We have not heard from the PRC yet.

In the meantime, Americans too have some excessive baggage of their own to get rid of. Our love-hate relationship with the emperor's China, Sun Yat-sen's China, Chiang K'ai-shek's China, and now Mao Tse-tung's China—China by whatever name and by whomever—has alternately caused Americans to romanticize it (Mandarins, Cathay, quaint Confucian aphorisms in fortune cookies), curse it (Communism and atheism), stereotype it (hardworking but cunning), victimize it (opium, missionaries), discriminate against it (immigration exclusion laws, coolies), respect it (the family), protect it (Open Door, Wilson, World War II), politicize it (McCarthy and all that), fight it (Korea), be puzzled by it (men wore gowns, women trousers; the Chinese character and no alphabet; read right to left, chopsticks) and fear it (its population constitutes about one-fourth of all mankind today).

A good place to begin our bicentennial celebration with China is in the public schools, and the sooner the better. Sadly, the public schools mirror America's ignorance of China. Approximately 90 percent of all high school graduates in the United States never take a course in a culture markedly different from their own.[36] In 1970–71 only 1.5 percent of students in the seventh through twelfth grades were enrolled in courses with Asian content.[37]

For prologue, the past is necessary.

China: A Slavic Manchukuo?

In the domestic furor following the outbreak of hostilities in Korea, it became fashionable among high administrative officials, politicians, and generals to assume that Peking's sneeze was Moscow's cold. Secretary of State John Foster Dulles, preferring family to medical metaphors, said:

> By the test of conception, birth, nurture and obedience the Mao Tse-tung regime is a creature of the Moscow Politburo, and it is on behalf of Moscow, not of China, that it is betraying the friendship of the Chinese people toward the United States. . . . We should treat the Mao Tse-tung regime for what it is—a puppet-regime.[38]

Under Secretary of State for Far Eastern Affairs Dean Rusk adds some genealogy: "The Peiping regime may be a colonial Russian Government—a Slavic Manchukuo on a larger scale. It is not the Government of China. It does not pass the first test. It is not Chinese."[39]

Rusk did not reveal the sources of his genealogical investigation, but one thing was certain, the "creature" was not Russian. One of the major themes developed here is the role which the Soviet Union played in China's turbulent history from 1919 to 1949. What is generally not known about the Soviet Union's role in Chinese domestic politics is that for a time Stalin compounded the formula that Mao Tse-tung and Chiang K'ai-shek both took. Not only were the Nationalist and Communist parties modeled after the Communist party of the Soviet Union, but in the first decade of Soviet participation in the Chinese revolution (1920–30) both parties followed Stalin's "estimate of the situation" in China. Both were also subsidized by the Comintern. In this early period, there were as many Russian advisers in China as there were Chinese revolutionaries, Nationalist or Communist. This is probably where Rusk's genealogy got confused.

What Rusk and so many others conveniently overlooked were

the efforts by both Chiang and Mao to sever the umbilical cord with the Soviet Union. Chiang took the first step toward independence in 1927, and he did so in the best tradition of Cain and Abel. Chapter 6 tells something about this story in which he not only turned against the Chinese Communists but he also expelled the Soviet advisers from China. Mao waited until 1942 to declare his independence, and Chapter 9 tells something about the time Mao made Marx, Lenin, and Stalin honorary Chinese citizens, and began directing the Communist portion of the revolution without interference from Moscow. Both simply stopped listening to Papa Joe since the late 1920s and early 1930s when much of what he said about the Chinese revolution was wrong—dead wrong.

For the Chinese Communists all was well that ended well. In 1949, the People's Republic of China was established "leaning to one side," the side of socialism and the Soviet Union. The Slavic Manchukuo myth received its impetus at this time when in late 1949, Chairman Mao took his first and only trip outside China when he and Stalin signed a treaty of mutual assistance in Moscow. By 1957, there were over 200 new industrial complexes built with Soviet aid and with the advice of over 7,000 Soviet technicians. When the treaty was renewed in 1958, the monolithic nature of world Communism, and Peking's puppet status, was confirmed.

The still waters, however, hid the raging currents below. Unknown to most observers, an ideological family quarrel had been developing since the Twentieth Congress of the CPSU met in February 1956, when Nikita Khrushchev delivered his famous "de-Stalinization" secret speech. In this speech Khrushchev made peaceful coexistence a fundamental principle of Soviet foreign policy, declared that war was not necessarily inevitable, and suggested that the transformation of capitalism to socialism could be accomplished nonviolently. Up to that speech, the Chinese had supported the exact opposite from what Khrushchev was now proposing. "Revisionism" became as dirty a word in Chinese Communist rhetoric as any American four-letter word. There was also a classic case of a failure to communicate between the two, for just before Khrushchev delivered his speech, Chu Teh, the Chinese Communist representative to the congress, had just finished delivering a speech praising Stalin.

In the next few years the ideological split worsened, as one issue after another arose, including the question of communization (how soon and how fast), nuclear weapons (why was the Soviet Union hesitating to share its knowledge and arsenal with the PRC?), the offshore islands (where was the support promised by the Soviet Union?), the Sino-Indian border dispute (Moscow was providing military support to both India and the PRC), the Cuban missile crisis (after the pullout, the PRC labeled the Soviet Union a "capitulationist"), and territory (border provocations were reported in 1963).[40] In 1959, the Soviet Union abruptly pulled its technicians from the PRC, leaving projects half-finished throughout the country.

In April 1966, the Chinese Communist party boycotted the Twenty-third Soviet Party Congress, the first time it had ever missed a congress. By late August 1966, Peking's ideological hostility turned into physical violence as hundreds of thousands of Red Guards demonstrated outside the Soviet embassy in Peking causing property damage and threatening Soviet diplomats with bodily harm.

Whoever heard of a puppet turning against its master?

In September the PRC expelled all Soviet students from the PRC, and in October the Soviet Union retaliated by expelling all Chinese students from Moscow. The excesses of the cultural revolution led the central committee of the Soviet Communist party to denounce Mao by name for the first time ever. In 1967, both withdrew their ambassadors thus bringing to an end both party-to-party relations as well as government-to-government relations.

The worst was yet to come. In 1968, the Soviet Union began to retaliate directly and indirectly. First, the Soviet Union suppressed the Dubcek reform movement in Czechoslovakia. Peking was visibly shaken, as we shall see. At this point, Peking stopped talking and began a serious mobilization effort to prepare for what Mao called the "inevitable war." State department officials were 99 percent sure of a war between the two, an analysis helped by the Soviet military buildup along the 5,000 mile common border and frequent violations of Chinese airspace.

Second, the Soviet Union launched a major diplomatic offensive from Japan to India, culminating in Secretary General Brezhnev's proposal for an Asian collective security system designed to contain a China which had apparently gone mad during the cultural revolution.

By late 1968 and early 1969 both were accusing each other of border violations and both continued their troop buildup along the border. The situation was perfect for the self-fulfilling prophecy to work or for state department analysts to predict with a 99 percent assurance.

In March 1969, the "inevitable" happened. Violent fighting broke out in a small island located in the Ussuri River which separates Manchuria from the Soviet Union's easternmost province, the Maritime Province. Chen Pao island (Damansky to the Soviet Union) was a throwback to the imperialist penetration of China in the midnineteenth century. Czarist Russia got into the act in 1860.

In 1860 a joint Anglo-French expedition of 100 warships and 17,000 troops was approaching Peking to force the ratification of another treaty giving foreigners more commercial rights in China. Just before the expeditionary force reached Peking, a Russian official offered to mediate a peaceful settlement. He sparred the annihilation of Peking and at the same time lopped off the Maritime Province, by treaty, of course. In 1969, the Chinese insisted that the treaty was null and void because it had been signed under duress. The law of nations was clear: treaties were binding whether or not they were signed under duress, or, to the victors went the spoils. Diplomacy having failed, the participants moved to the battlefield.

The PRC immediately put its civil defense plans into action. The plans called for increasing the country's grain reserves, asking the peasants to contribute 10 percent of their monthly rice ration to collective granaries, and requesting that the people store at least a six-month supply of food for the "protracted war." Urban factories were dismantled and reassembled in the interior as part of a "strategic redeployment" of the industrial base. Air raid shelters were built in the major cities, and the 7 million member people's militia was reactivated and most of it assigned to the border area.[41]

Soviet bellicosity further heightened Peking's anxieties of the inevitable war. The Chinese learned rather vividly that they had not cornered the market on bellicosity. For example, one Soviet deputy bluntly warned Peking that the Soviet Union had the capability to launch a "blitzkrieg" against China. The Soviet publicist, Victor Louis, wrote an article disclosing that Soviet missiles were already zeroed in on Chinese nuclear installations in Sinkiang Province, the PRC's major nuclear test site along the common border. Louis also warned that "the Kremlin would not hesitate to act against China as it did against Czechoslovakia."[42] In September 1969, Chou En-lai and Soviet Premier Kosygin met at a rare meeting during the funeral for Ho Chi-minh. Premier Kosygin suggested to Chou that they should resume their talks on the border dispute, perhaps while Kosygin was on his way home. Somewhere on his way to Moscow, Kosygin received Chou's invitation to come to Peking to discuss the border situation. The Chinese, however, refused to allow Kosygin to enter the city, so the meeting was held at the airport lounge. During their four-hour meeting, Kosygin reminded Chou that the Soviet Union had the "military muscle to bomb China back to the Han dynasty."[43] The Han dynasty existed between 206 B.C. and 220 A.D.

Since October 1969, an unsteady truce has prevailed between Moscow and Peking. A border commission has met approximately twenty times to solve the boundary issue, but as yet, to no avail. In the interim, the Soviet Union continues to perform its version of the mating dance of the peacock, occasionally firing a test missile across China, if not to woo it, at least to keep it interested.

The Soviet Union's military, diplomatic, and verbal offensives have led to what most observers agree is a major reassessment of Peking's foreign policy, especially its policy toward the United States. Before the actual outbreak of hostilities along the border, Peking had formally proposed at Warsaw that it might not be a bad idea for the PRC and the United States to discuss matters of mutual concern one month after President Richard M. Nixon took office. One month, the Chinese reasoned, was plenty of time for the Nixon administration to make up its mind about China. Quite possibly, then, and contrary to Soviet expectations, the border conflict may have hastened the Chinese Communists to a new United States policy, confirming what most students of international relations generally believe: politics does make strange bedfellows.

Detente

In the past two years the issue of détente has brought together the United States, the People's Republic of China, and the Soviet Union in still another example of the politics of strange bedfellows. Ideologically the Chinese believe that détente is a two-headed monster created by the superpowers to camouflage their intense rivalry for hegemony in the world. Peking's ideological attack focuses on two points: Europe and the arms race. Europe, according to the Chinese press, is what détente is all about. In the past few years, the Chinese say, the United States and the Soviet Union have been bitterly contending for the flanks of Europe—the Middle East, the Mediterranean, and the Balkans—for whoever controls the flanks, controls Europe.[44] Strategically, Europe is important to the Soviet Union for it has been the area where the Soviet Union has been the most vulnerable to invasions in the past. To accomplish its domination over Western Europe, the Chinese have accused the Soviet Union of using the Warsaw Pact to hide its aggression in Europe. Citing unspecified Western news reports, the Chinese claim that at present the Soviet Union has thirty-one divisions in Eastern Europe (twenty in Germany, two in Poland, four in Hungary, and five in Czechoslovakia), three-fifths of its ground forces, three-fourths of its air force, three-fourths of its intermediate range missiles, three-fourths of its surface naval ships and over one half of its submarines poised to attack Western Europe.[45]

The Chinese also believe, as a large segment of Americans believe, that the Soviet Union is using détente to increase its nuclear arsenal while the United States slows its own development. The Chinese note that while the Soviet GNP is about half that of the United States, its military expenditures are as big, if not bigger, than those of the United States.[46] Détente, the Chinese warn, is a policy intended to lull the United States into a complacency which could have global repercussions.

Pragmatically, détente has been both a blessing and a frustration for Peking. During the last quarter of 1975, Chinese leaders were questioning the United States ability to maintain a balance of power with the Soviet Union as a result of détente. The concerns were of such nature, apparently, that Secretary of State Henry Kissinger went to the PRC to reassure Peking that the United States would not be lulled into the complacency Peking feared. Kissinger's assurances must have jolted Peking when two months later Defense Secretary James Schlesinger was fired from his job. Secretary Schlesinger was viewed by the Chinese as being tough on the Soviet Union. Quoting Senators Henry Jackson and Barry Goldwater, Peking made it clear that Schlesinger's removal was a victory for the Soviet Union and a defeat for détente.[47]

The PRC was damned if it did and damned if it didn't where détente was concerned. If it accepted the United States' assurances on détente, it was putting itself in a position of having to trust a country which just a few years before was China's number one enemy. If it did not accept the policy of détente, it stood to alienate itself from the only country with the power to stymie Soviet expansion in Asia. The Soviet Union is China's number one enemy today, so the choice was painfully clear.

It was of course to Peking's advantage to keep the ideological accusations and political pressures alive. If anything, the Chinese might harbor the secret hope that détente might just work by slowing the arms race between the superpowers. Publicly, the PRC criticized both for speeding up the arms race, but in the meantime, it had set off its seventeenth nuclear test since 1964, developed reconnaissance satellites (until the past year the United States was providing Peking with space reconnaissance photos of the Sino-Soviet frontier and Soviet military troop movements and installations along the border), and launched some satellites in preparation for a space program which will enable it to send a manned spacecraft into orbit soon.

Where Confucius' China had its eye on the past, Mao's China has its eye on the future.

2

The Revolutionary Environment in Nineteenth-Twentieth Century China

We [the U.S.] recognize that China's long historical experience weighs heavily on contemporary Chinese foreign policy. China has had little experience in conducting diplomacy based on the sovereign equality of nations. For centuries China dominated its neighbor, culturally and politically. In the past 150 years it has been subjected to massive interventions.[1]

If it be true that the past is prologue, where does one begin in order to understand the conditions which gave rise to communism and nationalism in twentieth-century China? President Nixon's *U.S. Foreign Policy for the 1970s* makes a reference to the "past 150 years." A. T. Steele believes that the nineteenth century laid the foundations for the "huge and conglomerate edifice of truths, half-truths, assumptions, legends, prejudices, and contradictory opinions that make up our present-day outlook in China."[2] John K. Fairbank believes that "decisive differences in cultural traditions have underlain the political problems of our relations with East Asia during the last hundred and fifty years."[3] President Chiang K'ai-shek dates the "deterioration of China's national position" back to the last one hundred years,[4] while Chairman Mao Tse-tung, singles out the "middle of the nineteenth century" as a key point in China's revolution.[5]

Since President Nixon, Steele, Professor Fairbank, President Chiang, and Chairman Mao reaffirm the primacy of the past as a factor influencing the present, then we too shall attempt to ease our troubled minds and generalized anxiety by attempting to understand the present in an historic context, beginning sometime in the nineteenth century and examining certain aspects of China's economy, government, and society.   29

THE ECONOMY

China, to be sure, has traditionally been characterized as a poor country. Its immense population, natural disasters, wars, and famines have undoubtedly contributed to its poorness. In 1850, the population was estimated to be 429,931,034[6] and despite poor government statistics, the population by 1911 was estimated at 341,913,497. The huge population decrease in the sixty-one-year span has been largely attributed to the T'ai-p'ing rebellion which took an estimated 20 to 30 million lives.[7]

Famines contributed greatly to China's destitution. Famines were recorded in 1862, 1876–79, 1898–99, 1901, 1902, 1906, 1910–11, and 1911–12. The 1876–79 famine reportedly took 9.5 million lives.[8]

"Economic development in this economy of scarcity," wrote Lucien Bianco, "was further hobbled by the Chinese social structure."[9] Quoting statistics provided in Ch'en Han-seng's study of China's peasantry, Bianco shows that over 50 percent of China's rural land was owned by about 10 percent of the upper classes (including rich peasants). China's landlord-tenant system further thrust the economic control of rural China into the hands of a small elite class, for when tenants were forced to borrow money due to a poor crop year or famine, the tenant generally paid extremely high interest rates, ranging from 50 to 70 percent of the main crop. The land owner could count on the government in enforcing the tenant system. According to Bianco:

> Not only was the legal arm of the government always at the landlord's disposal (recalcitrant tenant farmers were promptly clapped into prison), but the landlord could also take back his land and rent it to a more docile tenant.[10]

The peasant's rural misery was further aggravated by the government's or the landowner's propensity to raise taxes without advanced notice.

In China, there was, nonetheless, prosperity amid poverty. This generalization will become clearer as we consider the growth of foreign investments and the growth of the modern and traditional sectors of the Chinese economy from the time of the Opium War (1839–42).

Foreign Investments

Foreign investments played a major role in shaping the Chinese economy. Beginning with the Treaty of Nanking in 1842, foreign investments gradually increased first around the treaty ports[11] and then into the Chinese interior. These investments had both a catalytic and sustaining effect on the economy before the revolution.[12] Table 2.1 shows the amount of foreign investments in China between 1902 and 1914.

Table 2.1
Foreign investments in China, 1902–1914
(U.S. $ millions: percent in parentheses)

Type of Investment	1902	1914
Direct Investments	503.2 (64)	1067.0 (67)
Obligations of Chinese Government	284.7 (36)	525.8 (33)
Loans to private parties	0.0	17.5 (1)
TOTAL	789.9 (100)	1610.3 (100)

Source: Hou, *Foreign Investments*, p. 13.

Table 2.1 shows that investments in China had nearly doubled in the period prior to the revolution. Direct investments accounted for the greater share of foreign capital in China, and since investments increased on a continuous line, it can be said that the economy was rising prior to the revolution.

Table 2.2 shows that the British, Russians, Germans, and French were the principal foreign investors. The foreign investors, in turn, invested their capital primarily in transportation (railroads accounted for 33 percent of foreign capital in 1914), import-export trade (8.8 percent), manufacturing (6.1 percent), real estate (6.5 percent), and mining (3.7 percent).[13] Table 2.2 dramatically illustrates the vast expansion in foreign investments, increasing from $787.9 million in 1902 to more than $1.5 billion in

Table 2.2

Foreign investments in China by country, 1902–1914

(U.S. $ millions: percent in parentheses)

Country	1902	Rank	1914	Rank
Great Britain	260.3 (33.0)	1	607.5 (37.7)	1
Japan	1.0 (0.1)	7	219.6 (13.6)	3
Russia	246.5 (31.3)	2	269.3 (16.7)	2
United States	19.7 (2.5)	5	49.3 (3.1)	6
France	91.1 (11.6)	4	171.4 (10.7)	4
Germany	164.3 (20.9)	3	164.3 (16.4)	5
Belgium	4.4 (0.6)	6	22.9 (1.4)	7
Others	0.6 (0.0)	8	6.7 (0.4)	8
TOTAL	787.9		1,511.0	

Source: Hou, *Foreign Investments*, p. 17.

1914. The effects were notable on the modern sector of the Chinese economy.

Modern Sector

According to Chi-ming Hou, the modern sector of the Chinese economy grew "continuously, not sporadically" from 1840 through the revolution.[14] Table 2.3 shows the "linear trend" in the growth of the economy, despite the revolution of 1911.

It would be misleading, however, to regard foreign investments as being solely responsible for stimulating the Chinese economy. Government spending in munitions, both at the national and provincial levels, helped to develop the modern sector. Furthermore, Chinese merchants invested in the modern sector for profit-making motives.[15]

Traditional Sector

Finally, the rise in the Chinese economy prior to and during the revolution can be examined by looking at the annual rates of growth in the traditional sector. The traditional, or premodern, Chinese economy was predominantly agricultural, with land equated with capital wealth. Land, in turn, could be bought and

Table 2.3

Rates of growth of the modern sector of the
Chinese economy

Indicator	Period	Annual rates (in %)
Physical quantity of imports	1867–1932	2.5
Physical quantity of exports	1867–1932	2.4
Railroad mileage	1894–1911	22.1
Tonnage of Chinese-owned foreign steamers	1882–1910	5.1
Pig iron production of modern mines	1900–1937	9.8
Cotton yarn spindles	1890–1936	11.6

Source: Hou, *Foreign Investments,* p. 126.

sold, and was a major factor in social mobility. Manpower was, as might be expected, the chief form of capital equipment. Alongside this farm economy, such handicraft industry as tea, silk, and cotton existed quite well. Because this premodern economy was locally oriented, market towns were the primary centers of domestic trade. "In general," wrote Fairbank, "the methods for the application of abundant manpower to all the processes of the economy—irrigation, rice culture, transport, handicraft production of consumer goods—had been thoroughly worked out within the limits set by the inherited prescientific technology."[16]

What were the effects on the traditional economy with the introduction of the West's vastly superior scientific technology?

According to Chi-ming Hou,

> The effects on the traditional sector of the development of the modern sector need not always be destructive. In the case of China, there is ground to believe that the modern sector in some ways actually helped the traditional sector to survive. The building of railroads, for instance, created a demand for many goods and services provided by the traditional sector. Many modern products such as matches, soap, and cigarettes were imitated by the handicrafts. . . . For certain industries the most important contribution of the modern sector had to do with supply. It provided the traditional sector with certain goods and services necessary for its

growth and also with certain technological improvements that strengthened its competitive power.[17]

Table 2.4 shows that the traditional sector functioned adequately in the period before and after the revolution.

Table 2.4

Annual rates of growth for selected indicators of the traditional sector of the Chinese economy (percent)

Indicator	Annual rate of growth (+)
Chinese junks entered and cleared in Chinese Customs:	
1864–1903	+6.3
1904–1914	+2.4
Tonnage of Chinese junks in the Yangtze:	
1890–1919	+0.7
Exports of selected handicrafts:	
1875–1928	+2.6
Exports:	
1873–1930	+2.6

Source: Hou, *Foreign Investments*, p. 171.

The state of the Chinese economy as a factor or cause of the Chinese revolution presents a paradox. On the one hand, there was the destitution among the masses caused by population problems, natural disasters, wars, and famines. On the other hand, the economy was growing prior to the revolution. There was then poverty amid prosperity. China's poverty was concentrated among 80 to 90 percent of the masses, the peasants, while China's prosperity was concentrated among the entrepreneurs, both foreign and Chinese, especially those Chinese who resided in the treaty ports. Indeed, the Chinese merchant and the foreign merchant needed each other, and the success of the economy was due mainly to their cooperation. But the treaty ports were only one facet of the overall economic index, and thus it is not difficult to imagine that the goods and services available in the treaty ports were not available to the vast majority of the Chinese people. Yet the preponderance of the treaty ports was such that they did affect the overall performance of the economy—statistically at least.

When the roles of foreign investments, the modern and traditional sectors of the Chinese economy, destitution, population problems, famines, wars, and the treaty ports are considered totally, it is difficult to disprove Crane Brinton's contention that revolutions are not born in societies economically retrograde. In China, the revolution occurred in an economically progressive environment. The gap between the poverty-stricken and the prosperous, however, was an important factor in the successful economic programs and propaganda first of the Nationalists led by Sun Yat-sen and then those of the Chinese Communist party.

THE GOVERNMENT

In this section, the government's role in the last fifty years of the Manchu dynasty will be discussed in order to further highlight the revolutionary environment in nineteenth-century China. Five developments are discussed: (1) the Chinese government's financial indebtedness and financial mismanagement, (2) the inability (or unwillingness) of the government to control opium trafficking, (3) the scramble for concessions and subsequent division of China by the foreign powers, (4) the failure of the government to reform itself, and (5) the inept ruling elite.

Financial Indebtedness

Prior to 1895, the Chinese government was financially solvent. But after the Japanese victory over China in 1895, the Chinese government was forced to borrow heavily to pay the indemnity (U.S. $206 million) imposed by Japan. Thirty-one months after the Sino-Japanese war, the Chinese government had managed to pay the entire sum, but not before the government had incurred a serious debt. According to one highly placed and influential government official, Li Hung-chang, "the amount demanded [was] beyond the ability of China to pay under her present system of taxation. To increase the internal or domestic taxes at this time would lead to great discontent and probably to insurrection."[18]

The Boxer indemnity of 1901 further thrust the government into financial indebtedness. The Boxer uprising cost the Chinese government $334 million, payable in forty years at an interest rate which would eventually double the principal amount borrowed. Between 1902 and 1913, its outstanding obligations totaled nearly $835 million, and of this total the government still owed $309.2 million by 1913.

Railroad financing accounted for further government indebtedness. Nearly 90 percent of all the foreign loans contracted during the period prior to the revolution (disregarding the Boxer indemnity) were for the construction of railroads. Table 2.5 shows the distribution of foreign loans up until 1911. Table 2.5 also shows that for the period prior to the revolution, 70 percent of foreign loans were for military and indemnity purposes, 26 percent for railroads, 2 percent for administrative purposes, and a negligible amount for industrial purposes. The dramatic decrease in military and indemnity loans between 1898 and 1899–1911 (89.5 percent down to 3.7 percent) reflects China's payment of the indemnity to Japan. In the same period, foreign loans were diverted from indemnities to railroad building (10.5 percent in the 1894–98 period up to 88.7 percent for the 1899–1911 period). Military loans, which were used to pay the troops before 1893 and to fi-

Table 2.5

Distribution of foreign loans to the Chinese government
by use, 1861–1911

(£ millions; percent in parentheses)

Period	Military and Indemnity	Adminis-trative	Railroad	Indus-trial	Total
	In 1913 Prices				
1861–1893	29.1 (87.7)	2.5 (7.6)	1.6 (4.7)	0.0	33.2
1894–1898	80.2 (89.5)	0.0	9.5 (10.5)	0.0	89.7
1899–1911	1.2 (3.7)	0.7 (1.9)	29.5 (88.7)	1.9	33.3
	110.5 (70.8)	3.2 (2.1)	40.6 (26.0)	1.9	156.2

Source: Remer, *Foreign Investments,* p. 29.

nance the 1894 war, were not used to modernize the army or build up the military in general.[19]

It cost the Chinese government to borrow. Between 1895 and 1911, the government paid between 4.5 and 5.2 percent on foreign loans. While the rate is considered low, it was still higher than that paid by other countries borrowing similar amounts. The government paid a higher price for the loans in other respects also. For example, foreign banks agreed to charge low interest rates in return for construction rights in China, and in some cases monopolized the supply of materials for construction.[20]

The financial burden of China's foreign loans was so severe that the republic started on shaky grounds. Table 2.6 and 2.7 show the extent of the government's indebtedness and the areas of indebtedness. Table 2.6 supports the generalization that the government was in debtor status at the time of the revolution. Clearly, it was paying out more than was coming in. In fact, from the disastrous Sino-Japanese war on, outpayments were the rule.[21] Table 2.7 shows a detailed accounting of China's balance of international payments, demonstrating again that for the representative period 1902–13 more money was going out of China than was coming in. The net result establishes the indebtedness of the Chinese government.[22]

Taken together, Tables 2.5, 2.6, and 2.7 are but a small representation of the inability of the Chinese government to meet its debts. Working capital simply was insufficient before 1911. Clearly, the Chinese government was ineffective in the economic field. The implications of the government's financial indebtedness became more manifest after the establishment of the Chinese republic in 1912.

Inability to Control Opium Activity

There was opium in China long before the foreigners brought more in, but initially, opium was used mostly for medicinal purposes. With the introduction of tobacco-smoking in China (an American innovation which spread to China by way of Manila in the seventeenth century), opium-smoking—and addiction—increased. According to Fairbank, by the early 1830s there were

Table 2.6

Inpayments and outpayments, 1894–1913

(In millions of Chinese dollars)

Period	Total in payments	Total out payments	Average annual in	Average annual out	Total net in	Total net out	Average annual net in/out
1894–1901	170.2	167.2	21.3	20.9	3.0		0.4
1902–1913	731.8	1,070.3	61.0	89.2		338.5	28.2

Source: Remer, *Foreign Investments*, p. 160.

Table 2.8

Trade in foreign opium after 1858

(1 picul = 133 lbs.)

Source	1863	1867	1879	1888	1897	1905	1911
Open ports	50,087	60,948	82,927	82,612	49,309	51,920	27,758
Other channels	20,000	20,000	20,000	5,000	5,000	5,000	3,000
Total	70,087	80,948	102,927	87,612	54,309	56,920	30,758

Source: Morse, *Trade and Administration*, p. 351.

Table 2.7

Balance of payments for the period 1902–1913

(In millions of Chinese dollars)

Outpayments			Inpayments		
Current items			Current items		
Government debt		89.2	Overseas remittances		150.0
Business investments		69.3	Unrecorded land		
Merchandise imports		631.3	frontier trade		20.0
Gold and silver			Merchandise exports		443.0
imports		2.5	Correction of		
	TOTAL	792.3	exports (5%)		22.2
				TOTAL	635.2
			Capital items		
			Loans of the Chinese		
			government		61.0
			New business		
			investments		52.8
				TOTAL	113.8
Net outpayments on current items		157.1			
Inpayments on capital items		113.8			
Unexplained difference		43.3			

Source: Remer, *Foreign Investments,* p. 220.

"somewhere between two and ten million habitual smokers [in China], many of them government personnel."[23]

The importation of foreign opium hit a peak during the waning years of the Manchu dynasty. Table 2.8 shows the extent of imported opium after 1858. Prior to the revolution, 1879 was the peak year with an estimated 102,927 piculs (1 picul = 133 pounds) of foreign opium imported mainly through the major ports. Between 1863 and 1911, Bengal opium from India accounted for 47.8 percent of all foreign opium, followed closely by Malwa opium (India) at 47.6 percent, and, at a distance, Persian opium at 4.6 percent.[24]

In time, the Chinese themselves became involved in heavy

opium trafficking. Between 1863 and 1906, *native* production was estimated around 376,000 piculs, but more telling, by 1906, native production was six to eight times more than the quantity of imported opium.[25]

The central government's willingness to stop the traffic was questionable since the central government drew revenues from the traffic, officially or unofficially. As Fairbank so aptly puts it:

> The incapacity of the Chinese government to stop the trade was illustrated by the opposite courses following in Ch'ing policy and official practice. Selling and smoking opium had been prohibited by imperial edict in 1729, its importation or domestic production in 1796, and after 1800 these bans were frequently repeated. But official connivance had grown as the trade had grown. Opium paid its way, becoming a new source of corruption.[26]

The Scramble for Concessions

A more threatening situation than the opium traffic was the foreign encroachments of 1898. This development threatened the very existence of the empire and nearly turned China into an international colony.

The scramble for concessions was initiated after the end of the Sino-Japanese war in 1895 basically by Russia's quest for an ice-free port and domination of Manchuria. Playing on Chinese fears of Japan, Russia obtained from China concessions to build the Chinese Eastern (1896) and South Manchurian railways (1898), a secret defensive alliance against Japan (1896) and the lease of the Liaotung Peninsula for twenty-five years with the right to establish a naval base at Port Arthur (1898). Other major powers secured similar leases and spheres of influence. In some cases, the foreign powers simply made a de facto situation legal by invoking a distorted notion of squatter's rights backed by the threat of military repercussions. For example, Russia had in fact occupied Port Arthur without Chinese consent as early as December 1897. Germany had as early as November 1897, forcibly occupied Kiaochow Bay, and thereafter "negotiated" a lease on March 1898, for ninety-nine years, and in April–July, 1898, Weihaiwei

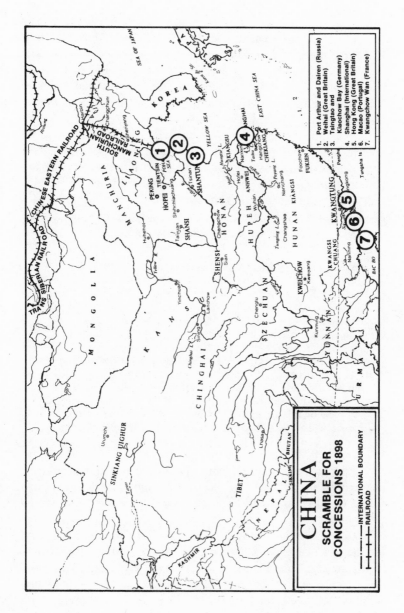

CHINA

SCRAMBLE FOR
CONCESSIONS 1898

---- INTERNATIONAL BOUNDARY
+-+ RAILROAD

1. Port Arthur and Dairen (Russia)
2. Weihai (Great Britain)
3. Tsingtao and
   Kiaochow Bay (Germany)
4. Shanghai (International)
5. Hong Kong (Great Britain)
6. Macao (Portugal)
7. Kwangchow Wan (France)

was leased to England for so long as Port Arthur should remain Russian. In June, England also leased Kowloon, opposite Hong Kong, for ninety-nine years.

The "imperialist penetration," according to Fairbank, "used loans, railways, leased areas, reduced land tariffs, and rights of local jurisdiction, of police power, and of mining exploitation to create in effect 'spheres of influence.' "[27]

In addition to the open ports, leased areas, and spheres of influence, one other practice by the foreign powers indicated the helplessness of the Chinese government: extraterritoriality. By this practice, foreign citizens in China were removed from the jurisdiction of the Chinese judicial system. While the practice dates back to early times, it grew in China as a result of the unequal treaties. An 1843 general resolution, for example, read:

> Whenever a British subject has reason to complain of Chinese he must first proceed to the Consulate and state his grievance. The consul will thereupon inquire into the merits of the case, and do his utmost to arrange it amicably. In like manner, if a Chinese has reason to complain of a British subject, he shall no less listen to his complaint and endeavor to settle it in a friendly manner.... Regarding the punishment of English criminals, the English government will enact the laws necessary to attain that end, and the consul will be empowered to put them in force; and regarding the punishment of Chinese criminals, these will be tried and punished by their own laws, in the way provided for by the correspondence which took place at Nanking, after the concluding of the peace [1842].[28]

Prior to the revolution, there were nineteen countries enjoying the rights and privileges of extraterritoriality,[29] with the United States, Great Britain, and France renouncing the practice between 1943–46.[30]

Extraterritoriality was in effect a slap at Chinese sovereignty, for the practice applied not only to foreign citizens, but also to their property. Thus foreign businesses took advantage of the practice to enlarge the scope of their activities with the minimum amount of Chinese interference and to evade paying taxes to the Chinese government; such as sales taxes, stamp duties, and wine and tobacco taxes. Chinese officials were prohibited from claiming any taxes in the area under foreign control. It is not without reason that Morse labels the period from 1894 to 1911 as a "period of subjection."[31]

Failure of Government Reform Programs

It would be misleading to think that foreign activities in China or the central government's own problems did not produce some changes in the Chinese political system. In 1860, for example, Chinese diplomatic relations were upgraded from provincial control to central control with the establishment of the Tsungli Yamen (Office in General Charge of Affairs Concerning All Foreign Nations). According to Li Chien-nung, "The inauguration of the new Yamen [and other offices] may be considered an unprecedented action, an indication of the Ch'ing [Manchu] government's change of attitude toward foreign countries."[32] In fact, between 1864 and 1894, Chinese statesmen were primarily preoccupied with imitating Western methods in order to save the Chinese empire. China "profited only slightly" from this experience.[33]

The reform program which caught the imagination of China's scholar-officials began in 1894 under the leadership of the Confucian Master, K'ang Yu-wei. It flourished for "One Hundred Days" between June 11 and September 16, 1898, and ended in failure by September 21, 1898. Acting on the advice of the two leading reformers and unwitting forerunners to the revolutionary tide in China, K'ang, and Liang Ch'i-ch'ao, Emperor Kuang Hsu issued a number of reform edicts which would have changed the civil service exam system, promoted agriculture, industry, and commerce, abolished the sinecure appointments in key offices of the central government, encouraged study abroad and would have modernized the army, navy, police, and postal systems. This was K'ang Yu-wei's finest hour.

The thrust of the reform edicts, however, did not go unnoticed by the retired Empress Tz'u Hsi, for the reforms struck at the very existence of the Manchu dynasty. Court and political intrigue followed on the heels of the reform edicts, until finally on September 21, 1898, the empress and her eunuch military bodyguards seized the emperor. When she summoned him to her, she scolded him saying:

> "I have been feeding you and taking care of you for more than twenty years, and yet you listen to the words of these churls to plot against me." ... The empress dowager spat at him. "Stupid son! If I do not exist today, how can you exist tomorrow?" And then the empress' decree was issued to the effect that the emperor was so ill that he could not manage affairs of the state and thus it was necessary for her, the empress, to attend court affairs and to instruct the administration.[34]

At the same time, the arrests and executions of the reformers, K'ang and Liang, were ordered, but both managed to escape to Japan, later to become advocates of a constitutional monarchy in China. Six others including K'ang's brother, were not as fortunate: they were executed. The reform edicts were abrogated.

The reform ideal, nonetheless, was implanted and there being nothing as persistent as an ideal whose time has come, a second far-reaching reform program was initiated in 1901.

The catalyst for the second major reform effort within three years was the failure of the Boxer Rebellion. Some reforms were immediate, such as the creation of still another office for foreign affairs and the reorganization of the military. Other reform edicts were long range in nature, such as the move toward a constitutional monarchy. By 1908, the dynasty had begun a nine-year program which included convening consultative provincial assemblies in 1909 and a national assembly in 1917, which was actually held, however, in 1910.

One other far-reaching reform area involved the educational system. Not only was there an emphasis on training and selecting better government officials, but education abroad was encouraged. This facet of the program was to have dire consequences for the dynasty: most of the students going abroad were destined to fall under the influence of the revolutionaries already overseas, especially in Japan, and returned to form the vanguard of alienated intellectuals *cum* revolutionaries. Finally, in 1905, the traditional civil service exam system was abolished, leading some to conclude that Imperial China really ended at this time and not in 1911.

The reforms of 1901 produced more problems than they could solve. The central government did not have the qualified personnel to man the various facets of the reform program. More importantly, each part of the reform program had an obverse effect on the goal of the empress: the educational program produced revolutionaries; the military reform program produced military forces which later contributed to the rise of warlordism; the administrative program produced a power struggle between the Manchu princes and the Chinese bureaucrats; and, the move toward constitutionalism produced a conflict between a constitutional monarchy and a republic.

The immediate aim of the reform program was to save the Manchu dynasty. The immediate result was revolution. There is some merit in the historian's verdict that "reformers, not revolutionists, mainly prepared the ground for revolution" in China.[35] In the five years preceding the revolution, however, no fewer than seven attempts were made to overthrow the weak Manchu government. That the uprisings were put down was due not to the strength of the central government, but rather to bad planning, timing, or other circumstances. The government was weak and disunited, and the disorganization of the government had its counterpart in the organization of its opponents led by an alienated group of intellectuals.

Inept Ruling Elite

Finally, historians have not been kind in their evaluation of the Manchu emperors' abilities as leaders. Table 2.9 shows some historians' evaluations of the ability of the major Manchu emperors between 1667 and 1912.

In the last ninety years of the dynasty, only one ruler, the Empress Tz'u Hsi, has been considered as a competent ruler, but in a traditional sense—she too was unprepared for the events of the 1890s. During the critical period between China and the West (1840–60), the emperors were considered incompetent.

THE INTELLECTUALS

Revolutions are born in the mind, or, as Crane Brinton succinctly puts it, "no ideas, no revolution."[36] Table 2.10 shows the

Table 2.9
Major Manchu Emperors
(1644–1911)

Name	Reign Dates	Historical Evaluation of Ability to Reign
K'ang Hsi	1667–1722	brilliant and very competent
Yung Cheng	1723–1735	competent
Ch'ien Lung	1736–1796	very competent
Chia Ch'ing	1796–1820	competent
Tao Kuang	1821–1850	incompetent
Hsien Feng	1851–1861	incompetent
Empress Dowager, Tz'u Hsi (Regent)	1861–1871	very competent
T'ung Chih (Empress' son)	1862–1875	incompetent; Empress ruled
Kuang Hsu	1875–1908	incompetent; government actually in hands of Empress
Hsuan T'ung	1908–1912	incompetent; the last Manchu

names of fifty leading Chinese revolutionary intellectuals.[37] Among the fifty revolutionaries identified, two were doctors, one was a philosopher, fourteen were teachers, six were authors or writers, two were scientists, four were poets or painters, fourteen were editors or publishers, and six were lawyers (the count includes some who made their reputations in one, two, or more fields). Table 2.10 needs further explanation of two of the categories: indicator of government allegiance, particularly those designated as "government sponsored students;" and, finally, a word on Sun Yat-sen's revolutionary organization, the Common Alliance Society (T'ung-meng hui).

Government Sponsored Students

Japan's victory over China in 1894–95 served as the catalyst for the creation of a new kind of education and educated man in China. Prior to the introduction of Western learning, Chinese education was determined by Confucian principles. Generally, Con-

Table 2.10

Some Chinese revolutionary intellectuals

Name	Intellectual Background	Indicator Government Allegiance	Revolutionary Behavior
K'ang Yu-wei			see fn. 37
Liang Ch'i-ch'ao			Organizer of Tung-meng hui
Sun Yat-sen	West. educated; M.D.		
T'an Ssu-t'ung	philosopher	high cabinet post	urged revolt against emperor; executed, 1898, reform failure
Ch'iu Chin	Japan ed; teacher; journalist	husband held official post	leader of revolutionary society; beheaded
Huang Hsing	*sheng-yuan* (B.A.)	government sponsored student at military academy	founded and belonged to various revolutionary organizations; led uprising; second only to Sun Yat-sen in T'ung-meng hui
Tsou Jung	Japan ed; author		wrote books and articles on revolution
Chang Ping-lin	philologist; teacher; editor	staff member of famous provincial governor	editor of revolutionary newspaper; T'ung-meng hui member
Wen T'ing-shih	*chin-shih* (Ph.D.)	expositor at Hanlin Academy	conspired against Empress
Wu Wo-yao	novelist		critical of government in novels
Wu Chih-hui	Japan ed; *chu-jen* (M.A.)	helped government establish college and a military school	helped to form an educational society which fronted as a revolutionary center; member of T'ung-meng hui

Table 2.10   (continued)

Name	Intellectual Background	Indicator Government Allegiance	Revolutionary Behavior
Chang Chi	Japan ed.	government sponsored student	member of T'ung-meng hui
Feng Tzu-yu	journalist; Japan ed.	government sponsored student	charter member of T'ung-meng hui
Chang Shih-chao	editor	government sponsored student	editor of revolutionary journal
Ts'ai Yuan-pei	Hanlin scholar *chin-shih*	Hanlin Academy	member, T'ung-meng hui
Sung Chiao-jen	editor; translator; Japan ed.		co-founder, T'ung-meng hui
Liao Chung-k'ai	U.S. & Japan ed.; *sheng-yuan,* translator	staff of border defense commission	member, T'ung-meng hui
Ma Chun-wu	chemist; Japan ed.		supporter of Sun Yat-sen; wrote speeches advocating overthrow of Manchu
Liu Shih-p'ei	editor; teacher, *chu-jen,* publisher	staff member of secretariat	member, T'ung-meng hui
Chu Chih-hsin	teacher; Japan ed.	government sponsored student	member, T'ung-meng hui
Wang Ching-wei	*chu-jen,* law degree from Japan	government sponsored student	member, T'ung-meng hui
Hu Han-min	writer; teacher; lawyer; Japan ed.	government sponsored student	member, T'ung-meng hui
Wang Ch'ung-hui	LL.M., Yale editor; translator; Japan ed.	diplomatic aide to Hague conference, 1907	drafted revolutionary statements for Sun Yat-sen
Chen Chiung-ming	*sheng-yuan* lawyer, editor	advisory council for provincial govt.	member, T'ung-meng hui
T'ang Hua-lung	*chin-shih* teacher; Japan ed.	clerk in ministry of civil affairs	belonged to revolutionary organization

Table 2.10 (continued)

Name	Intellectual Background	Indicator Government Allegiance	Revolutionary Behavior
ᴋu Ying-fen	*sheng-yuan* teacher; Japan ed.	government sponsored student	member, T'ung-meng hui
ᵀsou Lu	teacher		participated in uprisings
ᴄh'en Ch'i-mei			member, T'ung-meng hui
ᵉng K'eng	teacher	dean of Whampoa military school	member, T'ung-meng hui
ᴌi Lieh-chun	Japan ed.	director of provincial military school	member, T'ung-meng hui
ᵀai Chi-t'ao	journalist; teacher; Japan ed.		member, T'ung-meng hui
ᴴsiao Fo-ch'eng	lawyer; editor		member, T'ung-meng hui
ᴄh'en Shao-pai	editor		established the first Chinese newspaper to openly advocate revolution against Manchus
ᴄhan Ta-pei	editor		wrote revolutionary articles
ᴄhang Chi-luan	editor	government sponsored student	member, T'ung-meng hui
ᴄhang Mo-chun	feminist; educator; poet	father, a govt. official	member, T'ung-meng hui
ᴄhang Shih-chao	editor; lawyer; teacher		published radical revolutionary articles
ᴄhao Heng-t'i	Japan ed.		member, T'ung-meng hui
ᴄh'en Shu-jen	painter		member, T'ung-meng hui
ᴄhu Cheng	lawyer; teacher; Japan ed.		member, T'ung-meng hui

Table 2.10 (continued)

Name	Intellectual Background	Indicator Government Allegiance	Revolutionary Behavior
Ho Hsiang-ning	painter; Japan ed.		member, T'ung-meng hui
Hsieh Ch'ih	*sheng-yuan* teacher	asst. secretary bureau of trade	member, T'ung-meng hui
Li Shih-tseng	biologist; France ed.	attache in France	member, T'ung-meng hui
Lin Sen	ed. by missionaries	Chinese Maritime Customs	member, T'ung-meng hui
Ma Hsu-lun	teacher; poet		belonged to various revolutionary organizations
Su Man-shu	teacher; Japan ed.		wrote revolutionary articles
T'an Chen	Japan ed.		member, T'ung-meng hui
T'ang Erh-ho	Japan-trained physician		joined various revolutionary organizations
Ting Wei-fen	publisher; Japan ed.		member, T'ung-meng hui
Wu Yu-chang	publisher; Japan ed.		member, T'ung-meng hui

Source: Boorman (Ed.), *Biographical Dictionary,* 4 vol. This list, of course, is not all-inclusive.

fucian learning was a tool of imperial ideological control. The aim was to preserve the status quo generation after generation. The Sino-Japanese war began to change ideas about education in China.

Prior to the revolution, the reforms which were attempted in various areas which we have noted had repercussions against the central government. Education produced one such obverse result. As early as 1872, the government began sending students abroad in hopes of developing both the sciences and technology. Between 1872 and 1875, 120 students were sent to the United States for such education.[38]

Chinese students sent abroad were dependents of the government and were awarded official ranks and appointments to the government upon their return. Once accepted to study abroad, students could not withdraw before their education was completed, nor could they seek naturalization abroad. Students could not hold a job without the government's consent.

In 1904, there were thirteen hundred students abroad (mainly in Japan), but after the traditional civil service examination was abolished in 1905, the number jumped to fifteen thousand. By 1906, as the number of students studying abroad increased, the need for regulating the government's system of financing also demanded attention. After 1906, a uniform annual stipend was established. For example, students sent to England received £192; those sent to France and Belgium, fr.4,800; to Germany, RM3,840; and to the United States, $960. The stipend included tuition and medical and travel expenses.[39]

What effect did education abroad have on the returning students? Table 2.10 shows that twenty-six of the fifty revolutionaries had some contact with Western or Japanese learning prior to the revolution. In the sample, in only one case, that of Liu Shih-p'ei, did a returned student not follow through by participating in the revolution against the Manchus.[40] From the data, this is all one can say. However, the literature does suggest at least three other important developments.

First, foreign-educated students experienced a sense of frustration once they returned home. Some apparently were dissatisfied with the treatment they received at home or else they were dissatisfied with the jobs to which they were assigned. The returned students expressed their dissatisfaction through a journal, the *World Chinese Student's Journal,* in which they bitterly criticized the old regime. By 1910, the *Journal* was calling for the complete reorganization of the system by which students were assigned to particular jobs.[41]

A second point perhaps implicit in the statistics of the authoritative Y. C. Wang is the discovery of the social sciences by the students abroad. At the outset, the government stressed the physical sciences so much so that by 1909, 33.9 percent of those educated in the United States were engineers, medical doctors, and agriculturists. Up until 1906, only 5.6 percent chose a field within the social sciences, but by 1909, 19.7 percent had indicated an interest in these disciplines. Law (1.5 percent in 1905, but 8.2 percent in 1909) and political science (1.6 percent in 1905, but 7.7 percent in 1909) were the more popular fields of study in the social sciences. In the list of revolutionaries, only two, Ma Chun-wu, a chemist, and Li Shih-tseng, a biologist, had scientific backgrounds, and if the two physicians, Sun Yat-sen and T'ang Erh-ho, are included, then only four of the fifty had a nonsocial science educational background.

Third, Chalmers Johnson has suggested that one possible indicator for measuring dissynchronization of a social system on the verge of revolution is the sales and circulation figures for ideological newspapers.[42] Between 1903 and the revolution, and as a consequence of foreign education, student publications flourished throughout China. Most of the revolutionary publications were written by returned students from Japan, including the *Hupeh Student's Circle,* the *New Hunan,* and *Twentieth-Century China.* In Shanghai alone there were more than one hundred revolutionary journals published in 1904 and 1905.[43]

According to Gasster:

> There were scores of these journals. Some were published for several years, others for only one or two issues. Most were run on a shoestring; a few had wealthy backers. A magazine would run out of funds or be closed by the police and then start again with a new support or under a new name. Copies were circulated among the students in Japan or smuggled back into China. . . . These journals had no single message and elicited no single response. But there were passionate, and they aroused passions.[44]

One of the most famous of the revolutionary writings was Tsou Jung's *The Revolutionary Army,* in which he passionately declared:

To sweep away thousands of years of despotism, to throw off thousands of years of slavery, to wipe out the five million barbarian Manchus, to wash away the shame of two hundred and sixty years of cruelty and oppression, to make the China mainland clean once again, if every descendant of [the legendary emperor] Huang Ti [becomes a] George Washington there will be a return to life from the eighteen layers of hells, and a rising to heaven . . . the most revered and exalted, the one and only, the supreme and unparalleled goal that we call revolution.[45]

Recalling the English, American, and French revolutions, and also the writings of Rousseau, Montesquieu, Mill, Washington, and Napoleon, Tsou concluded:

Revolt! Revolt! If successful, we live; if not, we die. Do not retreat. Do not stand neutral. Do not be irresolute. Now is the time. Now is the time. . . . Let us, hand in hand, comrades together, carry out this revolutionary principle.[46]

Liang Ch'i-ch'ao

The unwitting resident-intellectual of the Chinese revolution was K'ang Yu-wei's protégé during the abortive 1898 reform movement, Liang Ch'i-ch'ao. Liang was a precocious child, raised and educated in the classics. At age sixteen, he had received the *chu-jen* (M.A.), and one year later (1890), he met K'ang Yu-wei in Canton and enrolled in K'ang's school. By 1893, he had become K'ang's teaching assistant, and in that year, both went to Peking to take the *chin-shih* (Ph.D.) examination, and both failed. Remaining in Peking, he became a secretary to the influential English missionary, Dr. Timothy Richards. From Richards, he learned of the achievements of science and technology in the West—and the world. Wrote Liang:

God was breaking down the barriers between all nations by railways, steamers, and telegraphs, in order that all should live in peace and happiness as brethren of one family.[47]

Prior to 1898, Liang began to make his career as a journalist-editor. Richards' influence was clear: Liang's editorials pleaded for rapid industrialization, Western education, the translation of Western books, and the implementation of a constitutional form of government. During the short-lived "One Hundred Days Reforms," he became the director of the translation bureau. Until 1898, he was nothing more than K'ang Yu-wei's alter ego.

After 1898, K'ang withdrew from politics and devoted his remaining years to writing about the advantages of a constitutional monarchy patterned after the British system. In time he founded a society for constitutional government. K'ang's effect on the revolution is difficult to determine. While it has been suggested that reformers, not revolutionaries, paved the way to revolution, a statement with much merit, K'ang's role is difficult to assess especially since his major work relegates a constitutional monarchy to second place behind the "rule of the people." By 1902 at the earliest and by 1911 at the latest, he was preoccupied with developing his ideas on utopianism of which no more need be said. What is important is that he generally stopped being a force in the reform movement after 1898.

Liang Ch'i-ch'ao thus became the main force behind the constitutionalists. First his protégé, and then his peer, Liang eventually replaced K'ang Yu-wei as the spokesman for the reformers. While it is difficult to characterize Liang as a revolutionary because of his loyalty to the emperor and his membership in the Emperor Protection Society, his ideas were very revolutionary. Personal rights, popular representation, and voting, for example, were unheard of in traditional Chinese society and politics. But more than this, after a trip to the United States, he began to question whether the Chinese people were ready for self-government. He eventually came to the conclusion that China's survival was dependent not on new institutions, but on a political awakening of the people. A constitutional monarchy seemed the perfect compromise, and so in 1902 he founded the *Renovation of the People,* the constitutional monarchists' periodical. By 1905, the battle of the words began between Liang's *Renovation* and Sun Yat-sen's Common Alliance Society's *People's News.*

Intellectually, Liang rationalized his shift from revolutionary views to moderate views thusly: "If my viewpoint guided by my

conscience today is like this, then I do according to my conscience of today; if my conscience of tomorrow receives some
further enlightenment, then I will do according to my conscience
of tomorrow."[48] After the abortive reform movement, he had
turned to Hobbes, Spinoza, Rousseau, and others for tomorrow's
enlightenment. He felt strongly against despotism, but he seriously
doubted the Chinese people's ability to govern themselves. Liang
was clearly inconsistent up to the revolution, but his influence and
his pen made him a formidable opponent of the revolutionists.
Wang has summarized Liang's weaknesses and failures well, and
thereby reveals something about Liang's inconsistencies. First,
Liang possessed an excellent writing style, mixing Chinese history
with Western experiences masterfully. The 120 pages of his periodical, however, betray his preference for Western civilization. A
second reason for his popularity lay in his ability to discern what
China's growing intellectual class wanted. One issue, for example,
contained the following:

> ... three pictures of Garibaldi, Cavour, and Mazzini; two
> pictures, with notations, of Chinese schools in Japan; selec-
> tions from "Discourses on the New People" from a history
> of Western economic thought, a history of Chinese despo-
> tism, and a history of Chinese thought; biographies of Gari-
> baldi, Cavour, and Mazzini: an article on Chinese histori-
> cal geography; a study of Chinese classics, penned by Chang
> Ping-lin, seeking partly to elucidate ancient Chinese usage
> by way of Japanese grammar; editorials on current world
> events; historical notes based on Gibbons' *Decline and Fall
> of the Roman Empire*; literary criticism dealing with Homer
> and Chinese poets; a Reader's Forum with replies to inqui-
> ries about Herbert Spencer and medieval Europe; current
> events, Chinese and Western, and a review of Japanese
> publications.[49]

Third, Liang was initially critical of the Manchu dynasty,
first advocating revolution and then a constitutional monarchy.
Fourth, he was a master tactician. As a political propagandist urging revolt, he felt that certain symbolic words were necessary to
keep the image of revolution passionately alive. During this phase
of his propagandizing, words such as "revolution," "political assassination," and "democracy" helped him to achieve the shock effect

which he sought. The revolutionaries, however, distrusted him, and they broke up one of his meetings. Someone threw a sandal which hit him on the cheek.[50] Nonetheless, between 1898 and 1903, Michael Gasster believes that Liang probably did more to push the revolution than even Sun Yat-sen himself.

Sun Yat-sen and the Common Alliance Society

One person not given to ambivalence was Sun Yat-sen. From the founding of the first truly revolutionary organization dedicated to the overthrow of the Manchu dynasty, the Hsing Chung-hui (Revive China Society: 1894), through the T'ung-meng hui (Common Alliance Society), and finally, the Kuomintang (Nationalist party), Sun Yat-sen "served as the rallying center; he was both midwife and guardian to these antidynastic bodies."[51]

Born of a farming family in south China in 1866, and educated initially in the Confucian classics, Sun was exposed to Western learning by the time he was thirteen years old. At thirteen, he left China for Hawaii, where his brother was living, and at age seventeen, he was converted to Christianity. In 1892, when he was twenty-six, he graduated "with great distinction" from the Hong Kong College of Medicine for Chinese. By now, Sun was steeped in revolutionary propaganda.

Shortly after graduation, Sun attempted to work for change within the system, but rebuffed by Chinese officials and dismayed by China's initial failures against the Japanese in 1894, Sun organized his first revolutionary organization, the Revive China Society on November, 1894. According to Lyon Sharman:

> In Hong Kong they opened a shop, which was really a sub-office. They then proceeded with the risky business of buying ammunition and enlisting. In Hong Kong they bought pistols, rifles, even dynamite. There also they recruited men. A consignment of six hundred pistols, shipped as casks of cement, was discovered . . . and the secret was out. . . . Their headquarters were raided September 9, 1895.[52]

Sought by the Manchu authorities, Sun met Dr. James Cantlie as he was about to set sail for the United States. Dr. Cantlie had taught Sun medicine. In June 1896, Sun Yat-sen sailed for San

Francisco, and for the next sixteen years he was forced to carry on his revolutionary activities outside of China. Sun was disappointed with the Chinese living abroad, finding them too conservative in the United States and inactive elsewhere. From the United States he went to England where an attempted kidnapping by the Manchu legation helped to make him an internationally known figure. In July 1897, he returned by way of Canada to Japan.

Japan proved to be the battleground for two groups which dominated Chinese politics in the next two decades: K'ang Yu-wei and Liang Ch'i-ch'ao's reformers (constitutional monarchists) and Sun's Revive China Society (republicans). Sun was able to recruit heavily among the Chinese students studying in Japan. With the help of students, secret societies, and convinced revolutionists, Sun's organizational activities spread to Southeast Asia, especially Hanoi, Saigon, and Siam. Propaganda journals were established, the most influential being the *Chinese Daily* founded by Ch'en Shao-pai in Hong Kong in 1899. The next phase was direct action, but here Sun was not as successful: his only attempted revolt ended in failure in 1900. In the next few years he again took up traveling, first for recruiting and then for raising funds. In San Francisco, for example, he sold revolutionary bonds for $10, raising $4,000 from the local Chinese community.[53]

In 1904–5, Japan was again the catalyst for the revolution abroad. Japan's victory over Russia in 1904–5 stimulated Chinese students in Japan, and especially the revolutionary intellectuals already in Japan, such as Huang Hsing and Sung Chiao-jen. Acting on Sun's suggestion, the various organizations in Japan amalgamated into one revolutionary alliance, the Common Alliance Society. When the alliance held its first formal meeting in Tokyo on August 20, 1905, it counted more than three hundred students and young revolutionaries among its members.

The alliance's manifesto contained four main provisions: (1) drive out the Tartars (Manchus), (2) restore China to the Chinese, (3) establish a republic, and (4) equalize land ownership.[54] Members had to sign an oath which read:

The person joining the alliance from _____ province, _____district, by name _____, has sworn before heaven

to drive out the Manchu barbarians, restore China to the
Chinese, create a republic, and equalize land rights, and keep
his good faith, and maintain his loyalty from beginning to
end. If he should break his promise, he will be punished by
other members as they see fit.[55]

The organization of the alliance included a department of
general affairs, a judicial department, and a deliberation department. The director-general was Sun Yat-sen. A council of
thirty oversaw the local branches established in China's various
provinces. With headquarters in Tokyo, the alliance established
a division to oversee alliance activities overseas, with emphasis being on Hong Kong and Southeast Asia (Singapore, Kuala Lumpur,
Penang, British Malaya, and the Dutch East Indies). By March
1907, Hanoi had become the center for military training. Supplies
were sent to Hanoi by the alliance office in Tokyo. In the five
years before the revolution, the alliance unsuccessfully tried no less
than eleven times to overthrow the Manchus by military coups.[56]

The value of these military uprisings is questionable. Sun Yat-
sen himself did not believe that the Chinese revolution was won
by military insurrections, but one historian writes that "these immature armed attempts had one wholesome effect: they served to
arouse the people to the necessity of revolution."[57]

With the improved organization of the alliance came improved propaganda techniques. The new propaganda journal was
known as *The People* (*Min-pao*). Chang Chi was appointed as its
publisher, a natural choice since the paper was published in Japan
and Chang was fluent in Japanese. Chang was an intellectual
whose allegiance to the government came as a result of being a
government-sponsored student, but who later joined the revolution.
The major points stressed by the propaganda machine of the alliance included learning from the Japanese experience with modernization, pointing out the corrupt and extravagant ways of the
alien Manchus, weak reform attempts, foreign encroachments,
wars, and of course, the advantages of a republican form of
government.

The People's greatest moment came when it discussed Sun
Yat-sen's blueprint for the republic, the *San Min Chu I,* or the
Three Principles of the People. The *Three Principles* was Sun's

major propaganda effort, so much so that propagandizing was considered as one of his two major contributions to the revolution. Raising money was the other. Although the *San Min Chu I* was not published in complete form before the revolution, the principles guided Sun's actions and so can be discussed here briefly.

The *Three Principles* were known as nationalism, democracy, and the people's livelihood. According to Sun, he received his inspiration from Abraham Lincoln's Gettysburg Address: "government of the people, by the people, and for the people."[58] The principle of nationalism dominated the pages of *Min-pao* from 1905 on. The other two principles were mentioned, but never fully elucidated.[59] Nationalism at first simply meant the overthrow of the Manchus, and democracy was something that Western countries had. If China were to become a democratic country, however, it could be accomplished by going through three stages: stage one was the military phase by which the alliance would continue to direct the revolution; stage two was the period of political tutelage during which the military government would educate the Chinese people in the meaning of democracy; and stage three, the final and constitutional phase. During the third stage the military government would be replaced by a national government. The third principle, livelihood, was an amalgam of Western ideas, especially socialist ideas, and those of Henry George and his thesis that social ills could be traced to the private sector's appropriation of land values.[60]

This, then, is the outline of his principles before the revolution. After the revolution, he modified them as his knowledge of each one increased. His personal magnetism, rhetoric, self-assurance, and selfless dedication to the revolution cannot be denied, although his political and military leadership qualities have been questioned.

As may be expected when intellectuals band together, the alliance was plagued by internal conflict. In its formative years, disagreements arose over ideology, personality conflicts, and tactics. The major problem, however, was the struggle for the leadership of the revolution.

Sun Yat-sen's main challenger was the classical scholar turned revolutionary, Chang Ping-lin. Chang was the editor of *The*

People, the alliance's propaganda periodical. In his capacity as editor of *The People,* Chang carried the revolutionary party's verbal conflict with Liang Ch'i-ch'ao's *Renovation. The People* was also a major instrument for recruiting members for the alliance.

In the area of tactics, Sun disagreed with Chang's fervent belief in political assassination. Chang, in turn, was greatly dissatisfied with Sun's leadership as a result of the unsuccessful revolts attempted by the alliance. Chang held Sun personally responsible for the military defeats, but even more scathing was Chang's attack on Sun's integrity: Chang accused Sun of misappropriating party funds for his own use.[61] Chang eventually joined a rival faction while maintaining his membership in the alliance. The net effect of this internal conflict was that Chang's faction gained ascendancy in Southeast Asia, eclipsing Sun's influence there to the extent that Sun was expelled from the region. In mid-1909, a disillusioned Sun underwent his usual therapy when things were going badly: he left on a fund-raising tour of Europe and the United States. In his absence, the revolution fell into the hands of two other capable intellectuals, Hu Han-min and Huang Hsing.

Sun's problems were not over yet. Feeling that the revolution needed a dramatic event, he summoned Hu and Huang to Penang, Malaysia, and planned a new military uprising: the Canton coup of April 27, 1911. When the Penang officials found out what Sun was up to they expelled him, and again, in late 1910, he set off for another fund-raising trip to Europe and the United States. Sun raised $77,000 for what resulted in an abortive revolt, but again his fund raising was outstanding.

The Canton uprising was the alliance's biggest and most costly affair. Not only had it taken place in one of the most important cities in China, but it had also bouyed the enthusiasm of the overseas Chinese. After the failure of the Canton uprising, Sun remained in the United States and continued to raise funds for the revolution. Alliance headquarters were shifted from Japan to Shanghai, where the revolutionaries enjoyed protection in the foreign settlement. In time, the revolutionaries also used the Russian concession in Hankow for their activities. It was in the Russian concession, in fact, that the accidental explosion set off the revolution. Sun Yat-sen read about the revolution in an American newspaper while traveling by train from Denver to Kansas City.[62]

The conflict among the intellectuals never endangered their objective. While most of their disagreements were over tactics and personality conflicts, they nonetheless agreed that overthrowing the Manchus was the major objective. However, while they did bring about the revolution, the roots for dissension were already present when the republic was proclaimed.

THE SOCIETY

Racial Antagonisms

Genealogically, the Manchus were related to the Jurched tribes of Tungusic stock, and so perhaps distant cousins of such other alien rulers of China as the Mongols. Geographically, the Manchus lived in the area known today as Manchuria, and were primarily hunters and fishermen. In 1644, the Manchus, who had established a close relationship with Ming China, invaded China, and ruled until 1911. That the Manchus were not Chinese racially was not lost on the revolutionaries. This distinction had first been noted by Wang Fu-chih (1619–92) and other anti-Manchu intellectuals during the early years of the Manchu conquest of China.[63] The distinction was rediscovered by the revolutionaries, and thus became a major component of alliance propaganda: "Prejudice is mightier than reason in stirring people to action."[64] Racial solidarity became an effective propaganda weapon of the revolution, pitting the Chinese against the Manchus. According to one source:

As far as the Revolution of 1911 was concerned, the doctrine of racial unity was the chief weapon the revolutionists used against the Manchu government. It was a sharp wedge driven between the Manchus and the Chinese, and was the cornerstone of the theory of revolution preached in the early years. There were at that time a host of revolutionary writers who daily inculcated in the minds of the Chinese people the racial distinction between the governing and the governed classes. These men published dailies and pamphlets on the central thesis of racial distinction. . . . The success or failure of the movement relied on whether or not the revolutionary leaders were able to bring home to the people the idea of racial unity or solidarity of the Chinese.[65]

The first two statements in the alliance's manifesto reflected this prejudice: drive out the Manchus and restore China to the Chinese.

The Manchus were a minority ruling elite in China, and because of this, they never relaxed the distinction between conquerors and subjects. Military garrisons subdued the native Chinese, and interracial marriages were forbidden. The main arena of conflict, however, was in the government, where the Manchus dominated the inner circles. Prior to the revolution, tensions between Manchu and Chinese officials in government increased appreciably. Thus, it was reported that:

> On the waiting list for each ministry are more than a thousand persons, and the Manchu and Chinese office seekers will not even talk to each other. In the offices, the Manchus are very domineering and arrogant toward their Chinese associates, and the latter can only bear their insults in silence.[66]

The intellectuals bitterly criticized the Manchu government for its reluctance in following through with various reform programs. They warned the Chinese people from becoming duped by the pseudoefforts of the Manchu government to establish a constitutional monarchy. Such a move would provide for the equality of Manchus and Chinese, something the Manchus would never allow as conquerors of China. According to one intellectual destined to play an important role in the Chinese Revolution, Wang Ching-wei, the proposed constitution was really a move to remove power from the provinces and local levels and to concentrate power in the hands of the central government. The reason, Wang offered, was ominous: it was the "inevitable result of a minority race controlling a majority race."[67] On the surface, Wang's charge had a ring of truth to it. Since the Opium War, there had been a steady decentralization of power, a devolution of authority from the central to provincial areas. Both the T'ai-p'ing and Boxer rebellions had further weakened the central government's ability to govern, accelerating this phenomenon. With this background in mind, a constitutional monarchy made sense to the Manchus, for the problem of growing regionalism would be stemmed. Above all, it would insure the survival of Manchu domination of the native Chinese. Actually, Wang's analysis stretched some historical truths. Decentralization was a way of life in China even when dynasties were in the hands of native Chinese monarchs, but propaganda being propaganda, history was used to feed a passion, a prejudice, not truth.

The revolutionaries' propaganda, however, was eventually overtaken by history. In 1908, a constitution was adopted, and the first article gave an indication of things to come. The emperor or empress was considered sacred and inviolable, and was to enjoy all of the traditional despotic powers under a constitutional framework. Petitions for establishing a national parliament were rejected. As if to lend credence to the revolutionists' arguments that the constitution was intended to keep a minority race in power, the first cabinet appointed by the regent in 1911 consisted of eight Manchus, one Mongol bannerman, and only four Chinese. Five of the eight Manchus belonged to the royal family, making plausible the designation as, "the royal cabinet." According to Li Chiennung, "Had the members of the royal family been men of ability, the selection still might have been justified, but practically all of them were inane, unprincipled, muddlers, ignorant of world affairs."[68]

The Ignorant Nobility

One of the major functions of the nobility was to provide the throne with heir-apparents. But once an heir-apparent was designated, the remaining princes were kept ignorant of state affairs. They were prohibited from any contact with high provincial officials for fear of collusion. Complete ignorance certainly diminished their interest and influence in political matters.[69] Princes were not allowed to exercise any of the emperor's powers, share his confidences, nor participate in policy matters. They also were kept out of high offices in the government structure. Their titles, however, did entitle them to privileges far greater than their duties or responsibilities. They were given room and board by the government. In sum,

> More than three hundred and fifty years of propagation, well protected from the acute attack of economic insufficiency to which common people were subjected, gave the House of Nurachi [the founder of the Manchu dynasty] thousands of

rice eaters with most of them making rice consumption their principal life work.[70]

The education of the princes was under complete control of the central government. Supervised by an Imperial Clan Court, the princes were given special examinations which meant next to nothing. The court, in fact, was more of a social instrument than an educational institution. By keeping the princes well fed and amused, the government thus hoped to divert their attention from policy matters. In the end, the government succeeded beyond its expectations. After the Boxer catastrophe, the Kuang-hsu emperor said of the princes:

> Since the beginning of the Imperial Dynasty, the number of serviceable men from the Imperial Clan has surpassed all other previous dynasties. All the Imperial Clansmen would abide by laws and add glories to the records of the Clan. But, unfortunately, of late, the tendency is toward decadence. . . . Those not holding positions often indulge themselves in loafing and are even influenced by political rebels and religious heresy and act fanatically without restraint. This is a disgrace to the Imperial Clan. The Court of Imperial Clan is hereby ordered to supervise them strictly and at all times. If there be those who voluntarily believe in political and religious heresies, heavy punishment shall be their lot.[71]

What were the political and religious heresies of the princes, and how could anyone accused of such misdeeds be allowed to assume a major role in the movement to oust militarily superior foreigners from China? This question may be answered by taking into account China's political, economic, and social environment in the years between 1898 and 1900. We have already discussed the foreign encroachments upon China in 1898, and we cited the economic condition of the central government. We have also mentioned in passing that China is a famine-prone country, and in the years preceding the Boxer uprising, the country was devastated by a famine. By late 1897, vagabonds were roaming throughout China, forming gangs and mobs wherever they went. Unemployment and an increase in opium smoking and the opium trade further increased the consternation of the central government.

It is against this background that a secret society, called the Boxers (supposedly because they practiced their own form of Chinese boxing) arose. The Boxers were noted for their reliance on magic based on Taoistic sorcery. One of their rituals called for reciting an incantation three times, breathing through clenched teeth, foaming at the mouth, and supposedly becoming possessed by the spirits. Their attraction to the princes, however, was in their claim to supernatural powers which gave them immunity to bullets.[72] While they were initially antidynastic (thus some writers have referred to the event as a rebellion quite correctly), in time they changed to support of the dynasty and became decidedly antiforeign. Their slogan was "Support the Ch'ing; destroy the foreigner."

It was the Boxers' beliefs that primarily attracted the princes initially and the court subsequently to the Boxers' cause. When the uprising began, and pillaging and murder increased, especially the murder of Chinese Christians, the antiforeign princes convinced the empress dowager of their invulnerability. Fully involved with obtaining leases in China, the foreign governments took seventeen months before they recognized the Boxers' intentions. By that time, in late 1899, the Boxers had swept through north China, burning missionary places and slaughtering Chinese Christians. The Boxers, however, still were not actively supported by the Manchus who put up token opposition to them. But there were some princes and other high officials who encouraged the Boxers.

By June 1900, the foreigners had had it with Boxer atrocities and Manchu appeasement. On June 13, the Boxers entered Peking and wantonly slaughtered sixty-one foreigners and Chinese Christians and wounded one hundred fifty others.[73] Still the empress hesitated. Finally, on June 17, Prince Tuan convinced her that the foreigners were intent on replacing her with the emperor, and two days later, the court ordered the Boxers organized under the government, and to continue their resistance to the foreigners. War, in effect, had been declared between China and the foreign powers. The pro-Boxer princes were given command of the Boxers, and logistical help was provided.[74]

Neither the Boxers nor the Chinese government was any match for the international forces of the foreign governments. On

September 7, 1901, the Boxer Protocol was signed ending the diplomatic phase of the war. However, in anticipating the demands of the allies for punishing the superstitious princes, the Chinese

Table 2.11

Manchu Princes and their fate

Title and Name	Penalty Determined by Protocol
Prince Tuan	imprisonment with possibility of decapitation
Prince Chuang	sentenced to commit suicide
Prince I	imprisoned
Prince Tsai Ying	imprisoned
Prince Tsai Lien	placed under house arrest
Duke Tsai Lan	imprisoned with possibility of decapitation
Duke Ying Nien	sentenced to commit suicide
Imperial High Commissioner Kang I	died before sentencing
Governor Yu Hsien	decapitation
Grand Councillor Chao Shu-ch'iao	sentenced to commit suicide
Minister Li Ping-heng	died before sentencing
Minister Hsu Tung	died before sentencing
High Official Hsu Ch'eng-yu	executed
High Official Ch'i Hsui	executed

Source: Tan, *Boxer Catastrophe*, pp. 137–43 and 215–23.

court, in deliberations with the allies, decreed various punishments for the participants. Among the provisions of the protocol were such items as prohibition for five years of the importation of arms and ammunition; the legation quarter in Peking was to be reserved for the exclusive residence of foreigners; Chinese and Manchus were prohibited, upon pain of death, from joining any antiforeign societies; and monuments were to be erected in each of the foreign international settlements which had been "desecrated" by Boxer atrocities.

Finally, China was assessed a $333 million indemnity, which it was expected to pay from such internal revenue producing sources as the maritime customs tax, internal customs tax, the salt gabelle, increasing import duties by 5 percent, and tax on any other goods which had not been taxed. The indemnity was payable in forty years, in gold, at an interest rate which would eventually double the principal amount owed.[75] "The Boxer rising," wrote Fairbank, "and the Protocol marked the nadir of the Ch'ing dynasty's foreign relations and left little hope for its long continuance."[76]

For its part the United States began remitting a part of its share of the indemnity for the expressed purpose of helping China finance student educational programs abroad. The funds were to be the source for sending abroad students who would later become the vanguard of the Chinese revolution. The remission of parts of the Boxer indemnity also were used to establish Tsinghua University in Peking, which along with Peking University formed the focal point of higher education in China during the period of the revolution and thereafter.

Part Two:
The Turning Point

3

Republican and Warlord Interregnums

REPUBLICAN POLITICS, 1912–1916

The Revolution of 1911

The revolution finally came to China—accidentally.[1] The area of Wuhan (composed of the cities of Wuch'ang, Hanyang and Hankow) was the site selected by the alliance for the uprising. Initially planned for October 6, 1911, it was postponed to October 16 because local officials discovered the plot. However, the revolution was prematurely launched on October 9 when a bomb accidentally exploded in the Russian concession at Hankow where some alliance members had hidden. Worse yet, the premature explosion found the alliance without any leaders present to direct the revolt.[2] The business of directing the uprising fell into the hands of some Manchu and Chinese soldiers who had secretly joined the alliance, and whose names had become known to the loyal Manchu army. On October 10, the anti-Manchu soldiers, fearing for their lives and without too much hope of succeeding, attacked and captured a major ammunition depot. This unexpected turn of events frightened the loyal army which just as unexpectedly abandoned the city and fled in disorder and retreat. Now, instead of a Sun Yat-sen (who was in the United States) or some other revolutionary leader, the leadership of the revolution fell to a former Chinese officer, Li Yuan-hung. Instead of a civilian government succeeding to leadership, a military government was established. In time, Li's military government brought some semblance of stability to the area, gaining for itself the general approval of the foreign consulates in Hankow. For these reasons, one can agree with Yu's assessment that the "leadership in the revolutionary movement passed from the hands of the [alliance]. The revolutionists had won the battle but lost the war."[3]

The initial success of the uprising led provincial authorities in south and west China to declare their independence from the Manchu government. With the exception of six provinces in north China still under the control of the Manchu government, the remaining provincial authorities declared their allegiance to the "Republic of China." Unable to transport fresh troops throughout the country now in revolt, a weary Manchu army fought stubbornly for two months. By November, the Manchu navy surrendered to the insurgents. On December 12, Nanking fell to the revolutionaries, whereupon the city was selected as the site of a new provisional government. By early December the Manchu court was negotiating a settlement with the revolutionaries, and after receiving assurances from the rebels that the imperial family would be treated favorably, the Manchu rulers officially abdicated the Chinese throne on February 12, 1912.

Yuan Shih-k'ai and the Restoration of the Monarchy

Establishing the republic was headier business than dealing the death-blow to two thousand years of imperial rule in China. That the "revolution of 1911 failed," as the historians have so judged, was due in part to the ambitious, self-serving, but politically astute machinations of one man: Yuan Shih-k'ai.

Born into an influential military family and having experienced initial failures in the examination route, Yuan Shih-k'ai burst into prominence as a young (twenty-three) and able military instructor in the Korean crisis of 1882. Between this crisis and the first Sino-Japanese war in 1895, Yuan's military career experienced its ups and downs. China's defeat in Korea during the Sino-Japanese war reflected heavily on Yuan's rising star: "the once powerful [Yuan] became a pathetic figure."[4] It didn't take Yuan long to recover his prestige. Between 1895 and 1900, he resumed his duties in the army as a military instructor. At thirty-six, he had impressed the Manchu court sufficiently to be appointed a commander of the New Army. By 1896, British Rear-Admiral Lord Charles Beresford proclaimed: "By Western standards, Yuan

Shih-k'ai's troops were the only completely equipped force in the empire."⁵ Yuan's power base, both politically and militarily, was assured.

Yuan's political fortunes were rising concommitantly with his military career. Having held several minor offices in the government, he assumed the position of governor of Shantung province in 1900. He naturally took his army to Shantung, in time to suppress the Boxers there. Although Yuan balked at sending his troops into the center of the Boxer uprising in Peking, he nonetheless ingratiated himself to the Manchu court. Given the strength of his army, Yuan was appointed governor-general of Chihli (modern-day Hopei, where Peking is located). Better still, he was also appointed commissioner of trade for the northern ports, thus bringing him into direct contact with the powerful Peiyang (northern fleet) military clique. The Peiyang clique was a composite of the most powerful military generals in north China. Most were Yuan's cohorts. Thus, by 1902, Yuan's "power was second to none but the throne's."⁶

Yuan's "second to none but" position was at best a tenuous one. It rested solely on his extraordinary relationship with the empress dowager. As long as she was alive, Yuan's political and military fortunes remained likewise. Yuan's main opponent in the Manchu court was the emperor, Kung Hsu, whom Yuan had helped depose during the abortive 1898 reform movement.

In 1908, both the empress and emperor died, only one day apart. At this point, Yuan's normally astute judgment failed him. In choosing the heir-apparent, Yuan sided with the loser. The winner, P'u-yi (Henry Pu-yi, the last Manchu emperor), arranged for Yuan to fall ill with "an affection [sic] of the foot" thus making it "hardly possible for him [Yuan] to discharge his duties adequately."⁷ Yuan proceeded to convalesce for the next three years, sitting out the revolution of 1911. When the court pressed Yuan into service shortly after the Wuch'ang uprising, Yuan responded: "My foot is not yet healed."⁸ The revolutionaries also attempted to enlist Yuan's support, offering him, no less, the presidency of the republic. Yuan skillfully began to play both ends against the middle.

Yuan finally succeeded in assuming the position of mediator

(and prime minister) between the emperor and the revolutionaries in a series of cunning moves. On November 13, Yuan had accepted the imperial decree appointing him premier of the cabinet, and now his power truly was second to none.

Just when the notion of "emperor" crossed Yuan's mind is difficult to say, but surely it was fully developed between November 13, 1911, when he was appointed premier, and February 12, 1912, the date of the official abdication of the last Manchu emperor. By February 12, he was *convinced* that he had been chosen successor to the throne. In the emperor's abdication decree, the emperor conferred on Yuan "full power to organize a provisional government to negotiate with the revolutionary army for unification measures."[9] Yuan, of course, had helped draft the abdication decree.

Yuan, however, had to contend with two other formidable individuals: Sun Yat-sen, who had been elected as the provisional president of the Chinese republic, and Sung Chiao-jen, Sun Yat-sen's successor as leader of the T'ung-meng hui and the real moving force in the creation of the Kuomintang (the Nationalist party). Yuan resolved both problems by maneuvering Sun Yat-sen out of the presidency and presumably ordering the assassination of Sung after Yuan became president.

Sun Yat-sen was elected as the first provisional president of the Chinese republic by sixteen of the seventeen provincial representatives gathered in Nanking to organize the provisional government. On January 1, 1912, the Republic of China was officially inaugurated. On January 2, the republic was steeped in conflict. The major issue involved the form of government which the republic should adopt: a presidential form (favored by Yuan) or a cabinet form (favored by Sun and Sung).

Sun's election had angered Yuan, who regarded this action as a "breach of agreement" by the revolutionaries. Sun, however, knew that neither a decision on the form of government nor a republic itself would be forthcoming if Yuan were not brought into the proceedings—indeed, if Yuan were not the president. Sun was no doubt aware of what the gesture of sixty-eight officers of the Peiyang army meant when they declared their allegiance to the Manchu dynasty.[10] Sun wasted no time in preserving the republic; on the very day of his election, he offered to abdicate the office in favor of Yuan. After an initial round of sparring between Sun and Yuan, Sun reiterated his offer:

> Your telegram of the second has been received. Since I could not bear to see a war between the South and the North because the people would suffer so tremendously, I have no objection to peace negotiations. . . . If war can be avoided through your efforts and the people's desire for peace can be satisfied . . . it would certainly be only fair for me to give you full credit and to yield [the presidency] to you as the most capable person. Since I have been elected by the representatives of all the provinces and have been formally sworn in, my sincere intention for peace should thus be made plain before both God and our people. If you think that I am trying to tempt you with this offer, you are certainly laboring under a misconception.[11]

Yuan was unanimously elected provisional president of the republic on January 14, 1912. One other problem was resolved at this time which illustrates the mutual distrust between Yuan and the revolutionaries. In Sun's letter of resignation, Sun insisted that the capital of the provisional government be located in Nanking. Peking, it was believed, symbolized everything that the revolution intended to destroy. Since Yuan's military power was concentrated in the north, he had no inclination to move southward, away from his power sources, and so displaying a deft hand for politics once again, a riot coincidentally broke out in Peking which attracted foreign troops to the area. Sun Yat-sen's delegation to Peking wired back to Nanking:

> The military riots in Peking greatly excited the foreigners and Japan has already sent many soldiers to the capital. Should such incidents recur, the foreigners will certainly take free military action. Observing this situation, we have decided that the crux of the problem is the need for establishment of a unified government. Other objectives may be compromised.[12]

On March 10, 1912, Yuan Shih-k'ai was inaugurated *in Peking* as the first president of the Chinese republic. Though nationalistic in outlook, Yuan had not fully accepted the concept of republican government. In fact, he was still deeply possessed of the Confucian tradition, proclaiming:

> Politics is the basis of founding a country, and the replacement of old politics with new always depends on political theories. [The Confucian doctrines are] great principles contained in a few words, and their validity becomes more evident as time goes on. The present democracy is the result of the ferment of these doctrines. Heaven gave Confucius [to us] to be our teacher for thousands of generations. [By his teachings] the empire came to a glorious end as [the system] of selecting the wise and talented [to govern] began. By the application of these principles, the people will be at peace. These principles can be applied to any country in the four seas.[13]

Yuan's monarchical aspirations were clearly evident. Yuan, however, still had one issue to resolve, the form of government within the republic, and one more individual to eliminate, Sung Chiao-jen. Yuan's problem with Sung revolved around the nascent political party structure emerging in the equally nascent republic. Political parties were, Sung believed, the essence of republican politics: "Politics is the life of political parties and political opinion is its pinot [sic]."[14]

Beginning in August 1912, Sung began widening the base of the alliance by proposing mergers with several other growing but still minor political parties. The several parties finally adopted the title Kuomintang (National People's party, or simply, the Nationalist party or KMT). From December 1912 through January 1913 China held its first parliamentary elections. As one observer noted, however, the elections were "absolutely unreal . . . the public took no part and exhibited no interest in the proceedings."[15] Nonetheless, what voting did take place was sufficient to send 269 Nationalists to the House of Representatives and 123 to the Senate. The Kuomintang's plurality in both houses was about 45 percent.[16] Sung Chiao-jen himself took to the hustings, severely criticizing Yuan's administration and advocating a cabinet form of government. The KMT's overwhelming victory strengthened his convictions. The KMT, in turn, suggested that Sung be appointed premier in charge of the cabinet. His prominence within the KMT was underscored by his election as the party's general-director, replacing Sun Yat-sen.

April 8, 1913, was the date selected for the convening of the republic's first national parliament in Peking.

Two months before the parliament opened, Sung had begun the series of talks throughout China generally critical of Yuan's administration. According to Yu, "He advocated a cabinet system because it could easily be changed [while] under a presidential system, [change] would be impossible, for a president served for a fixed term."[17] Sung's criticism was timely in that Yuan was especially preoccupied with correcting the financial indebtedness he inherited from the Manchu court. Yuan was operating a government burdened by a monthly deficit of about 15 million *yuan*. To make matters worse, "the government's credit was poor, and loan negotiations were arduous,"[18] a situation which by now should be understood.

Sung's political journey had reached Shanghai by March 20, 1913. Just as Sung was about to board the train for Peking, "a short man in black emerged from the crowd on the platform and shot Sung."[19] Two days later, the thirty-one-year-old Sung died, just as much from the government's refusal to give its consent to an operation as from the assassin's bullet.

Was Yuan Shih-k'ai involved in the assassination? During the Shanghai hearings, telegrams between the assassin and Yuan's premier were presented implicating Yuan. One particular undated letter from Yuan's premier to his confidential secretary read:

> Mr. Ying's [the assassin's] accomplice asks for money. Will you please deal with him directly and pay him when I [the premier] have obtained the president's permission.[20]

There were at least four persons in a position to implicate Yuan in the assassination. Within nine months, three principals were dead: the assassin, mysteriously; Yuan's premier inexplicably; and one through action by the police. The fourth was arrested during the May Fourth Incident (1919), charged, convicted, and executed.[21] His arrest was instigated by Sung's son. Yuan was suspected of having a hand in the deaths of the other three.

Yuan's alleged role in the assassination and his total disregard for the parliament in mortgaging China's taxes to a consortium of foreign bankers led Sun to call for a war against Yuan. Sun's call was taken up by one military governor, Li Lieh-chun of Kiangsi. On July 12, 1913, Li's troops engaged Yuan's in battle. Four months later, Yuan's superior military power (backed as it was by the powerful Peiyang generals) and the financial support of the foreign powers ended the "second revolution." Where once Yuan had feared traveling south from Peking, he feared no more: the KMT's influence in the south ended with Li's defeat. Only the southwestern provinces (Kwangtung, Kwangsi, Szechuan, Kweichou, and Yunnan) were precariously controlled by the KMT. On November 4, 1913, Yuan ordered the dissolution of both the beaten Kuomintang and shortly thereafter the Kuomintang-controlled parliament. By February 1914, Yuan ruled absolutely.

Yuan's grand design for the restoration of the monarchy began inauspiciously at the end of 1914 when he passed a declaration in support of the worship of Confucius, and followed the declaration with the ceremony to worship Heaven, which by Confucian ritual only an emperor could perform.[22] In August 1915, his monarchical ambitions surfaced openly with the establishment of a Peace Planning Society, founded by one of Yuan's henchmen. Under the auspices of this society, the merits of both republicanism and monarchism were "debated," culminating in the convocation of the National Congress of Provincial Representatives in Peking ostensibly for the purpose of voting for a form of government. Not surprisingly, the 1,993 members *unanimously* voted for a monarchical form of government, and even less surprising, voted Yuan to the throne. The assembly then declared:

> Reverently representing the public opinion of the nation, we request that the president, Yuan Shih-k'ai, be made emperor of the Chinese empire. He will have the highest and most complete authority and sovereignty over the nation. The throne will be handed down in his royal family from generation to generation through ten thousand generations.[23]

The assembly met on November 20, 1915, but plans for Yuan's investiture had already been in progress as early as September.[24] The dynasty was to be named *Hung-hsien,* which Yuan translated to mean, "Grand Constitutional Era." The actual accession to the throne was set for January 1, 1916.

Yuan's imperial aspirations, however, ran head-on into the firmly imbedded notion of a republic. On the date of his enthronement, the antimonarchist movement re-emerged full force. On New Year's Day 1916, the antimonarchists, led by dissident warlords, Liang Ch'i-ch'ao, and various political parties (KMT and the Chinese Revolutionary party), issued a declaration calling for the establishment of the republic, calling Yuan a traitor. By the end of January, China was again locked in civil war. Sustaining some surprising setbacks in the civil war, and engendering bitter criticisms from influential politicians and generals, Yuan abolished his short-lived (eighty-three days) empire on March 22. Two and a half months later, Yuan died, and with the exception of one last futile attempt by the militarist, Chang Hsun, to restore the last remaining Manchu emperor, P'u-yi, to the throne on July 1, 1917, the imperial tradition ended in China once and for all.

WARLORD POLITICS

Yuan Shih-k'ai's Legacy

Historians have been harsh in assessing Yuan Shih-k'ai's regency. He has been variously accused of being the "Brutus" of Chinese politics,[25] "disloyal,"[26] a "cheater,"[27] and a "great" betrayer.[28] Yuan's most bitter epitaph and his "most powerful single legacy," however, is that he "fathered" the immediate rise of warlordism in China.[29] If Yuan had dealt the republic a lethal blow during his presidency, the warlords nearly dealt the republic the death blow.

Yuan was not a warlord,[30] but the charge that he fathered the growth of warlordism is based on the fact that the men destined to become warlords after his death had been trained, educated, and made officers by Yuan. In 1901, Yuan had been named the commissioner of trade for the northern ports and was, at the same time, commissioned by the throne to develop an army,

trained, educated and organized along modern professional bu-
reaucratic lines. The Japanese army served as Yuan's model. According to S. MacKinnon, the "criteria for qualification as an officer or soldier in the Peiyang army emphasized education and
professional military training over personal and regional connections."[31] By 1904, the army reached its maximum size, 60,000,
divided into six divisions of 10,000 men each. Yuan's division
commanders and senior officers included, in turn, Feng Kuo-
chang, Tuan Ch'i-jui, Wu P'ei-fu, and Ts'ao K'un, all destined to
become key military governors (*tuchuns*), or warlords, in the
period after Yuan's death.

The revolution of 1911 further allowed the professional officers of the Peiyang army to assert themselves within the geo-
graphic boundaries or provinces assigned to them initially. In time,
they converted their positions into military satrapies in the wake
of the political power vacuum created by the demise of the
monarchy. Yuan assumed the presidency in a country divided between the northern and southern provinces,[32] and his tumultuous
reign continued to facilitate the growing strength of the military
governors in the period between 1912 and 1916. His death in
1916 removed the last restraint upon the military governors.

The Nature of Warlordism

Military regionalism and military governors were not a new
development to China inspired by Yuan. This feature of Chinese
history has been endemic in Chinese political and military life. Indeed, "in no country in the world have soldiers dominated politics
as extensively or for so long as in China. Modern Chinese politics
has revolved around armies and military figures."[33] What, then,
is a warlord? Who were they? How did they emerge from the
rubble of the Chinese republic? According to Sheridan,

> a warlord exercised effective governmental control over a
> fairly well-defined region by means of a military organiza-
> tion that obeyed no higher authority than himself.[34]

Between Yuan Shih-k'ai's death in 1916 and the reunification
of China under Chiang K'ai-shek's Kuomintang in 1928, there

were no fewer than thirteen hundred such militarists who fit Sheridan's definition.[35] There were so many warlords, in fact, that it was not unusual to find some petty or minor warlords controlling some areas presumably under the control of a major warlord.[36] These warlords, in turn, engaged in more than one hundred forty provincial and interprovincial wars in the sixteen year period between 1912 and 1928.[37]

The majority of the warloads were illiterates or semi-illiterates whose socioeconomic backgrounds were equally poor. Of the thirteen hundred warlords counted by Ch'en, approximately 30 percent could be considered educated, with the greatest number trained in Japan (117). Most were superstitious. At least twenty-three began their careers as bandits, while others started as page-boys, bodyguards, doormen, peddlers and "hawkers."[38] The major warlords such as Chang Tso-lin, Yen Hsi-shan, Wu P'ei-fu, Tuan Ch'i-jui, and Ts'ao K'un began their careers in the regular army.

Warlords and warlordism were characterized by several factors. First, warlord armies were conscripted and held together by personal loyalties between the warlord and his men, especially the officers. "Personal authority over one's troops . . . implied the capacity for independent military action."[39] Because of the continuous chaos in China dating back to the T'ai-p'ing rebellion in 1854, recruits were plentiful. The lines of the unemployed and the hungry were the primary recruiting grounds for the warlords.

A second characteristic of warlords and warlordism was control over territory for the construction of military bases and the generation of resources and money. Money was their life blood, and the warlords created taxes to fit the occasion. In one area, there were no fewer than seventy types of taxes which the warlord could impose to raise revenues.[40] On the giving end, obviously, was the impoverished peasant.

A third characteristic flows from the second. The power to tax implied some form of civil administration. In this sense, warlordism took an institutional characteristic. Warlord organizations generally began as armies which gradually metamorphosed into political entities. This transformation was not without its problems. The central question emerged: to retain the military character or become effective administrative units replete with competitive political or party organizations? Thus,

> the multiple demands on the warlords' organizations greatly compromised their effectiveness, yet, as the dominant organizations, indeed almost the sole effective public organizations in the country, they were expected to perform a wide variety of functions, more certainly than any single structure could reasonably do. The entire dynamics of warlord politics was shaped by this contradiction between presumed strength and actual weakness. It encouraged the notion that the only salvation of China lay in a single warlord expanding his organization to form a new Chinese state. Warlord organizations were thus expected to have the potential of becoming the nucleus of a modernizing Chinese state but recognized as being in fact ineffectual in almost all the functions associated with a modern state.[41]

With more than one hundred forty wars fought among themselves, it is not difficult to suggest that warmaking was still another feature of warlordism in China. In north China, Peking was the coveted prize, symbolizing as it did the seat of China's legitimate government, empowered to enter into relations with foreign powers, and to control revenues and loans.[42] Other coveted possessions included key railroads from Peking to Hankow in central China and Peking and Nanking. Whoever controlled these railways controlled China's heartland.[43]

Finally, Chinese warlordism was characterized by alliances, cliques, or faction-building. While this feature of warlordism in China has not been adequately researched,[44] the rise of cliques was tied to disputes between north and south China. After Yuan's death, the disputes between north and south focused mainly on the form of government and the adoption (or readoption) of a constitution for that particular form of government. One persistent problem, it will be recalled, was the question of adopting a strong executive form of government or a strong parliamentary form of government. By 1917, the northern warlords dominated the parliament, successfully placing their men in the top positions of the central government.

The ideological split over the form of government best suited for China gave way to a geographical split in 1917. In mid–1917,

Sun Yat-sen, in protesting the domination of the central government in Peking by the warlords, rallied two hundred fifty southern members of the parliament in Canton and formed a military government in Kwangtung province.[45] Sun's military government, paradoxically, was allowed to exist by the Kwangtung warlord. Thus, north and south China were under the mercy of the military governors. To compound the individual warlord stranglehold of China, warlord cliques were formed to balance their own power. North China was controlled by the Chihli clique, comprised of the military governors of Chihli (modern-day Hopei), Hupei, Kiangsi, Kiangsu, and Honan, while south China was controlled by the Anhwei-Fukien (An-Fu) clique comprised of the military governors of Anhwei, Shensi, Fukien, Chekiang, Hunan, Shantung and Shanghai.[46] In both cliques were the generals of the Peiyang army, splitting the once-dominant army for good. By July 1920, the various warlord cliques were at war with one another, and China, in the next six years, was to know no peace from warlord warfare.

The Warlords' Legacy

Although individual studies have placed the warlords' role in China in a socioeconomic perspective apart from the solely military one,[47] most historians have been critical. On balance, however,

> the warlords probably contributed more to the modernization of China than critics of their day recognized. Compared with military rule in some of the new states, that of the tuchuns permitted greater freedom for future-oriented groups to improve themselves. On the other hand, the warlords' failure to provide the Chinese with a more tolerable and respectable system of rule also set back whatever chances there may have been for China to develop a more open, competitive, and democratic system of government.[48]

The May Fourth Movement

4

ASIAN FOREIGN POLITICS, 1914–1919

Amid the turmoil caused by the warlords' warmaking and political intrigue, China's traditional poverty, foreign encroachments, and the breakdown of the Chinese social structure, China's dramatic turning point occurred. On May 4, 1919, in opposition to the Treaty of Versailles, a series of protests against the government's pro-Japanese policy and a wave of boycotts against Japanese goods inaugurated a national movement unprecedented in Chinese political and social history.[1]

The May Fourth incident begat a national effort against China's foreign and domestic ills which was to last roughly through the mid-1920s. In the interim, the movement facilitated the rise of student and labor movements, reinvigorated Sun Yat-sen's demoralized Kuomintang, inspired the rise of a new cultural and intellectual "revolution," accelerated the decline of China's traditional social structure, and provided the environment for the rise of feminism in China. The most far-reaching significance of the May Fourth Movement was its catalytic effect on the introduction of Marxism-Leninism in China. Finally, May Fourth gave rise to the development of the Communist Party of China.

For the general Chinese leadership, the movement is of great historical significance. According to Chairman Mao Tse-tung, it was the event which introduced a "new revolutionary process, that of the new democratic revolution."[2] Mao's main competitor in the early years, Chang Kuo-t'ao, called it "epoch-making,"[3] while Chiang K'ai-shek saw it as the "clearest evidence of . . . strong revolutionary sentiment" in China.[4] Truly, the May Fourth Movement represents the major turning point in China's troubled past since 1840.

Since the past and immediate catalyst behind the May Fourth Movement was Japan's interests in China, China's foreign affairs prior to 1919 need to be discussed, especially China's relations with Japan and the United States. Of Japan's interests in China, there was little doubt after 1895; of the interests of the United States, the only country openly committed to preserving Chinese territorial integrity, many questions arise. Both the interests of Japan and the United States were to converge at the Paris Peace Conference in 1919. Dramatics aside, the shape of international relations in Asia in the interwar period were largely determined by the events at Paris.

Japan and China

Japan's interests in China were clear since its stunning defeat of China in 1895. But Japan wanted more than simply economic "rights" in China: it wanted China's body and soul.

World War I inaugurated Japan's design for China. With an eye toward obtaining Germany's rights in Shantung province in general and the excellent base facilities in Tsingtao, located on the northeast shore of Kiaochow Bay, Japan declared war on Germany on August 23, 1914. Disregarding China's proclamation of neutrality issued two and a half weeks earlier, by November, Japan had successfully eliminated Germany's presence from Asia.[5] The worst, however, was yet to come.

On the dark and chilly evening of January 18, 1915, the Japanese minister to China presented Yuan Shih-k'ai "a few sheets of paper watermarked with dreadnoughts and machine guns," a euphemistic phrase coined by the American ambassador to China to denote the now infamous Twenty-One Demands which were to play an important role at the Paris Peace Conference four years later.[6] Because of their importance, the demands are presented in full below.[7]

The Twenty-One Demands Presented by Japan to China,
January 18, 1915 Japanese Statement

GROUP I.
    The Japanese Government and the Chinese Government, being desirous to maintain the general peace in the Far East and to strengthen the relations of amity and good

neighbourhood existing between the two countries, agree to the following articles:

Article I.—The Chinese Government engage to give full assent to all matters that the Japanese Government may hereafter agree with the German Government respecting the disposition of all the rights, interests and concessions, which, in virtue of treaties or otherwise, Germany possesses vis-a-vis China in relation to the province of Shantung.

Article II.—The Chinese Government engage that, within the province of Shantung or along its coast, no territory or island will be ceded or leased to any other Power, under any pretext whatever.

Article III.—The Chinese Government agree to Japan's building a railway connecting Chefoo or Lungkow with the Kiao-chou-Tsinanfu Railway.

Article IV.—The Chinese Government engage to open of their own accord, as soon as possible, certain important cities and towns in the Province of Shantung for the residence and commerce of foreigners. The places to be so opened shall be decided upon in a separate agreement.

GROUP II.

The Japanese Government and the Chinese Government, in view of the fact that the Chinese Government has always recognized the predominant position of Japan in South Manchuria and Eastern Inner Mongolia, agree to the following articles:

Article I.—The two Contracting Parties mutually agree that the term of the lease of Port Arthur and Dairen and the term respecting the South Manchuria Railway and the Antung-Mukden Railway shall be extended to a further period of ninety-nine years respectively.

Article II.—The Japanese subjects shall be permitted in South Manchuria and Eastern Inner Mongolia to lease or own land required either for erecting buildings for various commercial and industrial uses or for farming.

Article III.—The Japanese subjects shall have liberty to enter, reside, and travel in South Manchuria and Eastern Inner Mongolia, and to carry on business of various kinds—commercial, industrial, and otherwise.

Article IV.—The Chinese Government grant to the Japanese subjects the right of mining in South Manchuria and Eastern Inner Mongolia. As regards the mines to be worked, they shall be decided upon in a separate agreement.

Article V.—The Chinese Government agree that the consent of the Japanese Government shall be obtained in advance (1) whenever it is proposed to grant to other nationals the right of constructing a railway or to obtain from other nationals the supply of funds for constructing a railway in South Manchuria and Eastern Inner Mongolia, and (2) whenever a loan is to be made with any other Power, under security of the taxes of South Manchuria and Eastern Inner Mongolia.

Article VI.—The Chinese Government engage that whenever the Chinese government need the service of political, financial, or military advisers or instructors in South Manchuria or in Eastern Inner Mongolia, Japan shall first be consulted.

Article VII.—The Chinese Government agree that the control and management of the Kirin-Changchun Railway shall be handed over to Japan for a term of ninety-nine years dating from the signing of this Treaty.

GROUP III.

The Japanese Government and the Chinese Government, having regard to the close relations existing between Japanese capitalists and the Han-Yeh-Ping Company and desiring to promote the common interests of the two nations, agree to the following articles:

Article I.—The two Contracting Parties mutually agree that when the opportune moment arrives the Han-Yeh-Ping Company shall be made a joint concern of the two nations, and that, without the consent of the Japanese Government, the Chinese Government shall not dispose or permit the Company to dispose of any right or property of the Company.

Article II.—The Chinese Government engage that, as a necessary measure for protection of the invested interests of Japanese capitalists, no mines in the neighborhood of those owned by the Han-Yeh-Ping Company shall be permitted, without the consent of the said Company, to be worked by anyone other than the said Company; and further that whenever it is proposed to take any other measure which may likely affect the interests of the said Company directly or indirectly, the consent of the said Company shall first be obtained.

GROUP IV.

The Japanese Government and the Chinese Government, with the object of effectively preserving the territorial integrity of China, agree to the following article:

The Chinese Government engage not to cede or lease to

any other Power any harbor or bay on or any island along the coast of China.

GROUP V.

1. The Chinese Central Government to engage influential Japanese as political, financial, and military advisers;

2. The Chinese Government to grant the Japanese hospitals, temples, and schools in the interior of China the right to own land;

3. In the face of many police disputes which have hitherto arisen between Japan and China, causing no little annoyance, the police in localities (in China), where such arrangements are necessary, to be placed under joint Japanese and Chinese administration, or Japanese to be employed in police offices in such localities, so as to help at the same time the improvement of the Chinese Police Service;

4. China to obtain from Japan supply of a certain quantity of arms, or to establish an arsenal in China under joint Japanese and Chinese management and to be supplied with experts and materials from Japan;

5. In order to help the development of the Nanchang-Kiukiang Railway, with which Japanese capitalists are so closely identified, and with due regard to the negotiations which have for years been pending between Japan and China in relation to the railway question in South China, China to agree to give to Japan the right of constructing a railway to connect Wuchang with the Kiukiang-Nanchang line and also the railways between Nanchang and Hangchou and between Nanchang and Chaochou;

6. In view of the relations between the Province of Fukien and Formosa and of the agreement respecting the nonalienation of that province, Japan to be consulted first whenever foreign capital is needed in connection with the railways, mines, and harbor works (including dockyards) in the Province of Fukien;

7. China to grant to Japanese subjects the right of preaching in China.

While the overall intent of the demands was to make China Japan's vassal-state, a stunning turnabout of political relationships in Asian politics, the focal point in the negotiations was the status of Shantung province. At the outset of the negotiations (February 2), China had "agreed in principle" to the transfer of German rights in Shantung to Japan. By May, the Chinese had managed to forestall any definite agreement on the disposition of Shantung.

Its patience worn thin, Japan delivered an ultimatum on May 7 requiring the acceptance of the first four groups, reserving Group 5 "for future discussion." The last paragraph of the ultimatum read:

> In case the [Japanese] Imperial Government fails to receive from the Chinese Government, before 6 P.M. of May 9th, a satisfactory response to their advice, they will take such independent action as they may deem necessary to meet the situation.[8]

In accepting the ultimatum on May 9, and signing an agreement to that effect on May 25, Yuan Shih-k'ai had capitulated to Japan's interests in China in general and Shantung in particular. While the subject of the demands was to be raised four years hence at Paris, the news of the agreement had an immediate effect of far-reaching consequences for China.

In presenting the demands, Japan had insisted on absolute secrecy. However, Chinese officials leaked the substance and intent of the demands to both the Chinese and foreign presses with the hope that someone would come to China's aid. No foreign country did. However, the leaks did have some domestic repercussions: for the first time in modern Chinese history, Chinese public opinion asserted itself. Protests, mass rallies, and boycotts of Japanese goods erupted as the mass movement against a new enemy, Japan, developed. In the end, the news of the demands had two important consequences for China. First, a new nationalism developed around the theme of resistance to foreign aggression, and second, a spirit of national unity emerged which saw the region give way to the center.[9] The events surrounding the news of the demands truly were harbingers of the events surrounding the May Fourth Movement four years later.

Japan and the United States

The Twenty-One Demands also marked the turning point in U.S.-Japanese relations.[10] Three days after China had agreed to the ultimatum, the Wilson Administration informed Japan that the United States could not

recognize any agreement or understanding which has been

entered into or which may be entered into between the governments of Japan and China, impairing the treaty rights of
the United States and its citizens in China, the political or
territorial integrity of the Republic of China, or the international policy relative to China commonly known as the open
door policy.[11]

There was, however, no particular reason to expect the
United States to react differently. Since the U.S. acquisition of the
Philippines in 1898, relations between the United States and Japan
had been strained.

Between 1906 and the Paris Peace Conference in 1919, one
persistent problem, immigration, surfaced to strain U.S.-Japanese
relations immeasurably, while another immediate problem, China's
entry into World War I provided both countries with the opportunity to determine the extent of each other's influence in China
in particular and Asia in general.

The first Asian immigrants (mainly Chinese coolies) to the
United States reached California during the gold rush of 1848.[12]
By the mid-1880s, there were nearly one hundred thirty two thousand Chinese in California. Welcomed in the United States during
the labor shortages associated with the railroad building boom, the
industrious Asians soon lost their favored status in California and
the rest of the United States. By the mid-1890s, Asian exclusion
laws were enacted in some states.

Chinese formed the greatest percentage of Asians in the
United States. Where the Chinese population in the United States
neared one hundred thirty thousand in the early 1880s, there were
only 148 Japanese in the entire country. Japan's victory over Russia in 1904–5 heightened American anxieties over the now steady
influx of Japanese. By 1906, Asian immigrants in California were
legally segregated in Oriental public schools. The Japanese government protested. Despite the abrogation of the school segregation
order and efforts to cooperate between the two countries, California's legislature continued its harassment of Asian immigrants.

In 1913, the California legislature enacted a law prohibiting
Japanese from owning land and limiting to three years the tenure
during which time the Japanese could lease land. Despite Wilson's

attempt to prevent the passage of the law, Japan protested the enactment, calling it "unfair and insidiously discriminatory."[13]

Between 1913 and the Peace Conference in 1919, President Wilson found himself in a major dilemma, having gone on record opposing further Asian immigration,[14] and yet atttempting to head off the enactment of exclusion laws throughout the United States. At Paris, Japan was prepared to make racial equality into an international issue, a move which would influence Wilson to acquiesce to Japan's political demands during the conference. U.S. domestic politics would once again have a profound influence on U.S. foreign politics.

A second conflict between the United States and Japan prior to Paris concerned China's entry into World War I. With the U.S. declaration of war against Germany in 1917, the United States actively sought China's entry into the war. Japan greeted this effort by the United States as a threat to its special status in China guaranteed by the Twenty-One Demands.

China had favored joining the war effort as early as 1915, much to Japan's dismay. For China, participation in the war effort offered prospects that it would be represented in any postwar conference. Later, after continued insistence by the United States that it join the war effort, China finally declared war on Germany. Unable to continue its opposition to Chinese participation, Japan began behind-the-scenes maneuvers among the allies toward securing agreements recognizing its special interests in China, particularly those in Shantung province. Again, these secret agreements effected before the peace conference convened were to be a source of frustration in Wilson's efforts to aid China during the conference.

The Paris Peace Conference and the Shantung Question

The United States was the first country to recognize the new Chinese republic.[15] During his Presidency, Wilson received the Chinese republic favorably, and according to Wilson's minister to China, Paul Reinsch, Wilson's fondest hope was that China would find in the United States its political and moral model.[16]

Wilson's penchant for moralizing, as exemplified by his Four-

teen Points, was about the only hope that the Chinese had for re-
gaining Shantung province. Japan, on the other hand, had all the
legal instruments it needed to press its case for Shantung, including
the agreements based on the Twenty-One Demands, the secret
treaties with the allies (Great Britain, France, and Italy) recognizing Japan's special interests and claims in China and Shantung,
the Lansing-Ishii agreement of 1917 in which the United States
recognized that Japan's territorial propinquity gave it special rights
in China, and finally, Chinese agreements entered into in 1918
granting Japan certain claims in China in return for vast loans.

The Paris Peace Conference convened on January 12, 1919.
Japan was the lone Asian nation admitted as one of the five Great
Powers alongside the United States, Great Britain, France, and
Italy. The Chinese delegation was not given Great Power status
but it did play an active role in the proceedings of the conference.
The Chinese delegation, however, mirrored the division between
north and south China. Three of the five members were loyal to
the government in Peking while the remaining two represented the
government in Canton. Inevitably, the delegation was given to
internal dissension.

On January 27, Japan revealed its three-point program which
was to rock the conference and threaten the establishment of the
League of Nations. Japan claimed:

1. Germany's possessions in Shantung
2. Germany's possessions in the South Seas
3. Recognition and establishment of an international principle on racial equality.[17]

So as to insure the passage of its three-point program by the
conference delegates, the Japanese delegation threatened to divulge
the various secret treaties with China recognizing Japan's status
and rights in China, something as yet unknown to a confident Chinese public. The Chinese delegation, split on whether or not it
wanted the treaties revealed, asked for a stay of any decision by
the Great Powers. The Wilson administration, for its part, encouraged the Chinese delegation to "stand firm"[18] while the
United States searched for some solution.

Having succumbed to the euphoric environment created by
Wilson's Fourteen Points, especially the principle of national self-

determination, China invoked, at the suggestion of the United States, a tenuous principle of international law, *rebus sic stantibas,* to forestall Japanese claims in Shantung.[19] The principle of *rebus sic stantibas* holds that treaties cease to be binding when the basic conditions upon which they were founded have been essentially changed. The Chinese delegation, in accepting the suggestion, claimed that the conditions under which China had been forced to grant rights and privileges to foreign powers had changed sufficiently to abrogate any treaties entered into by China during the war.[20] Japan held firmly to the equally strong principle of international law of the binding force of treaties.

Wilson personally undertook to play the role of China's champion, but his consummate desire to establish the League of Nations finally forced him to sacrifice China for the larger cause. Japan forced his hand when it threatened to bolt the conference. Italy already had left the conference and Belgium was threatening to do so. Wilson's only consolation in the long run was to force the Japanese to give up their military designs on China and retain only economic rights in Shantung. "The settlement," Wilson is reported to have said, "was the best that could be had out of a dirty past."[21]

The resolution of the Shantung Question finally was agreed upon by the powers, including the United States, on April 30. By nightfall, the press was announcing the momentous decision at Paris to a shocked world.

THE MAY FOURTH MOVEMENT

The May Fourth Incident

By May 3, the Chinese public had learned that Japan's diplomatic maneuvering had gained for it Germany's possessions in Shantung. Further, the Chinese public also learned that its own government had "sold out" China to Japan through the loans contained in the secret treaties of 1918.

The resolution of the Shantung Question and the news of the secret treaties converged upon an indignant Chinese public at a time when students at Peking University had scheduled a mass demonstration for May 7, the anniversary of the ultimatum on the Twenty-One Demands. The students, reacting to the fever pitch environment of the first few days of May, moved the demonstration scheduled for May 7 up to May 4. Faculty members at Peking University adopted a hands-off policy lest they attract the attention of the hostile warlord government in Peking.[22] According to one student, Chang Kuo-t'ao, who was to play a major role in the rise of the Chinese Communist Party:

> About eleven o'clock on the morning of May 4 Peita [Peking University] students were assembled in the mall of the first campus at Ma-shen-miao, ready to start for the Gate of Heavenly Peace, when Chancellor Ts'ai Yuan-p'ei [of Peking University] tried to prevent us from marching. In a moving address he declared that the demonstration would not improve the situation. Because of Peita's insistence upon academic freedom, he said, it had earned the hatred of the government and of conservatives in general. It was looked upon as some sort of heretical monster. . . . We reached it [the Gate of Heavenly Peace] at last. Students from all other institutions of higher education in Peking had kept their promises and were waiting. There were more than three thousand students altogether. Promptly after a brief announcement of the objectives of the demonstration, we marched off in force to the Legation Quarter, intending to demonstrate before the Japanese Legation first of all. We shouted a wide variety of slogans and carried many different banners. Chief among them were "Return our Tsingtao," "Abolish the Twenty-one Demands," "Punish the Traitors," "Refuse to Sign the Peace Treaty," and "China for the Chinese." . . . A leading pro-Japan official—Chang Tsung-hsiang, who was then Minister to Japan—happened to be in the [Legation]. He had not managed to escape in time, so the students gave him a harsh beating. Meanwhile they turned their wrath against the house's furnishings and recklessly destroyed things. Some students set fire to a pile of this wreckage in one of the courtyards. . . . Thirty-two students who had failed to rejoin the main body of students were seized. And that was the stirring May Fourth Movement episode known as "the fire at Chao-chia-lou."[23]

The National Movement

The incident begat a national movement, if by movement is meant a series of related activities or actions which are directed toward a particular goal. According to the authoritative Chow Tse-tsung, the goal of the movement was to:

> achieve national independence, the emancipation of the individual, and a just society by the modernization of China. ... The most important purpose of the movement was to maintain the existence and independence of the nations, a goal which had actually generated all of the major reforms and revolutions in China since the latter half of the nineteenth century.[24]

In the months that followed the incident, the students at Peking University continued organizing demonstrations, strikes, and boycotts of Japanese goods. Student agitation also succeeded in mobilizing Chinese merchants, industrialists, and workers in the national movement. Women played a key role in the movement. For the first time in Chinese history, both men and women actively participated in Chinese politics.[25] The student movement had come of age in China.

The student demonstrators soon incurred the wrath of the warlord-controlled government in Peking. By June, about eleven hundred-fifty students had been arrested and imprisoned.[26] Both the mass arrests and the miserable treatment of the imprisoned students aroused the public's indignation. In Shanghai, for example, merchants, industrialists, and urban workers joined forces with the student movement. Shanghai was paralyzed subsequently by a commercial strike. According to Chow:

> The significance of the strike does not lie in its economic consequences, but in its nature. It was the first political and patriotic strike in Chinese history, one in which the aim of the workers was not to increase their wages or better their treatment. They were making a protest against the Chinese and Japanese governments.[27]

The series of demonstrations, strikes, and boycotts had an immediate effect on China's foreign and domestic affairs. In its foreign affairs, the Chinese delegation in Paris responded to nearly eight thousand telegrams from an irate Chinese public and refused to sign the peace treaty with Germany.[28]

Domestically, the demonstrations and strikes exerted great pressures on the Chinese government. In the end, the cabinet convened and accepted the resignation of the pro-Japanese Chinese officials. The movement had accomplished still another immediate goal.

From among the numerous events which composed the movement in the following years, two events in particular had far-reaching effects: the development of a new culture movement and the introduction of Marxism-Leninism. The new cultural movement, or Chinese renaissance, was characterized by the increased unity of the intellectuals, especially the professors from Peking University such as Ch'en Tu-hsiu, Li Ta-chao, and Hu Shih. In the nearly six hundred periodicals and newspapers which flourished in the aftermath of the incident, the new intellectuals discussed such Western ideas as democracy, science, liberalism, pragmatism, humanitarianism, anarchism, and socialism. Western scholars such as John Dewey and Bertrand Russell were invited to lecture extensively throughout China on Western ideas. In the next few years, the favorite topic among the intellectuals was the emancipation of the individual. For China, the doctrine of the emancipation of the individual was filled with the criticism of the traditional family system. "The destruction of tradition and convention by iconoclasm and criticism," writes Chow, "became the most colorful phenomenon of the movement."[29]

5

The Origins of
Marxism-Leninism in China

There is no contradicting the significance of the May Fourth movement in facilitating the introduction of Marxism-Leninism to China. Before 1919, Marxism-Leninism had received little attention in China. At most, parts of the *Communist Manifesto* had been translated, but no particular significance was attached to the translation. Until the May Fourth movement, Chinese intellectuals were caught up with the ideas of Adam Smith, Nietzsche, J. S. Mill, Tolstoy, T. H. Huxley, Darwin, Spencer, Rousseau, Montesquieu, and Kropotkin, among others. The omission of Marxist ideas by Chinese journals and periodicals, especially the leading journal for Western ideas, *New Youth,* is best explained by B. Schwartz, who suggests that:

> [for] the Chinese intelligentsia, immersed as they were in their own situation—the Chinese situation—*Marxism in its pre-Leninist form must have seemed irrelevant.*[1]

THE POLITICALIZATION OF MARX

Irrelevant? By the end of the nineteenth century, it was clear that Marx's predictions concerning the destruction of capitalism in Europe had not come true. As the conditions of the working class improved, and as wages rose, the theory of class struggle and its related doctrines lost their appeal. What was the Marxist explanation for the delay in the destruction of capitalism?

In 1916, Lenin published his answer—*Imperialism: The Highest Stage of Capitalism.* According to Lenin's thesis, capitalism had succeeded in extending its system to the entire world through the tentacles of imperialism. The extension of imperialism globally prevented the rise of proletarian revolutions. The Leninist approach to Communist theory and strategy shifted the emphasis away from Europe toward the underdeveloped countries, especially those in Asia. In the underdeveloped countries, Lenin reasoned, lay capitalism's weakest link.

How and by whom were the "permanent revolutions" to be initiated? Again, Lenin filled the largest single gap between European Marxism and his notions of revolutions by developing further the area of strategy and tactics. In the area of tactics, Lenin developed the twin ideas of a party and the professional revolutionary.

Interestingly, Marx showed little interest in organizing for a revolution. In the *Communist Manifesto,* Marx's only discussion of organization was to declare that Communists were not a separate party, but rather would be the leading members of the proletariat. In Marx's political scheme, the leadership of the revolution would develop spontaneously from the proletariat as the proletariat developed its own class consciousness.

Lenin, on the other hand, left nothing to chance, spontaneity, or man. The success of the communist revolution, he stated in his *What Is to Be Done,* depends on the Communists' ability to organize along two lines: (1) labor unions, operating openly, legally, and as publicly as conditions would allow, and (2) side by side with the development of the labor unions would come the development of small, select, secretive groups of professional revolutionaries. It was the professional revolutionary who would be sent into the underdeveloped areas to organize a party along Leninist disciplinary methods.

Who were the recipients of the messianic message of the Russian revolution?

Marxism-Leninism and the Chinese Intellectual

In the vacuum created by the chaotic situation in China between 1911–19, a new breed of revolutionary was in the making: the college professor and the student. It is quite understandable that only the educated (in contrast to the worker and peasant, who usually was uneducated) could see in Marxism a methodology for viewing China in a scientific and historical context. Indeed, the utopian appeal of Marxism explained for the Chinese intellectual not only where China had been, but where it could go; ideally, it gave him a vision of direction and mission, but, more than this, it made the linkage between Chinese nationalism and foreign imperialism a natural one.

In the formative years of Marxism in China, several individuals stand out for their contributions in *introducing* Marxism to China and several others stand out for their attempts to *apply* it to the Chinese situation. The two men who were most responsible for introducing the doctrine to China were Peking University professors Ch'en Tu-hsiu and Li Ta-chao. The two men who eventually took over from the college professors were two protégés, Mao Tse-tung and Chang Kuo-t'ao.

Ch'en and Li

Before their conversions to Marxism-Leninism, Li Ta-chao and Ch'en Tu-hsiu were caught up with such concepts as "democracy and science" (Ch'en) or "reality" (Li). In democracy, Ch'en saw the emancipation of the individual as attainable, while in science, he saw for man a weapon against superstition. In each concept, Ch'en was rebelling against a society in which the individual was subordinated to the group, a legacy, he believed, from Confucian, Buddhist, and Taoistic ideas.

For the metaphysician, Li, the individual also was seeking freedom, but unlike Ch'en, Li's individual spirit could find expression within the group (the world spirit). In effect, he believed that just as youth mirrors age, so China's worn-out spirit could renew itself in the context of the flow of history. In a historical context, China was relatively young. Both men, however, were not quite sure how China could gain its individuality or its renewal.

Li was the first intellectual to attempt to put down his understanding of the Russian revolution and of Marx. The revolution answered his long-awaited "cosmic act of liberation," but Li offered very little evidence in his essay ("The Victory of Bolshevism"—October 1918) that he either understood Marx or that he was a Marxist.

Whether he really understood Marx or not may well be an academic question in retrospect. What is important is either that

Li believed he understood Marx or that he had to do something to understand Marx. To this end, Li promoted the first societies for the study of Marxism at Peking University. Ch'en acknowledged the study groups, but apparently did not take an active part in them. Two enterprising students who did actively participate, however, were Mao Tse-tung and Chang Kuo-t'ao.[2]

Mao Tse-tung and Chang Kuo-t'ao

We have seen that one of the immediate and profound effects of the May Fourth movement was that it released the fury and the stirred-up energies of the students, especially the students at Peking University. In time, student federations were formed in various major cities, including Peking, Tientsin, Nanking, Hangchow, and Shanghai. By June 1919, a National Student Federation was formally established in Shanghai. From among the many student activists who later went on to gain fame in the turbulent years from 1919–49, the most notable included: Mao Tse-tung, Chang Kuo-t'ao, and such recent party leaders as Tung Pi-wu (d. April 1975) and Chou En-lai (d. January 1976).

Two of the most active students who would struggle for control of the future direction of the Chinese revolution were Mao Tse-tung and Chang Kuo-t'ao. Chang Kuo-t'ao's role in the development of the Chinese Communist Party has heretofore been minimized, partly because the main sources of information on the rise of the CCP have concentrated on Mao, but also because of a lack of information on Chang himself. Since the publication of his autobiography, however, it is now possible to compare the roles of these two men in the revolutionary politics of the mid–1930s. Much had already been written about Mao's leadership of the revolution,[3] but in the mid–1930s, "it was possible that (Chang Kuo-t'ao), rather than Mao Tse-tung, might emerge as the party's predominant leader, and Mao achieved primacy only after a power struggle in which he defeated Chang."[4] It should be interesting to follow the rise of the party through the lives of these two students caught up in the events of the 1920s and 1930s. In the process, it will become apparent that the men were of quite different backgrounds and revolutionary temperament.

Mao Tse-tung (December 26, 1893) was born of a poor

peasant family while Chang (1897) was born into the lauded gentry-scholar class, truly a member of China's ruling elite. Both had good relationships with their mothers. Mao's relationship with his father was a tempestuous one (his father constantly beat him), while Chang's relationship with his father was a cordial one, at least until the May Fourth incident. Both were tutored early in Confucian texts, but Mao seems to have been turned away from the classics sooner than Chang. While Mao had to quit his traditional Confucian education at the age of thirteen, Chang was considered a model student. At early ages, both fell victim to the custom of arranged marriages; however, Mao apparently never consummated his and Chiang succeeded in breaking the engagement before the marriage actually took place.

Chang, at fourteen, seems to have been better informed of the events surrounding the revolution of 1911 than Mao was at eighteen. This again reflects their different family environments. "My uncles, brothers and cousins," wrote Chang, "frequently gathered in the family hall for heated discussions of current affairs."[5] Mao, on the other hand, did not learn of the deaths of the empress dowager and the Kuang-hsu emperor until two years after the fact. Both attended primary schools (roughly junior high by U.S. standards), but again under quite different circumstances. Mao was ridiculed for his appearance, and as the son of a peasant, chided for having the temerity even to enter a school normally attended only by the sons of big landlords. Chang was among his peers in primary school, and despite one altercation which led to his dismissal, he was nonplused by it all: he simply moved on to a "better middle school" in Nanch'ang, the provincial capital. Both were exposed to Western learning in middle school. Both experienced their first personal moments of rebelliousness by cutting off their pigtails, the symbol of Chinese submission to the alien Manchus.

Chang seems to have narrowed his educational objectives to science and engineering by the time he entered Peking University. Mao, on the other hand, was indecisive and unsure of his calling. He went from school to school (which one could enroll in by sending in a coupon and one dollar), and from vocation to vocation. He tried a soap-making school because an advertisement "told of the great social benefits of soap-making, how it would enrich the country and enrich the people."[6] He was then attracted to a police academy, a law school, and an economics school operated by the government. He expressed the most interest in the economics school, but withdrew in disgust because the classes were taught in English, and he "knew little English; indeed, scarcely more than the alphabet."[7] Chang had apparently attained a good command of English, busying himself after his arrival at the "better middle school" to "catch up to a much higher level of English and science" than before.[8] By 1920, Chang was reading either the Chinese or English translations of *Das Kapital, Critique of Political Economy* and other Marxist works. In fact, English was the medium by which Chang and the Comintern agent, Voitinsky, conversed prior to the official establishment of the Chinese Communist Party.[9]

Mao apparently began reading Western literature, translated into Chinese, during a self-education program in the summer of 1913 when he was nineteen. He undertook the self-education program because he was dissatisfied with the narrow curriculums of the various schools which he had briefly attended in the Ch'angsha school system.

At nineteen Mao was broke and having his usual family problems. Chang, however, always had money, and it was apparently easy for him to "replenish" his purse when it ran low.

Their paths finally crossed in the library at Peking University sometime in late 1918 or early 1919. Chang recalls the meeting parenthetically, while Mao simply mentions it, attaching no particular significance to it. More important is their relationships with Li and Ch'en. Mao was given a menial job under Li Ta-chao. This job should have been exciting, but according to Mao, his "office was so low that people avoided me. . . . They had no time to listen to an assistant librarian speaking a southern dialect."[10] Chang, on the other hand, writes of a special relationship with Li Ta-chao. Chang writes of "we" throughout, and summarizes the relationship thusly: "I respected Li Ta-chao. . . . In the beginning our friendship was not connected with the study of Marxism. Although he was often my mentor, both of us seemed to have grown up together."[11]

Mao credits Ch'en Tu-hsiu with influencing him "more than

anyone else," but in time Mao was to break with Ch'en over the role of the peasants in the revolution. Here, too, Chang's relationship with Ch'en seems to have been a richer one. Chang had lived with Ch'en in Shanghai during the period when the formation of the party was being discussed. "He was elated and announced that he was eager to discuss the Communist Movement with me," Chang wrote.[12] Ch'en and Chang continued their close relationship even after Ch'en relinquished or was forced to give up the position of secretary of the Communist Chinese Party in 1927 and went into seclusion.

The differences in their backgrounds and their relationships with the future leaders of the Chinese Communist Party were to become magnified immediately upon the establishment of the Chinese Communist Party in 1921.

Part Three:
Political History
of the CCP, 1921–1947

Russia, the Founding of the Party & the First Revolutionary Civil War, 1921–1927

RUSSIA

Any understanding of the early successes and failures of the Chinese Communist Party must take into account the newly established Soviet Union's three-point China policy adopted in 1918. First, the Soviet government was interested in securing an ally in China to stem Japan's expansionist policy in Asia. The Bolshevik government had every reason to fear Japan. In 1918, Japan took advantage of the power vacuum in Siberia, created by the Russian Civil War and the subsequent Allied intervention in the war against Germany in the eastern front, to occupy not only parts of Siberia (until 1922), but also Northern Sakhalin island and Northern Manchuria. Japan had also fought the Bolsheviks to gain partial control of the railway network in Manchuria and Siberia. Second, the Soviet government sought diplomatic recognition from China as well as other countries. Third, the Soviet government sought to eliminate Western influence from Asia in general. This facet of its China policy was influenced not only by the Soviet quest for an ice-free port but also by the Allied intervention in the Russian revolution.

The implementation of its China policy included establishing contacts with the four dominant political groups in China, any one of which might emerge as the victor in the unstable China situation: (1) the Chinese central government with whom the Soviets wished to establish diplomatic relations, (2) Sun Yat-sen, whom the Soviets regarded as a potential rallying symbol of the Chinese revolution, (3) the warlords, especially Wu P'ei-fu in central China (Peking) and Ch'en Chiung-ming in south China (Canton), and (4) the left-wing intellectuals such as Ch'en Tu-hsiu and Li

Ta-chao, who had discovered Marx and Lenin shortly after the May Fourth incident. In a testament of sympathy, the Soviet Union declared on July 25, 1919, in the Karakhan Declaration (the Soviet foreign minister was Leo Karakhan), that it was ready to give up rights and interests acquired by Czarist Russia through the unequal treaties. It did not.

The first direct contact with the Chinese by a Russian came sometime in 1920 when the eastern bureau of the Communist International (Comintern), with headquarters in Irkutsk, Siberia, sent Gregory Voitinsky to Peking. In Peking, Voitinsky contacted Li Ta-chao and Li, in turn, referred Voitinsky to Ch'en Tu-hsiu who was then in Shanghai. Voitinsky went to Shanghai where he established his headquarters and began his work toward the founding of a Chinese Communist Party. In his initial efforts, Voitinsky established Marxist Study Societies in Shanghai, Peking, Hunan (under Mao's guidance), Hupei, Chekiang, Anhwei, Shantung, and Kwangtung. Similar organizations also were being established abroad, as in France where Chou En-lai was studying, Japan, and Germany, where the future commander-in-chief of the Red Army, Chu Teh, was a college student.

Voitinsky also financed the Socialist Youth Corps, an organization which was made up of a motley group of individuals, including Communists, anarchists, and anti-Confucianists. Ch'en Tu-hsiu was later to dissolve the corps because its heterogeneous nature made it unworkable as a Marxist front.

One of Voitinsky's major contributions, however, was as Marxist educator of China. It was Voitinsky who guided both Ch'en and Li through the intricacies of Marxist-Leninist philosophies. When Voitinsky left China a year later, he left behind the nucleus of a Communist movement in China.

THE FOUNDING OF THE PARTY

On July 1, 1921, twelve delegates representing seven centers of Communist activity in China met at a girls' school in the French concession in Shanghai to establish a Communist party. Among the delegates were Mao Tse-tung representing Hunan province,

Chang Kuo-t'ao from Peking, Tung Pi-wu from Hupei, and the Comintern representative, Maring. The twelve delegates, in turn, represented the total membership of the party at that time, fifty-two, which included such recent party stalwarts as Chou En-lai, Chu teh, Li Fu-ch'un, and Nieh Jung-chen. Ch'en Tu-hsiu and Li Ta-chao were absent from the founding meeting. Ch'en, however, was elected party secretary and Chang Kuo-t'ao head of the important organization department. Mao was elected secretary of the congress and then appointed secretary of the Hunan branch of the CCP.

Among its first decisions, the party declared that: (1) its chief aim was to form industrial unions and imbue the unions with the spirit of the class struggle, (2) establish propaganda outlets, (3) establish nightschools among the workers to raise the political consciousness of the working class, (4) maintain an attitude of independence, aggression, and exclusion from other existing political parties, and (5) maintain close relations with the Comintern.[1]

Each decision was adopted only after heated debate. For example, the decision to imbue the workers with the spirit of the class struggle (Mao, Chang) was opposed by those (Ch'en Kung-po) who felt that the party should pursue such legitimate activities as research and propaganda. Indeed, where this decision was concerned, the militant wing not only succeeded in establishing the Secretariat of the All-China Labor Union but also in organizing strikes against China's endemic social conditions. At one such strike, Mao met the man destined to become, in 1958, the party's second leading theoretician and chairman of the People's Republic of China, Liu Shao-ch'i (purged, however, during the cultural revolution, 1966–68).

A second argument erupted over the decision to establish the CCP's independence and autonomy from the other existing political parties, especially Sun Yat-sen's KMT. The delegates voted not to ally themselves with any party, but they did endorse the spirit of Sun Yat-sen's activist policies. While this question was not as important as the academic vs. militantism one, the CCP's relationship with the KMT was destined to become the key question by 1923.

THE FIRST UNITED FRONT

From 1921 to 1923, the CCP was all dressed up but with no place to go. True, the party had adopted a program, elected its leadership, and allied itself with the reliable Comintern, but it had failed during the two-year interim to penetrate the Nationalist movement, nor had it made impressive strides in party membership, having grown from 52 in 1921 to only 432 in 1923. One of the sharpest criticisms against the CCP came from the Comintern itself, when it charged that the CCP had not even succeeded in penetrating the labor movement, thus failing to accomplish its "chief aim" of 1921.

The question of the CCP's future was formally decided at the Fourth Congress of the Comintern in late 1922. At this historic congress, the Comintern adopted a resolution to have the CCP join the KMT. Ch'en Tu-hsiu, who was present at the congress, opposed the alliance on two grounds: (1) ideological, arguing that the Communist party was the party of the working class and an alliance with the bourgeois-dominated KMT was contradictory to Marxist-Leninist doctrine, and (2) political, for he believed that the Chinese working class was emerging as a viable factor capable of sustaining the revolution as an independent force. Ch'en's ideological reservation was answered by the Comintern with Lenin's 1920 thesis that under certain circumstances Communists may have to form temporary alliances with their class enemies providing the Communists preserve their independent status in the proletarian revolution. Ch'en's second reservation was answered by the February 7, 1923, worker's massacre. The massacre, detailed below, destroyed his conviction that the labor movement in China was sufficiently developed to carry on the leadership of the proletarian revolution. Before discussing the growth of the Chinese labor movement and the events leading up to the massacre, we must consider the Comintern's role in convincing a hesitant Sun Yat-sen that the KMT should agree to the united front.

Sun Yat-sen

It will be recalled that the Comintern had singled out Sun Yat-sen as one of its contacts in China. In November 1921, the

Comintern agent, Maring, visited with Sun. Maring, who had established himself as a master of united front tactics, proceeded to point out to a reluctant Sun the similarities between his "Three Principles of the People" and Communism, and between the Russian and Chinese revolutions. Maring argued, for example, that both countries were noncapitalist and backward; both had foreign and domestic enemies; and both were interested in liberating the masses from oppression. It was, however, in the area of ideological similarities that Maring made his most convincing argument. Generally speaking, his description of the dictatorship of the proletariat sat well with Sun, who had by now become disillusioned with parliamentary democracy and was leaning toward the idea of a one-party government. Specifically, Maring discussed each of the "Three Principles of the People," equating them to Marxist-Leninist doctrine. Thus, Sun's principle of nationalism was expanded to embody the Soviet concept of anti-imperialism; the principle of democracy was said to embody the Soviet concept of political tutelage under one-party rule and a democratic process guided by Sun's KMT toward the third-stage, constitutional government; and, finally, the principle of people's livelihood was equated by Sun to the Soviet "land to the tiller" policy and even "communism."[2]

Sun was fairly well convinced by Maring that Russian communism was very similar to his own beliefs.

Maring was not, nonetheless, entirely successful in this initial meeting with Sun. In January 1922, a delegation of KMT members attended the First Congress of the Toilers of the Far East held in Moscow. Zinoviev, the chairman of the congress, called again for an alliance between the CCP and KMT. In August 1922, Maring again came forward with the formula which was to cement the alliance and receive Sun's acceptance: Communists would be allowed to join the KMT as individual members but not as Communists. To counter Ch'en Tu-hsiu's ideological reservations, Maring argued that the KMT was not a bourgeois party but rather a coalition of all classes, and thus it was incumbent on the proletariat to transform the KMT in the long run. Maring exhorted the Comintern to pressure Sun into accepting the alliance.

The Comintern did not have to apply too much pressure. It

would be difficult to understand Sun's eventual acceptance had it not been for his disillusionment with Western ideas and behavior and his own loss of vitality and popularity. As has already been mentioned, Sun had lost faith in Western parliamentary practices and was, in fact, tending toward the notion of a one-party government. Further, the foreign powers had ignored him, refused him financial aid, and believed him (of all people) of being an obstacle to national unity. Domestically, Sun was frustrated by warlord politics, especially those of the southern warlord, Ch'en Chiung-ming, for whom Sun had implemented reforms in Kwangtung. In July 1922, Ch'en Chiung-ming chased Sun out of Canton, and in the process, Sun was advised by friends to forget about politics. Thus, when Dalin, a delegate of the Russian Communist Youth League, reintroduced Maring's formula, Sun agreed.

With Sun in a more agreeable mood, the Comintern sent Adolf Joffe to Shanghai to conclude a formal agreement with Sun. Joffe arrived in Shanghai where Sun was in exile after Ch'en had chased him out of Canton in December 1922, and discussed the components of the united front. Finally, on January 26, 1923, both issued a joint statement in which Sun held that:

> the Communistic order or even the Soviet system cannot actually be introduced into China ... [and] this view is entirely shared by Mr. Joffe [who] ... had reaffirmed the [three] principles ... [and has] categorically declared ... that the Russian government is ready and willing to enter into negotiation with China on the basis of the renunciation by Russia of all the treaties and exactions which the Tsardom imposed in China.[3]

Treating Sun Yat-sen as an equal assured the Comintern of the support of one of the two important political parties needed to forge the alliance and assure itself of a badly needed ally in Asia. Where the CCP was concerned, however, the Comintern received its help from China's chaotic domestic politics.

The Chinese Labor Movement

The leaders of the CCP continued to question the propriety of the proposed alliance through 1922 and early 1923. What made the CCP leaders change their minds was not the ideological arguments advanced by the Comintern or even the kinds of pressures brought on Sun Yat-sen by the Comintern. What made the CCP leadership change its mind was a miscalculation of the growing strength of the Chinese labor class.[4]

Again, it was the May Fourth movement which brought the Chinese labor movement to the fore. Up until the May Fourth movement, the Chinese labor force was mostly employed in foreign-owned large-scale industrial enterprises, but it was unevenly distributed throughout the country. Before the turn of the century, a nascent Chinese-owned industry was emerging. But as we shall see, foreign domination of China's economy was to become an important part of Chinese evidence of imperialism.

Prior to 1919, China's working class was distributed unevenly in roughly five regions: (1) Shanghai and along the Yangtze River, (2) Canton and Hong Kong, (3) Hupeh and Hunan, (4) Shantung, and (5) Peking. In these areas, foreigners owned 100 percent of the flour, tobacco, blast-furnace, cement, metal ore, and silk industries, 93 percent of all shipyards, and 84 percent of the coal mining industry. In these areas, there were more foreign-owned enterprises than Chinese-owned ones.

Jean Chesneaux has estimated the strength of the labor force in 1919 at 1.5 million (0.5 percent total population) with nearly 50 percent employed in foreign-owned businesses. Shanghai alone accounted for nearly three hundred thousand workers, or about 20 percent of the total labor force. Thus, around the time of the May Fourth movement, the Chinese labor force was numerically weak in relation to the total population of the country, and because of its uneven distribution, it was effective only within the limited areas where it was concentrated, such as in Shanghai and Hunan with its one hundred thousand iron workers.

Prior to May fourth, the political consciousness of the labor force was negligible. The young and inexperienced Chinese proletariat were unable to organize themselves; moreover, several official regulations were adopted restricting such labor activities as meetings or strikes. Despite the harsh treatment accorded the labor organizations by both Chinese and foreign companies, nearly one hundred fifty strikes and protests were recorded between 1895 and

1918. Most of the strikes were over wage increases, and most did not succeed in their objectives, with their failure generally explained by the repression of the workers by the Chinese government and/or the foreign-owned companies. Between 1917 and 1919, the frequency of strike activities increased, paving the way for the series of economic strikes which prepared the Chinese working class for its mass entry into the turbulent political situation.

The Chinese workers' militancy carried into the May Fourth incident. The strike activity, which initially was small but spontaneous and effective, eventually led to the growth of labor organizations. In June 1919, the All-China Industrial Federation was established followed shortly thereafter by the founding of other trade and labor organizations.

In time, the labor movement fused with Marxist-Leninist political activities. The May 1920, issue of *New Youth,* for example, devoted its entire issue to labor problems. The influential Marxist publication, *The World of Labor,* contained various discussions on Marxist theory. In Peking, Canton, and Ch'angsha, similar labor journals were founded. In Hunan, Mao founded night schools for the workers and also opened a "New Culture" bookstore as a front to pass out Marxist literature. Communist activities among the workers led to the first May Day celebration held in Shanghai in 1920.

By 1922, the Chinese working class was making impressive strides. Not only had a seaman's strike in Hong Kong rallied over one hundred twenty thousand workers, but by April 1922, the All-China Labor Congress attracted 160 delegates from twelve cities representing more than three hundred thousand workers. Ch'en Tu-hsiu expressed high hopes for this congress. In it, Ch'en saw the potential for a national labor union which would put an end to economic regionalism. According to Chesneaux, the economic barriers did come down and for the first time, "the labor organizations of the entire country made contact with one another."[5] The rapid strides toward organizing the working class and the number of successful strikes in 1922 explained Ch'en Tu-hsiu's euphoric assessment of the growing strength of the Chinese labor movement at the same time that the Comintern was proposing an alliance between the CCP and the KMT.

The Comintern and Warlords

When Maring was on his way to Shanghai for the First Party Congress, he stopped in Peking to secure the support of one of the four groups in contention for power in China: the warlords. He conferred with Wu P'ei-fu, who was then in control of Peking. Maring assured Wu of the Comintern's support and financial assistance in return for sanctuary for Communists in and around Peking. On at least one occasion, Maring made good on his promise of support. In 1922, Comintern agents helped Wu P'ei-fu defend Peking against the Manchurian Warlord Chang Tso-lin.[6] On the other hand, under Wu's protection, Communist labor organizers began their organizational activities among the railway workers.

The railway workers, however, soon incurred the wrath of Wu P'ei-fu. The strike waves of 1922 had damaged one of Wu's sources of revenue, the railway running between Peking and Hankow. This line linked Peking with British mines in Honan, some important military camps, and Wuhan, the most important economic center in China.[7] It was said that whoever controlled this important railway line controlled the heartland of China.

To protect this important railway system Wu ordered the formation of "railway soldiers" to guard the railway and to prevent strikes along the line. The railway workers, however, buoyed by successes in the 1922 railway strikes and by strikes against the British in Hankow, decided to organize themselves into the Peking-Hankow General Union of Railway Workers.[8] A founder's meeting was scheduled for February 2, 1923, in Chengchow, Honan, the center of the railway network. Despite Wu P'ei-fu's ban on the conference, the workers met, founded the union, and dispersed. Not, however, before some arrests were made.

Two days later, a general strike was called against the railway. On February 7, Wu P'ei-fu and other warlords attacked the workers, killing thirty-five to sixty of them during the strike.[9] On February 8, the British sent their marines to Hankow and there suppressed a sympathy strike declared after the February 7 massacre.

A new policy of suppression was ushered in by both warlords and foreign governments. The effects of the policy can be seen in the decreasing frequency of strikes, falling from ninety-one in 1922 to forty-seven in 1923 and increasing only slightly to fifty-six by 1924.[10]

According to Communist party-historian Teng Chung-hsia, "most of the labor unions so carefully built up by the Communist party during the previous two years . . . were crushed, and the Chinese Labor movement entered into a period of decline."[11] The new policy had its profoundest effect on Party Secretary Ch'en Tu-hsiu, who, after February 7, lost all faith in the power of the proletariat.[12] According to Ch'en, "the Chinese proletariat is immature both quantitatively and qualitatively. . . . They [the workers] do not feel the need for political action and are still full of ancient superstitions."[13]

New Leases on Life: The KMT,
the CCP, and the Soviet Union

The KMT. In January 1924, the First National Congress of the KMT was held in Canton, Sun Yat-sen's power base. The congress attracted 199 delegates from the leading factions. Sun Yat-sen was among those representing the KMT while Li Ta-chao and Mao Tse-tung were among those representing the CCP. Borodin, who had initiated the preliminary negotiations for the congress, represented the Comintern.

The five-member presidium which overlooked the proceedings of the congress included the rightist Hu Han-min, the leftist Wang Ching-wei, and the Communist Li Ta-chao. Li Ta-chao also was elected to the twenty-four-member Central Executive Committee with Mao as an alternate. The congress reorganized the KMT party along Russian Communist party lines, and Communists were elected to such key posts within the KMT as members of the organization, labor, peasant, women, industry, and propaganda (Mao) departments. Clearly, Communists had successfully infiltrated the KMT party organization and were biding their time for the take-over.

The delegates also adopted a manifesto which outlined the

KMT's policies and programs, including the cooperation of the KMT with Russia, the admission of Communists (as individuals) to the KMT and the emphasis on the organization of peasants and workers.

Sun Yat-sen's most important writings were adopted into the KMT's general program. The "Three Principles of the People" (San Min Chu-i) was adopted as the official ideology of the Chinese revolution. Equally important, the congress also adopted Sun's *Fundamentals of National Reconstruction,* in which he had outlined the three stages leading to China's political unification. Under this plan, the first stage was to be a military one. The second stage was to be a period of political tutelage during which the KMT was to prepare the masses for local self-government (this stage, although ultimately implemented, never accomplished its stated objective). Finally, once the people were sufficiently acquainted with the electoral process at the basic levels of government, the central government would proclaim the start of the third stage, during which a national assembly would be convened to enact and promulgate a national constitution. The adoption of a national constitution would mark the consummation of constitutionalism in China.

Despite the absence of clearly defined transitional time periods, the first stage (detailed below) was inaugurated in 1926 with the antiwarlord campaign called the Northern Expedition. This stage lasted until roughly 1928. The second stage was proclaimed in October 1928, when the standing committee of the KMT passed the "Essentials of Tutelage" program. The third stage was inaugurated on December 25, 1946 with the adoption of a national constitution by the national assembly. But, as we shall see, neither the second nor third stages was to prove advantageous to the KMT in its struggle with the CCP.

The congress, in 1924, adopted Sun's blueprint for the shape of the KMT's government. In his *Fundamentals of National Reconstruction,* Sun made it clear that his governmental blueprint would not be put into effect until the country had been declared as having successfully passed the military and political tutelage stages. The congress, however, disregarded Sun's qualification and on October 8, 1928, adopted the "Organic Law of the National Government," containing Sun's "Five-Power Constitution." It was Sun's erstwhile protégé, Chiang K'ai-shek, who pushed for the adoption of Sun's governmental blueprint.

Sun's "Five-Power Constitution" was built around five major branches (*Yuan*) of government. Sun's governmental structure included three branches inspired by Western models (executive, legislative, and judicial branches) and two branches inspired by traditional Chinese institutions (the examination and control branches). To the people, Sun reserved the four powers of election, recall, initiative, and referendum. In setting up his ideal political system, then, Sun was careful to distinguish between governmental function (the five branches) and political power (the four powers of the people).[14]

In effect, the congress had established the framework for a governmental and political system which despite its defects in later years, was to claim a greater degree of political unity for China than ever before. Herein lies the greatest significance of the congress and of Sun's organizational efforts.

The congress further adopted the Leninist techniques of party organization, structure, and discipline. Borodin was to play a central role in the reorganization of the KMT along Russian Communist party lines. Figure 6.1 provides a graphic representation of the form which the KMT took.

The structure of the KMT was pyramidical. At the base of the pyramid was the party membership. Recruitment was undertaken at the ward level. The party membership at the ward level then elected its representatives to the next higher level, the district. District congresses in turn elected their representatives to the next higher level, the county, while the county sent delegates to the provincial level. The provinces finally elected their representatives to the highest party level, the National Congress. The National Congress was (theoretically) the supreme authority within the party. Party congresses were to meet every two years. Because of its unwieldy size (First Congress: 200 delegates; Sixth in 1945; 600), a Central Executive Committee (CEC) ran party affairs when the National Party Congress was in recess. The NPC grew in size, so did the CEC (1924: 41; 1945: 312). Thus, when the CEC was

Figure 6.1
Kuomintang Party Structure

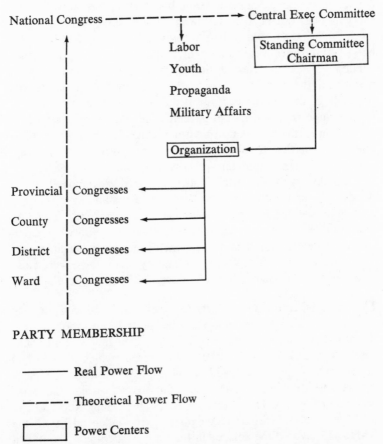

PARTY MEMBERSHIP

———— Real Power Flow

— — — - Theoretical Power Flow

☐ Power Centers

itself adjourned, a standing committee elected from the CEC
wielded the power. Real power resided in the standing committee,
at least until 1938, when Chiang K'ai-shek was elected party
leader. Prior to Chiang's ascendancy and after Sun Yat-sen's death
(1925), party leaders enjoyed whatever power the standing committee wished to bestow upon them.

The organizational principle which formed the basis of the
party ideology was "democratic centralism." The principle was

adopted from Leninist, and therefore, Soviet, party organization. On one level, the principle recognized the importance of free discussion prior to reaching a decision, but after a decision was made, everyone was obligated to follow it without dissent. At a higher level, the principle guided the selection and election of party members: "Authorities were to be democratically elected by the membership . . . and once elected, they were to have the power of command and the right to be obeyed."[15] "Democracy," under the principle of democratic centralism did not imply the presence of many democratic processes as generally understood by Westerners. For example, there were no provisions made for the right to form opposition parties, to obtain redress from government or freely participate in the nominating process of candidates.

Finally, with the establishment of the Whampoa Military Academy near Canton in May 1924, the Kuomintang completed its reorganization. The party now had its own military force. As noted earlier, Chiang was appointed president in 1925 while Chou En-lai headed the political department of the army. Galens represented the Comintern at Whampoa, and by 1925, there were close to a thousand Russian military advisers in China.

The CCP. When the Third Party Congress convened in Canton in June 1923, Ch'en Tu-hsiu and the other party leaders looked upon the proposed alliance in a new light. Indeed, the united front dominated the agenda of the Third Party Congress, which by now had 30 delegates representing 432 members. The issue at the party congress was not the alliance itself, but the role which the party was to assume in it. There were some, notably Chang Kuo-t'ao and Li Li-san, who favored keeping the party independent of the KMT, and favored the alliance in the form of a "bloc without." In the main, however, Ch'en Tu-hsiu, who counted Mao among his supporters, favored Stalin's formula of forming a "bloc within" the KMT organizational structure. Those favoring the "bloc within" formula saw the alliance as an opportunity to expand the party's propaganda and recruiting efforts, allying the party with the symbols of the Chinese revolution (Sun Yat-sen, for example) and more importantly, "gather the masses around [the CCP] and split the Kuomintang Party."[16]

Chang Kuo-t'ao's only consolation was his success in keeping the trade unions independent of joint CCP/KMT control, having lost in his initial proposal before the Third Party Congress, but ultimately gaining a reversal of the decision. This issue, however, widened the gap between Mao and Chang when Mao changed his support from Chang to Ch'en Tu-hsiu on this point.

In retrospect, the CCP stood to gain more from the alliance than did the KMT. First, the alliance gave the CCP full freedom of movement within the KMT, one advantage which the KMT did not enjoy with respect to the CCP. The infiltration of Communists in the KMT began what came to be known as the "left wing" movement of the KMT.

The infiltration of the KMT was modest at the outset, but it was important nonetheless. Communists were given key positions in key departments within the newly reorganized KMT. Three Communists were elected to the powerful Central Committee of the KMT, including Li Ta-chao. Mao was one of six Communists elected as alternates to the Central Committee, and one of three elected as secretaries to key departments (labor, peasant, and organization). From among the many departments which made up the KMT structure, only three did not have a Communist in them (youth, commerce, and military affairs).

Chou En-lai, however, was appointed as the political commissar to the Whampoa Academy, giving the Communists access to the primary military unit of the KMT.

The second important gain for the CCP was its identification with the symbols of the national revolution, such as Sun Yat-sen and with the reform programs of the KMT and the national revolution. The CCP's organizational activities became manifest in the labor movement (notably through Chang Kuo-t'ao) and peasant associations, especially in Kwangtung Province under the leadership of the first acknowledged Communist peasant organizer, P'eng P'ai.

The alliance also had some dire consequences for the CCP in the long run. The most notable setback to the CCP was in its leadership. The decision to join the KMT eventually caused internal divisions within the CCP, beginning with the removal of the party cofounder, Ch'en Tu-hsiu, shortly after the Shanghai Massacre of 1927 (to be discussed later) and the execution of the other party cofounder, Li Ta-chao, as a result of the events leading up to the Shanghai Massacre. From the disastrous losses of party leaders in 1927 until the ascendancy to power by Mao Tse-tung in 1935, the CCP was to suffer continuously because of leadership problems.

The Soviet Union. With the united front a fact and with the establishment of the Whampoa Academy and concomitant influx of Russian advisers, the C.P.S.U. had every reason to be optimistic about its chances for pushing the national revolution in China under Soviet control. For the next decade, at least, Stalin was to attempt to control the future of the Chinese revolution from Moscow.

The Stillborn Alliance

Stalin may have been the only one with any reason to be optimistic. The alliance, to paraphrase an old sophist saying, was dying at birth. As early as November 1923, some KMT members expressed the fear that the Communists would use the KMT for their own purposes. By April 1924, an attempt was made to censure the Communists for allegedly attempting to create a bloc within the KMT. Following Sun Yat-sen's untimely death on March 12, 1925, all that remained of the alliance was its form. It was, as shall be seen, devoid of content.

After Sun's death, a group of his loyalists, known as the Western Hills Group, unsuccessfully attempted to expel all Communists, Chinese as well as Russian, from China. The group also failed to transfer the Central Committee from Communist-infested Canton to Shanghai. The stopping force during these unsuccessful attempts was Moscow's influence within the KMT. In any case, the one issue which would split not only the KMT from the CCP but also the KMT itself into left- and right-wing factions was the issue of the alliance.

The May Thirtieth Movement

After the alliance was cemented, Mao went to Shanghai to assume the post of secretary of the organization department of the

KMT. According to Mao, he coordinated the measures of the Communist and Nationalist Parties. His counterpart in the KMT was Hu Han-min, and Mao's close associations with Hu led some of Mao's less friendly cohorts to refer to him as "Hu Han-min's secretary," a dig which Mao would just as soon forget and one which Communist historians understandably ignore.

By 1925, the alliance found itself facing an explosive situation in China. On the one hand, China reeked of foreign activities and foreign exploitations. The mid-1920s were characterized by foreign gunboats patrolling central China.

Domestically, warlordism had reached its peak. Wu P'ei-fu controlled central China; Chang Tso-lin dominated Manchuria; Sun Ch'uan-fang was in charge over parts of east and southeast China (headquarters in Shanghai); and Feng Yu-hsiang was the power in an area around the northwest.

It was in response to this highly volatile situation that China entered into a period of patriotic antiimperial and antiwarlord sentiment. To this end, the alliance responded to both developments with some successes against the warlords and some failures against the foreigners.

The first response by the Chinese was a patriotic anti-imperialist movement. This movement was to be especially beneficial to the Chinese Communist Party.

By the spring of 1925, a growing hostility to the foreign powers in China was evident. Strikes increased in numbers and intensity. In Shanghai and Peking, serious incidents occurred, involving clashes between students and police. Student rallies and rioting increased, with violence and even killings reported. It was because of the slaying of a Chinese worker by a Japanese foreman that a memorial service was planned for May 24. The memorial service attracted five thousand people.[17] The memorial service was ended by foreign police acting to protect the rights of foreign investors.[18]

In response to the actions of the foreign police, the Central Committee of the Chinese Community Party decided to stage still another demonstration in hopes of provoking a clash with the foreign police. The date for the demonstration was set for May 30 in Shanghai.

"Several thousand people" participated in the demonstration.[19] Soon, a clash occurred between British police and the demonstrators. Panicking, the British chief of police ordered his men to fire at the demonstrators. Ten persons were killed and over fifty injured. The major number of those killed or injured were workers.[20]

The clash and ensuing bloodshed had its desired effect: on June 1, all work ceased in shops, schools, and factories. Sparked by Tsai Ho-shen, a Communist and Mao's closest friend at that time, the Shanghai General Union was founded. It was controlled by the Communists. A future leader of the Chinese Communist party, Li Li-san, began his rise to the top during this period.

The May Thirtieth movement, as it came to be called, had three significant results. First, despite the failure to dislodge foreign interests in China, it did achieve a measure of national solidarity as the movement expanded to such places as Manchuria, Peking, Nanking, Wuhan, Chungking, and Canton. In the short run, however, the combined strengths of foreign police and the Chinese Chamber of Commerce forced the initial fervor of the national movement to subside.[21]

Second, the one group which profited significantly from its involvement in the demonstrations was the Chinese Communist Party. Party membership increased from 950 in 1925, at the time of the Fourth Congress of the CCP, to 57,967 when the Fifth Congress met in early 1927.[22]

Third, although he had not participated in the movement because of illness, Mao credits it with turning his attention toward the revolutionary potential of the peasantry. "Formerly," he told Edgar Snow, "I had not fully realized the degree of class struggle among the peasantry, but after the May Thirtieth incident, and during the great wave of political activity which followed it, the Hunanese peasantry became very militant."[23] Mao eventually was shifted to the peasant department of the KMT, where P'eng Pai, a Communist, served as secretary. During this time, Mao wrote an important essay, "Report of an Investigation into the Peasant Movement in Hunan," which Ch'en Tu-hsiu, the party secretary, refused to acknowledge. Mao and Ch'en began drifting apart as a result.

Chiang K'ai-shek

The second response by the Chinese to the situation of 1925 was directed internally at the warlords. As part of Sun Yat-sen's first stage leading to national unification, a military expedition was announced on July 1, 1926.[24] On July 9, Chiang's military forces took an oath and issued a manifesto proclaiming that it was "the purpose of the military campaign . . . to build an independent nation on the basis of the Three People's Principles and to protect the interests of the nation and of the people."[25] Before we discuss the campaign itself, Chiang's rise to power will be considered briefly at this point.

Chiang K'ai-shek was born on October 31, 1887, in Chekiang Province located in east-central China.[26] His parents were farmers, and salt merchants. Chiang was extremely devoted to his mother. He was educated along Confucian lines, but he showed the keenest interest in Sun Tzu's military classic, *The Art of War* (written in the fourth or fifth century B.C.). In 1907, he attended a military school where he spent an uneventful year, but succeeded in becoming a government-sponsored student in Japan. Chiang continued his military studies, but here he was to meet a cadre of revolutionaries who would greatly influence his life. In 1908, Chiang joined Sun Yat-sen's revolutionary Common Alliance Society. He apparently met Sun at this time.

In 1911, when he was twenty-four, Chiang was deeply involved in the revolution against the Manchus (Chiang had as early as 1905 cut off his queue as his own personal act of rebelliousness against the alien Manchus). At this time, he made his first contacts with the secret societies of Shanghai. During Yuan Shih-k'ai's attempt to restore the monarchy, Chiang played a minor role, preferring to continue his study of military works and military strategy. Between 1916, the year of Yuan's death, and late 1919, Chiang lived an undistinguished life. "He was," writes Linebarger, "simply one more among the dozens of bright young military men who were in the existing crudity of warfare, unneeded in China."

During this "unneeded" period, Chiang turned his attention to business. It was at this time (1919) that he is alleged to have established, on Sun Yat-sen's orders, a brokerage firm in Shanghai. Once again, Chiang continued to develop his close ties with the secret society called the Green Gang, which, in turn, had connections with the Shanghai underworld. Until 1922, Chiang's career and his role in the Kuomintang remained unimpressive.

Chiang's rise to power began with his selection by Sun to head a special mission to Moscow under the aegis of the first united front talks. Chiang's mission was to study Soviet political and military tactics and organization. In Moscow, Chiang met such Soviet leaders as Trotsky, Chicherin, Zinoviev, Maring, Joffe, and Voitinsky. He did not meet Lenin, who was ill at this time. He did, however, read Marx's *Das Capital,* to which he had a mixed reaction. He left Moscow on November 29, 1923.

Chiang's political and military fortunes continued rising when, in January 1924, he was appointed to the military council of the newly reorganized KMT. More importantly, he was appointed chairman of a study group to establish a military academy at Whampoa, a small island ten miles from Canton. When the academy was formally opened on May 3, 1924, Chiang was appointed as its first president. Many of the cadets who were to attend Whampoa were destined to become Chiang's closest advisers in the years ahead. Furthermore, both Chiang and his cadets distinguished themselves in early 1925 when they successfully routed the southern warlord, Ch'en Chiung-ming. From mid-1925 on, Chiang was clearly the military leader of the Kuomintang.

The Northern Expedition

Once the expedition against the warlords started, the KMT army moved rapidly. Starting in Canton in July 1926, the army captured Ch'angsha in the same month, Wuhan in October, Nanch'ang in November, Foochow in December, Hangchow in February 1927, Nanking in March, and it reached the outskirts of Shanghai in the same month.[27]

During the campaign, three significant events occurred. First, the KMT army established temporary headquarters in Nanch'ang, where Chiang remained from November 26 to March 27 to direct

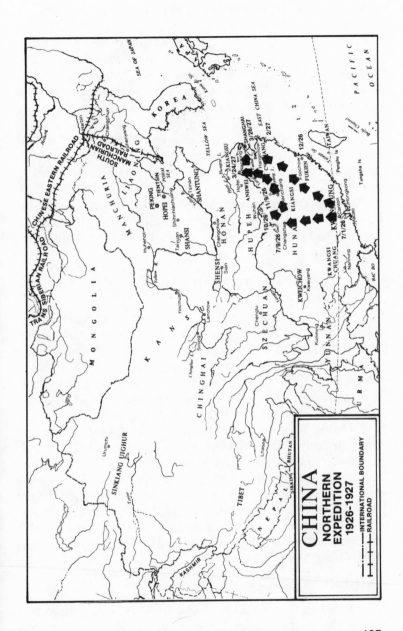

CHINA

NORTHERN EXPEDITION 1926-1927

- - - - - INTERNATIONAL BOUNDARY
+ + + + + RAILROAD

the military campaign. Second, the KMT government moved from the Communist stronghold in Canton to Wuhan in December 1926, where it became dominated by Wang Ching-wei, a leftist by reputation, and by the Communists. This government came to be known as the Left-Wing KMT. The shift was made by Stalin's order, an act which Chiang viewed with apprehension.[28] Furthermore, while in Wuhan the left-dominated KMT defined itself in such terms as to exclude the other wing of the KMT from being considered as an active participant in the national revolution.

The third event was the Shanghai Massacre of April 12, 1927, when Chiang entered Shanghai and destroyed the Chinese Communists who had fought alongside him during the campaign and who had just liberated the city from the Shanghai warlord, Sun Ch'uan-fang.

THE SHANGHAI MASSACRE

Why? This question will probably never be answered to anyone's satisfaction. Enough had been done by both parties to warrant some kind of confrontation at some point during the first united front. The only point which can be made with any kind of confidence is that Chiang struck first. There is a need now, however, to review some major events which may help us to understand the so-called Day of Infamy, April 12, 1927.

Chiang had every reason to be suspicious of the Communists from the time of the declaration of the alliance in 1923 right up to the moment when he struck in 1927. Three events may help to explain Chiang's frame of mind during the expedition: (1) the March 20, 1926, coup, (2) Chiang's demotion by the left wing of the KMT in March 1927, and (3) the discovery of incriminating evidence against Communists in China during the April 6, 1927, raid on the Russian military attache's office in Peking by the warlord, Chang Tso-lin.

The March 20, 1926, Coup

Relations between the CCP and the KMT were strained even during the inauguration of the alliance. Chiang was particularly worried about the secrecy and the ease with which CCP members moved inside the KMT, so he took the first step to counter the growing influence of the Communists and the Comintern within the KMT.

The growing tension between Chiang and the Communists was brought to a head first by the smear campaign which branded him a "counter revolutionary and a new warlord," but more importantly, by the "Communist plot" which he "sensed" was to be made against his life. The plot revolved around a gunboat, the *Chungshan*.[29]

According to Chiang, the gunboat had been moved from Canton to the Whampoa Academy without his knowledge. When the gunboat returned to Canton on March 19, it was loaded with "enough coal for a long voyage."[30] On March 20, Chiang moved. He declared martial law in Canton, arrested the Communists he suspected were out to harm him, and placed Russian officials under surveillance. Chiang wrote of the coup:

> Only after it was all over did I learn of [the Communist's] plan to seize me on board the *Chungshan* when I was to take it to go back to the Military Academy at Whampoa from Canton. They would then send me as a prisoner to Russia via Vladisvostok, thereby removing the major obstacle to their scheme of using the National Revolution as a medium for setting up a "dictatorship of the proletariat."[31]

Demotion of Chiang

Early in the Northern Expedition, a controversy emerged which was to be the test case between the left and right wings of the KMT. The controversy centered on the location of the Third Plenum meeting of the KMT Central Executive Committee. For the Communists, the faction which decided the location would indicate who was in control of the national revolution. The left wing, led by Wang Ching-wei, and supported by the Communists, won.

The Third Plenum of the CEC was scheduled to meet in Wuhan from March 10 to March 17, 1927. During the session, the left wing gained control of the highest offices within the KMT. Although Chiang was elected to the powerful standing committee of the Central Executive Committee, he was replaced by Wang Ching-wei as chairman of the equally powerful organization department. Furthermore, the CCP established its control over the military council headed by Chiang. The Communists had influenced the events leading to Chiang's demotion, and Chiang knew it.

Raid of the Russian Embassy

The third incident which led to Chiang's growing distrust of the Communists was the result of some evidence discovered during a raid of the office of the Soviet military attaché in Peking on April 6, 1927, less than a week before the Shanghai incident. The Soviet attaché's office in Peking was the point for directing Soviet activities in China.[32] The raid was led by the warlord, Chang Tso-lin, who was now in control of Peking. During the raid, he uncovered about a thousand documents (324 have been translated but their authenticity is doubted) which revealed that the Comintern was attempting to manipulate the Chinese revolution through the Chinese Communists. Following the discovery of the documents, Li Ta-chao, one of the cofounders of the CCP, was arrested, tried, convicted and on April 28, he and nineteen others were executed by strangulation.

Chiang's role in the raid is not clear, but it is possible that he helped to arrange it, knowing, or at least suspecting, what would be found in the embassy compound. According to Chiang's official biographer, Hollinton Tong, "After the disclosures based upon the documents taken in the raid at Peking, Chiang realized that it would be folly to wait longer, thereby giving time for the machinations of the Reds to mature."[33]

Shanghai Massacre, April 12, 1927

Shanghai was the center of labor activities in China. It was also the focal point for Communist infiltration of the labor movement. By the spring of 1927, the Communist-controlled Shanghai General Union, founded during the May Thirtieth movement, numbered approximately 1.2 million workers.[34] In Shanghai, the labor movement was one of the leading factions in the struggle against the Shanghai warlord Sun Ch'uan-fang.

On March 21, the Shanghai General Union rallied over a half-million workers and led an insurrection in the city, liberating the city from warlord control at this time. On March 22, Chiang's troops reached the outskirts of the city, and on that same day, the Provisional Municipal Government of Shanghai was formally inaugurated. Communists, such as Chou En-lai, were members of the body.

Because the provisional government included a well-armed workers militia, Chiang began to take precautions. His movements between March 22 and March 29 intensified. He held a series of meetings with foreign settlement authorities, police and the Shanghai underworld, ostensibly to seek aid and to reassure these groups of his impending action. Groups contacted by Chiang included the city's merchants and bankers who "rallied to his support" by raising $3 million for his "immediate needs."[35] Another group included the secret societies, notably the Green Gang, with whom Chiang had established relations eight years before. Chiang's troops included members from this secret organization based in Shanghai.

At 4:00 A.M., April 12, Chiang struck. The main target was the headquarters of the Shanghai General Union. The surprise attack led to the quick routing of the workers in Shanghai, during which about three hundred Communist and labor leaders were either killed or wounded.[36] On the following day, about one-hundred thousand workers demonstrated in protest of Chiang's actions, whereupon Chiang's machine guns killed several hundred more.[37] Chiang then declared all left-wing organizations in Shanghai illegal, including the various student associations.

As if to lend further credence to the charge that the coup was planned well in advance, the extermination of other left-wing organizations occurred simultaneously in such places as Fukien, Kiangsi, Szechwan, Chekiang, and Canton, where the right-wing KMT was in control. In the end, only the labor organizations in Hunan and Hupeh, where the left-wing KMT was dominant, survived. With Chiang's proclamation of a new government to be established in Nanking under his control on April 18, 1927, the Chinese labor movement and its Communist connection came to an end. From this point on, labor went underground and the Communists took to the hills.

The Period of the Second Revolutionary Civil War, 1927–1937

THE SHANGHAI AFTERMATH

The events surrounding the Shanghai Massacre had a profound impact on the three major participants in China in mid–1927. For Stalin and the Comintern, "Chiang's betrayal" of the alliance saw the intensification of the intraparty feud between Stalin and Trotsky and the concomitant shift of strategy by Stalin which was to have disastrous results for the Communist movement in China; for Chiang and the KMT, the end of the alliance and the gradual loosening of ties with the Comintern thrust Chiang and the KMT into the middle of the revolution; and, for a time, the Chinese Communist Party was turned into a pawn in the battle between Stalin and Trotsky and nearly ended the rise of communism in China.

Stalin, Trotsky, and the China Question

Following the Shanghai Massacre, Stalin continued to push for the continuation of the united front. Now, however, Stalin's strategy called for the capture of the KMT through the left-wing faction of the KMT led by Wang Ching-wei. By July 1927, Stalin's "estimate of the situation" in China was that both the workers and the peasants were ready for pushing the revolution from above, that is, through the alliance of workers and peasants as outlined by Lenin as early as 1905. Trotsky, on the other hand, took the opposite view, and in doing so, continued to question Stalin's judgment on events occurring in distant China.

Stalin could not, for example, advocate breaking the alliance since Trotsky had always been against it. To do so would be to prove Trotsky correct in his analysis of conditions in the Chinese revolution. Trotsky's own "estimate of the situation" was that the revolutionary tide was in "ebb-tide," and therefore the revolution from above should give way to the revolution from below. For Trotsky, the CCP's mission now was to organize soviets, raise an army, and arm the workers.[1] In rejecting Stalin's call for the continuation of the alliance, an impassioned Leon Trotsky said:

> We say directly to the Chinese peasants: The leaders of the Left Kuomintang of the type of Wang Ching-wei and Co. will inevitably betray you if you follow the Wuhan heads instead of forming your own independent Soviets. . . . Therefore Chinese proletariat, build up your workers' Soviets, ally them with the peasant Soviets, draw soldiers' representatives into the Soviets, shoot the generals who do not recognize the Soviets.[2]

But Stalin had the last word.

Chiang and the Left-KMT

Shortly after the Shanghai Massacre, Chiang K'ai-shek was expelled from the KMT by the Wuhan faction for his part in the massacre. A resolution, which was passed through the efforts of the left wing of the KMT accusing Chiang of various crimes, read:

> Whereas Chiang K'ai-shek is found guilty of massacre of the people and oppression of the Party and, Whereas he deliberately engages himself in reactionary acts and his crime and outrages are so obvious, The Mandate is hereby issued that the Central Executive Committee has adopted a resolution that Chiang shall be expelled from the Party and dismissed from all his posts and that the commanders and soldiers shall affect his arrest and send him to the Central Government for punishment in accordance with the law against counterrevolutionaries.[3]

In August 1927, Chiang "retired" from the KMT, and in the next few months was solaced by the arrangements for his marriage to Mei-ling Soong, the sister of Sun Yat-sen's widow. The marriage took place in December 1927. In the meantime, control of the KMT government was under the undisputed leadership of the left-KMT and Wang Ching-wei. This faction, as has been noted, became the focal point of Stalin's new strategy for controlling the revolution in China. However, events beginning in mid–1927 would deliver the left-KMT to a waiting and patient Chiang K'ai-shek.

The White Terror

The pursuit of Communists and other radicals continued after the April 12 incident. But, the intensity of the anti-Communist campaigns increased significantly after the disclosure of Stalin's intentions for gaining control of the left-KMT.

The preservation of the alliance headed Stalin's list of priorities in China. Thus, Stalin decided to put the left-KMT to the test and determine, once and for all, if the left-KMT was ready and vulnerable to Comintern control. On May 30, 1927, Stalin wired Borodin about his new radical line for taking advantage of the revolution's high tide. The CCP, Stalin ordered, was to (1) confiscate land, being careful not to touch the land of the military officers, (2) check the peasants' (and Mao's) overzealousness, (3) destroy any general in the KMT who proved to be unreliable or unwilling to accept the Comintern's directions, and (4) arm twenty thousand Communists and create a new army from the workers and peasants. As Jerome Ch'en has correctly noted: "Was it possible to carry out these self-contradictory measures at one time? Since 'all the landowners were directly or indirectly protected by the officers,' confiscation was bound to lead to a clash of arms with the officers as it had done before."[4] Borodin and CCP Party Leader Ch'en Tu-hsiu hesitated to implement Stalin's new policy, but the young Indian representative to the Comintern, M. N. Roy, did not hesitate. Eager to implement Stalin's new policy, Roy showed Stalin's telegram to Wang Ching-wei, believing that this was what Wang needed to bolster his confidence as the new head of the Wuhan KMT.[5] For one who was supposed to have already known the contents of the policy long before it was put down on paper,[6] Wang reacted in an unexpected way. Wang first contacted the warlord, Feng Yu-hsiang, who at this time "held the balance of power" in the China situation.[7] No agreement was reached, whereupon Feng then met with Chiang K'ai-shek, and in a joint statement reaffirmed the primacy of Sun Yat-sen's

Three Principles, anti-imperialism, and the goals of the Chinese revolution. Feng, in a show of strength, suggested that all Russian advisors, notably Borodin, either take trips abroad "for rest" or else join the right-wing KMT headed by Chiang.

Wang Ching-wei also undertook his own reappraisal of the situation. First, he reasoned that the CCP's chances for success were minimal since the masses were not responding to the CCP. Second, Wang reasoned that Chiang had by now become China's symbol of the revolution. The army was powerful and loyal to Chiang, and Wang concluded:

> To go with the masses means to go against the Army. No, we had better go without the masses but together with the Army.[8]

On July 13, 1927, Chiang and the right-KMT shut the door on Stalin's united front policy: Wang Ching-wei's leftist government at Wuhan expelled the Communists from the left-KMT. Following Wang's actions, Chiang ushered in the period of the White Terror, a policy of routing known Communists. Within six months, the CCP's membership declined from fifty thousand to between ten thousand[9] and twenty-five thousand.[10]

UPRISINGS AND DEFEATS

Events in China were slowly slipping from Stalin's control. Not only had his new radical program resulted in the White Terror, but he learned too late that the remnants of the CCP were planning armed revolts in the main urban centers of China. It is not clear whether Stalin approved the uprisings or not,[11] but this was another example of the extent to which events in China had overtaken him.

The location for the first armed uprising was the city of Nanch'ang, in Hunan province. The principal members of the CCP participating in the uprising included such party luminaries as Ho Lung, Li Fu-ch'un, Liu Po-ch'eng, Nieh Jung-chen, and Chu Teh. Lin Piao, now fallen in disgrace and the once designated heir (1969) to Mao Tse-tung, also participated in the uprising. The key figure, however, appears to have been Chou En-lai, whom

Chang Kuo-t'ao characterized as being angry at Stalin's stipulation that the uprising occur only if it could succeed.[12]

At three o'clock on the morning of August 1, 1927, the Communists struck the KMT garrison at Nanch'ang, and for four days held on to the city. However, the superior-armed and well-organized forces of the KMT reclaimed the city by August 5. In the wake of the defeat and retreat, the Red Army was born.

Following the defeat at Nanch'ang, an emergency meeting of CCP leaders was called on August 7, during which a small group of Chinese revolutionaries reaffirmed Stalin's radical line and a new leadership began to emerge from within the CCP. At this meeting, Ch'en Tu-hsiu was quietly excluded from any future leadership of the party, and in his stead, the radical Ch'u Ch'iu-pai assumed control of the party. Mao's stature within the party was growing, having been elected to the Central Committee, but he was, at this time, also being criticized for his insistence and emphasis on the use of peasants in the revolution. Mao's job as chairman of the All-China Peasant's Union was to curb the peasants' overzealousness, not to provoke them prematurely into active participation. Stalin had not yet declared this phase of the Chinese revolution be implemented.

Despite the criticism Mao was given the responsibility of coordinating the second major uprising in the provinces of Hunan and adjacent Kiangsi in September 1927. The CCP had selected the date to take advantage of the peasants' harvesting period. The party had hoped that the peasants would turn against the landlords when they came to collect their share of crop taxes.

Ch'angsha, the capital city of Hunan, was selected as the major target of the uprising. The choice must have been a painful one for Mao who had once captured his fondness for the city in one of his first poems, entitled "Ch'angsha." Mao wrote the poem in the autumn of 1925; his sensitivity for nature and the city is clear.

> I stand alone in the cold autumn,
> where the Hsiang River flows north.
> I see the Orange Island at the river's end,
> and see the thousands of mountains, red everywhere.
> The vast forest range exhausts the scenery . . .
> Eagles darting about in the sky,

fish roaming under the shallow waters . . .
I ask . . . who controls life's ups and downs?
My great many friends used to come here,
to recall times past, and raise anew
the fullness of the years
when we were young students,
blooming and bright. . . .[13]

Between September 8 and 13, Mao's motley collection of
miners, peasants, and KMT-deserters captured the city, but without reinforcements, Mao's "army" was soon routed. During the
fighting, the uprising became so chaotic that at one point Mao's
troops ended up fighting one another. Mao himself was captured
during the uprising, but was able to buy his release.[14] For his
failure, Mao was dismissed from the politburo of the party.[15]

Apparently undaunted by the failure of the uprisings in
Nanch'ang and Ch'angsha, other Communist uprisings were staged
in south, north, and central China. All failed. In the process, with
the party membership being decimated, Stalin continued to advocate attacking the cities, insisting the policy was the correct one.
Trotsky, of course, lamented the strategy, calling it a "lunacy."[16]
And, still another party secretary, Ch'u Ch'iu-pai, was removed,
for the party led by Stalin did not admit to mistakes; only individuals made mistakes. At this point, a third party secretary, Li Li-
san, took over the leadership of the CCP. Finally, two other important consequences arose as a result of the abortive uprisings.
One was that on August 1, 1927, the Red Army was founded, and
two, during the retreat from the cities Mao organized the retreating
stragglers and took sanctuary in the mountains of south central
China. A legend was in the making.

THE CHINESE SOVIET REPUBLIC

During the retreat into the Chingkang Mountains which span
Hunan and Kiangsi provinces, Mao's opposition to the Comintern
became manifest. The major area of contention between Mao and
the Comintern was over the appropriateness of establishing soviets,
the primary organs of government under Communism.

As late as July 28, 1927, Stalin had argued in an article published by *Pravda* that the establishment of soviets was not yet advisable since the CCP had not yet prepared the people for accepting the concept. Stalin wrote:

> If in the near future—not necessarily in a couple of months, but in six months or a year from now—*a new upsurge of the revolution should become a fact,* the question of forming Soviets of workers' and peasants' deputies may become a line issue, as a slogan of the day....[17]

The key link in Stalin's analysis of the Chinese revolution was between *using slogans* and the revolutionary estimate of the situation. Slogans, he argued, could only be effective if the masses were convinced of their correctness. In China, he therefore reasoned, the CCP had not prepared the masses on the correctness of establishing soviets, and to do so without advance preparation would further jeopardize the future of the revolution in China.[18]

According to Mao, the first soviet was established on the Hunan border in November 1927. Here, the soviet "promoted a democratic program, with a moderate policy, based on slow but regular development."[19] The soviet was criticized by hard-core Communists led by Ch'u Ch'iu-pai for its refusal to carry out a terrorist policy of raiding, burning, and killing of landlords.[20] In May 1928, Chu Teh joined Mao in the mountain stronghold, and with Mao's military strength increasing, began the two main tasks of the soviet: dividing the land and establishing more soviets. Further, Mao and Chu Teh began arming the masses to hasten the two tasks.[21] By the end of 1929, Mao had succeeded in expanding and consolidating what was to become the major soviet in south China, located in Juichin, Kiangsi province. By the end of 1930, there were at least fifteen other soviets (red bases) established throughout China. Chang Kuo-t'ao directed the Oyuwan red base which straddled the three provinces of Hupei, Honan, and Anhwei.

Mao's organizational efforts were finally realized on November 7, 1931, when the First All-China Conference of Soviets convened in what became the CCP's future headquarters in 1933, Juichin, Kiangsi. At this congress, 290 delegates elected Mao as chairman of the Provisional Soviet Government, Chang Kuo-t'ao as deputy chairman and Chu Teh as commander-in-chief of the Red Army. Chou En-lai was not elected to any governmental position, but he was elected to membership on the Central Executive Committee of the CCP.

The congress adopted a variety of laws, including a land distribution law which outlined the party's land reform policy. Land was to be confiscated from the rich landlords and distributed among the peasants. Moderately wealthy and rich peasants were allowed to keep some land, but had to give up any "excess" houses or farm implements.[22] A labor law was adopted to nourish the growth of labor unions and the development of a rural proletariat. These laws, however, were more propagandistic than real since the Provisional Soviet Government was interested in "creating the impression of a proletarian base where none existed."[23] Other laws and programs adopted by the congress provided for the nationalization of forests and mines; cooperatives were set up; hospitals, clinics, and schools were established; equality was declared between men and women; and finally, the soviets were declared to be antireligious and anti-imperialist.

In time, the organizational efforts of the Soviet government became apparent. When the remnants of the defeated Communist troops made their way into the mountains of central China, they controlled but a small village area of about ten thousand people and an army of around the same number,[24] but by the start of the Long March in 1934, the party controlled some 10 million people and an army of two hundred thousand. In addition to the growth of the party and the army, the soviet government provided the Chinese leadership with important administrative experience. Mao and his loyal followers were to capitalize on this experience when it became necessary first to dismantle the government in 1934 and then to reorganize it one year later in north China.

THE MAOIST STRATEGY

Mao also had learned an invaluable lesson in military tactics and strategy during the retreat into the Chingkang Mountains. During the flight into the mountains, the Red Army followed "three simple rules of discipline: prompt obedience to orders, no confiscations whatever from the poor peasantry, and prompt delivery directly to the government, for its disposal, of all goods confiscated from the landlords."[25] In time, the Red Army adopted eight other rules:

1. Replace all doors when you leave a house;
2. Return and roll up the straw matting on which you sleep;
3. Be courteous and polite to the people and help them when you can;
4. Return all borrowed articles;
5. Replace all damaged articles;
6. Be honest in all transactions with the peasants;
7. Pay for all articles purchased;
8. Be sanitary, and especially establish latrines a safe distance from the people's houses.[26]

Mao credited the now disgraced and dead former heir-apparent, Lin Piao, with formulating the last two rules.[27]

In addition to the rules of discipline, the Red Army adopted the following four slogans:

1. When the enemy advances, we retreat!
2. When the enemy halts and encamps, we trouble them!
3. When the enemy seeks to avoid a battle, we attack!
4. When the enemy retreats, we pursue![28]

In November 1928, Mao laid out the basic features of the strategy which would eventually become the model for the other soviets being established after the uprisings of 1927. In a report which he submitted to the Central Committee of the CCP on November 25, 1928, entitled, "The Struggle in the Chingkang Mountains," he analyzed the situation after the August defeats in detail, and wrote:

> The area stretching from northern Kwangtung along the Hunan-Kiangsi border into southern Hupei lies entirely within the Lohsiao mountain range. We have traversed the whole range, and a comparison of its different sections shows that the middle section, with Ningkang as its centre, is the most suitable for our armed independent regime. The northern section has terrain which is less suitable for our taking either the offensive or the defensive, and it is too close to the enemy's big political centres.... The southern section has better terrain than the northern, but our mass base there is not as good as in the middle section, nor can we exert as great a political influence on Hunan and Kiangsi from it as we can from the middle section, from which any

move can affect the lower river valleys of the two provinces. The middle section has the following advantages: (1) a mass base, which we have been cultivating for more than a year; (2) a fairly good basis for the party organizations; (3) local armed forces which have been built up for more than a year and are well experienced in struggle—a rare achievement—and which, coupled with the Fourth Red Army, will prove indestructible in the face of any enemy force; (4) an excellent military base, the Chingkang Mountains, and bases for our local armed forces in all the counties; and (5) the influence it can exert on the two provinces and on the lower valleys of their rivers, an influence endowing it with much more political importance than that possessed by southern Hunan or southern Kiangsi, the influence of either of which can reach out only to its own province, or only to the upper river valley and the hinterland of its own province. The disadvantage of the middle section is that, since it has long been under the independent regime and is confronted by the enemy's large "encirclement and suppression" forces, its economic problems, especially the shortage of cash, are extremely difficult.[29]

The final strand of Mao's military tactics and strategy was contained in a letter which he wrote in January 1930, entitled "A Single Spark Can Start a Prairie Fire." In this essay, Mao's major thrust was on the acceleration of the revolutionary upsurge throughout the country through the correct policies of "establishing base areas; building up political power according to plan; deepening the agrarian revolution and expanding the people's armed forces. . . ."[30] Uppermost in Mao's mind was the continuation of the encirclement of the KMT in the countryside. Party Secretary Li Li-san considered the encirclement thesis as "sheer nonsense."[31]

Mao's feud with Li Li-san was, in effect, Mao's feud with the Comintern. As early as the Autumn Harvest Uprising, Mao's independent decision to include the organization of soviets as part of his program was, according to Mao himself, "opposed by the Comintern," which had not yet authorized either the establishment of soviets nor the use of the slogan, "establish soviets."[32] The following table lists some of the issues on which Mao's new strategy differed from that of Li Li-san, and from the Comintern's.

Despite his differences with Li Li-san, Mao was not yet ready

Table 7.1

Mao v. Comintern

Issues	Mao	Li
1. Estimate of the situation	rev. tide rising peasants ready	pessimistic; rev. movement had not arrived in 1928; Urban Workers passive
2. Guerilla tactics	centralize Red Army	dispersal of troops into small, anti-guerilla units
3. Agrarian (Soviet) bases	organize soviets	opposed peasant soviets
4. Agrarian problems	land redistribution	postpone land redistribution
5. Military strategy	circle the cities with the countryside	attack the cities

Source: See Rue, *Mao in Opposition*, p. 141.

to declare his independence from the Comintern's line. Therefore, when in mid–1930, Li Li-san ordered the resumption of attacks on the cities, Mao obeyed. Chou En-lai was supporting the Comintern line. In late July 1930, the army under the command of P'eng Te-huai (purged in 1958–59) attacked and captured Ch'angsha, holding it for ten days. Mao then attacked Nanch'ang, while Chang Kuo-t'ao attacked Hankow. The short-lived successes of the attacks caused a euphoric feeling among the Comintern's leadership, which hailed the success of the attack-on-the-cities policy, but the uprisings were quickly quelled by the KMT. Not only did the combined armies of Mao, Chu Teh, and Chang Kuo-t'ao sustain large losses, but Mao himself suffered personal losses during the attack in Ch'angsha. His wife and younger sister were captured and executed by the KMT, while his two brothers were arrested but later released. In a show of great love for his wife, Yang K'ai-hui, whose "beauty, serenity, and intelligence were an oasis in Mao's otherwise arid existence in Peking" in 1919,[33] the poet Mao wrote a poem to a friend in 1957 in memory of their departed spouses, entitled (by Ch'en), "The Immortals":

> I lost my proud poplar and you your willow,
> Poplar and willow gently ascend to the Ninth Heaven.
> When they asked Wu Kang what he had to give
> He offered them cinnamon wine.
> The lonely moon-maid, Ch'ang O, spreads her ample sleeves
> To dance in boundless space for these loyal souls.
> Suddenly, a report from Earth of the tiger's defeat,
> Immediately, tears fall as torrential rains.[34]

The abortive "attack the cities policy" left a long-lasting impression on Mao. From this time until the civil war (1946–48) was all but over in 1948, Mao employed the "circle the cities with the countryside policy." Not once, according to Jerome Ch'en, did Mao deviate from this policy in the eighteen years between Ch'angsha in 1930 and Lin Piao's attack on Mukden in 1948.[35]

Finally, as was Stalin's policy during such failures, Li Li-san was removed from his position as party secretary, and in his place, the Comintern selected the Russian-educated Wang Ming and the Twenty-Eight Bolsheviks. The so-called Twenty-Eight Bolsheviks were Chinese students who had studied at the Sun Yat-sen University in Moscow and had ingratiated themselves with the Comintern. They were to become the staunchest supporters in the Comintern's efforts to control the destiny of the Chinese revolution. Between 1931 and 1935, the date of Mao's consolidation of power within the CCP, the returned students led by Wang Ming were to carry on a bitter struggle with Mao for control of the CCP.

CHIANG AND THE
COMMUNIST EXTERMINATION CAMPAIGNS

On October 10, 1928, Chiang's political fortunes reached a new zenith when he became chairman of the National Government established at Nanking. The military phase of Sun Yat-sen's blueprint was officially ended. The period of political tutelage was now in effect. Politics in China, however, were not conducted by pieces of paper. From 1928 on, Chiang was faced with internal divisive forces including warlord remnants, other autonomous regional leaders, and the Chinese Communist Party. Externally, Chiang had to contend with continued Japanese attempts to expand existing interests and power bases in China.

Chiang's final consolidation of power began with overcoming his internal enemies. In 1929, his growing power alarmed some of his former allies during the Northern Expedition but there was nothing that they could do. In May of that year, not only did Chiang defeat one faction which had challenged his position, but in that same month, he expelled the major warlord, Feng Yu-hsiang, from the KMT, whereupon Feng sought the alliance of still another major warlord, Yen Hsi-shan. From mid-May 1929, until the end of 1930, Chiang was locked in battle with these formerly coopted KMT warlord-generals. Until the invasion of Japan in 1937, however, the handful of dissident warlords and former KMT generals made sporadic but unsuccessful attempts to dislodge him from power. That they did not succeed was due to his military genius, but also due to Japan's propensity for attacking China when Chiang got himself into trouble. For example, by September 1931, a group of important southern KMT leaders organized a government in Canton to oppose Chiang's government in Nanking. However, Japan's invasion of Manchuria in that year precipitated a national emergency which saved Chiang's government.[36] Japan, as we shall see, was also to aid, again unwittingly, the Chinese Communists, who by December 1930, had attracted the full force of Chiang's wrath.

Internal pacification was, to Chiang, a prerequisite to resistance against foreign aggression.[37] That the two problems were related is undeniable. Having experienced some measure of success against the dissident warlord-generals, he turned his attention toward achieving complete internal pacification by launching a series of extermination campaigns against the Communists. Confident that he could eliminate Communism once and for all within three months, he launched the first campaign in December 1930, with a force numbering one hundred thousand. As the KMT army advanced toward Mao's soviet, it treated the peasants brutally, either demanding food or information, behavior which would in time deliver the peasants into the hands of the more disciplined Red Army. Thereafter, the peasants led the KMT army into one trap after another in retaliation. The contrast between the discipline of the Red Army and the KMT was sharply evident from the inception of the campaign. Within five days, the Red Army not only turned back the KMT but captured in the process more than ten thousand KMT soldiers and six thousand rifles. Of the ten thousand captured soldiers, three thousand volunteered to join the Red Army. The poet Mao wrote of the first campaign:

> . . . two hundred thousand troops
> enter Kiangsi again,
> the wind and dust rise up to heaven. . . .[38]

The second campaign launched in February 1931, met with the same fate as the first, except that the booty captured by the Communist forces was larger. This time the Red Army took twenty thousand KMT soldiers prisoner.

Chiang immediately launched a third campaign in March 1931, and this time he assumed personal command of his forces in the field. From March 1931, until September 1931, a cautious and patient Chiang moved slowly toward Mao's enclave in Juichin, but just as he was about to enter Juichin, Japan invaded Manchuria.

In September 1931, Japan established the puppet-state of Manchukuo. Chiang was forced to cease operations, and, in a moment of self-evaluation and disgust, he resigned from the government, not because he wanted to nor because he had been asked, but because 2,000 years of cultural conditioning calls for China's leaders to assume personal responsibility for their failures as well as their successes. He returned within one year, but during his absence and the break between the third and fourth campaigns (June 1932), the Communists convened the First All-China Conference of Soviets in Juichin. By now the Communists could claim control of nearly 2.5 million people, and the Red Army's strength had grown to two hundred thousand men armed with one hundred fifty thousand rifles.[39]

Ironically, the combination of Mao's successful guerilla tactics and strategy, the respite from battle while Japan set up its government in Manchuria, and the continued growth of the CCP and Red Army was to lead to the demise of Mao's strategy, and for a short time, of his leadership. In June 1932, Chiang assembled five hundred thousand troops and pushed toward the soviets. Chiang's strategy was to concentrate his forces into larger attack units and push forward on all fronts. This new strategy forced the Red Army to reassess its strategy and tactics. Previously, utilizing guerilla tactics, the Red Army succeeded in forcing the KMT to disperse its troops over wide areas, stretching its supply lines, whereupon the guerillas isolated and annihilated one unit after another.

Chiang's switch to positional warfare forced the Red Army to reassess its own strategy. In August 1932, three months into the fourth campaign, the party and army leaders convened a conference where it was decided to counter Chiang's strategy. Despite Mao's resistance, the decision was made: switch from guerilla tactics to positional warfare. Whatever the real cause, Mao fell ill and was bedridden for the next four months. Chou En-lai replaced him during his illness as the political commissar to the Red Army. Chou, too, had favored the switch in tactics and strategy. In any case, with both sides adopting positional warfare, the fourth campaign settled into a stalemate. Chiang, acting on the advice of his German advisers, constructed block-houses around the central soviet and imposed an economic blockade of the soviet. Salt, a vital commodity, was soon in extremely short supply. In reassessing the events of the fourth campaign, Mao said, "It was a serious mistake to meet the vastly superior Nanking forces in positional warfare, at which the Red Army was neither technically nor spiritually at its best."[40]

This remark proved to be an understatement. With the stranglehold which he had applied during the fourth campaign taking its toll inside the soviet in August 1933, Chiang pressed the fifth campaign with 1 million men and four hundred airplanes. "This time," Chiang wrote, "the campaign was to be conducted on the basis of 30 percent military effort and 70 percent political effort."[41] Chiang had apparently learned a bitter lesson from the previous four campaigns, and especially the first two.

The Red Army continued to cling to its newly adopted strategy of positional warfare. With the KMT pressing closer and closer to the central soviet, Mao, well again, called for a return to guerilla warfare. Again, he was soundly rebuked, but perhaps no rebuke was so severe as that of his loyal friend, Chu Teh, the army commander-in-chief who exclaimed that guerrilla warfare was "useless in blockhouse operations."[42]

In January 1934, a lull in the fighting permitted the Communists to convene the Second All-China Conference of Soviets in Juichin. Mao's continued insistence on a return to guerrilla warfare was rejected again. From January 1934, ten months before the start of the Long March, Mao's voice was barely audible in party matters. In fact, it is possible that he had been actually expelled from the Central Committee of the CCP and also placed under house arrest.[43]

In April, Chiang mounted another major offensive which had startling results. In one encounter, Chiang's troops killed four thousand Red Army troops and wounded twenty thousand others. The tide was turning, and the Communists were running out of time and territory in which to maneuver; the area which they controlled by the early fall of 1934 was essentially reduced to that which they had held in 1927! On October 2, 1934, the party-army leadership made one of its most momentous decisions: the Kiangsi soviet was to be abandoned, and a retreat was to be implemented immediately. Mao, Chu Teh, and Chou En-lai, among others, were appointed to a military council in charge of planning the retreat. On October 16, one hundred thousand men, women (including Mao's new wife, Ho Tzu-chen, who was pregnant), and children stripped the arsenal, dismantled the factories, loaded the machinery on mules and donkeys, collected all available documents, gold and silver, and began that long trek from central to north China known as the Long March. Edgar Snow characterized this chapter in the rise of the CCP as a "nation emigrating," and truly, this is a correct assessment of what actually occurred.[44]

On November 10, a triumphant Chiang finally realized his

objective and entered Juichin. Among those who died in rearaction fighting was one of Mao's brothers and former Party Secretary Ch'u Ch'iu-pai. Paradoxically, after the Long March was already in progress, the Comintern approved it!

THE LONG MARCH

The decision to abandon the Kiangsi Soviet led to what most observers consider to have been the ultimate test of endurance and human suffering. This "epic of human endurance,"[45] lasted 370 days (October 16, 1934 to October 20, 1935) and covered a distance of six thousand miles.

The Communists were moving with no idea where they were going. Mao, back in good graces, claims not to have had any "exact plans," except, of course, to survive the KMT extermination campaign.[46] Indeed, the Communists did not even possess adequate maps during their break-through.[47] Nonetheless, the Red Army's breakthrough appears to have been executed relatively unhindered, for the magnitude of the escape was not known to the KMT for about four weeks.[48] Once the KMT realized what was happening, however, it wasted no time pursuing and catching up with the retreating communists. Mao's First Front Army, which was regarded as the "Central Red Army,"[49] engaged the pursuing KMT initially while the First Front Army was attempting to cross the Hsiang River, ostensibly in an effort to join the Second Front Army located at the Sangchih soviet, just slightly north of the Kiangsi soviet. Having this route blocked by the KMT, the First Front Army changed its direction to the next closest soviet, Chang Kuo-t'ao's soviet located in northwest Szechwan.

The Tsunyi Conference

On New Year's Day 1935, Lin Piao led his army into the city of Tsunyi, Kweichow province, where the historic reorganization meeting of the CCP and Red Army was to take place, and where, for the first time, Mao Tse-tung was to take full charge of the revolution. Mao, in fact, was the moving force behind the conference.

On January 8, 1935, the party adopted the Tsunyi Resolution

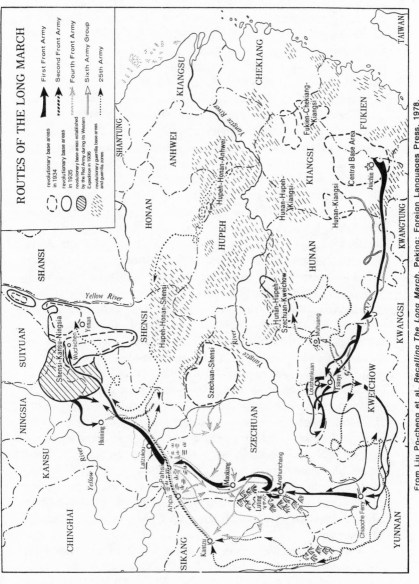

ROUTES OF THE LONG MARCH

First Front Army
Second Front Army
Fourth Front Army
Sixth Army Group
25th Army

revolutionary base areas in 1934
revolutionary base areas in 1935
revolutionary base areas established by the Red Army during its Western Expedition in 1936
revolutionary guerrilla base area and guerrilla zones

From Liu Po-cheng et al, *Recalling The Long March*. Peking: Foreign Languages Press, 1978.

entitled, "Summing up the Campaign Against the Enemy's Puni-
tive Encirclement Drive."[50] There were fourteen resolutions in
all. Briefly, the resolutions criticized the leadership of the Twenty-
Eight Bolsheviks, reaffirmed Mao's guerrilla warfare tactics, and
reviewed the disastrous fifth extermination campaign and the various military defeats suffered by the Red Army. Individuals who
were specifically singled out for criticism included Chou En-lai.

The real meaning of the Tsunyi Conference, however, was the
reshuffling of the party leadership and the ascendancy of Mao Tse-
tung as chairman of the politburo. From this time forward, despite some attempts to remove him from office, Mao was to guide
the destiny of the Chinese Communist Party.

Mao's views at the conference were supported by those generals who later were to form the leadership of the People's Liberation Army. Some, such as Nieh Jung-chen, Yeh Chien-ying, and
Liu Po-ch'eng, continued in Mao's good graces until his death,
while others such as Lin Piao and P'eng Teh-huai were much later
to fall in disgrace for various alleged crimes against Mao and the
revolution. Other present-day party stalwarts such as Ch'en Yun,
Li Fu-ch'un, Tung Pi-wu (d. 1975), and Teng Hsiao-p'ing
(purged 1967 and again 1976) also supported Mao at the conference. When the reorganization of both the Red Army and the politburo was announced, Chu Teh was named commander-in-chief
of the First Front Army aided by Lin Piao, Nieh Jung-chen, P'eng
Teh-huai, and Liu Po-ch'eng. Mao was named chairman of the
politburo and concurrently named chairman of the military council, replacing Chou. These two positions made him the dominant
figure in the party, and for the first time since the founding of the
party in 1921, its leadership was determined by the party itself and
not by the Comintern. Finally, the adoption of the slogan, "Go
North to Fight the Japanese," gave the newly reorganized party
army a sense of mission and direction. The decision to head north
followed, presumably to join forces with Chang Kuo-t'ao in northern Szechwan.

Unknown to the advancing First Front Army, however,
Chang Kuo-t'ao had decided to abandon his soviet without con-
sulting anyone, and marched to the aid of Mao's First Front
Army.[51] However valid his reasons for abandoning his soviet,

(Chang claims that he was forced out by a local warlord) and however sincere his motives, Chang was later labeled a "flightist" by other Communists.

Chiang K'ai-shek's strategy at this point was to force Mao's main army toward the perilous Yangtze River. He skillfully placed his superior forces at key points along the anticipated escape routes of the Red Army. By preventing the Red Army from crossing the river and pushing the Long March northward, Chiang had hoped to push the Communists into the wastelands of Tibet. "The fate of the nation and the [KMT]," he wired to his field commanders, "depends on bottling up the Reds south of the Yangtze."[52] Bottling up the Communists, Chiang found, was one thing; destroying them was something else. A master of guerrilla tactics, Mao sent Lin Piao and a diversionary squad to threaten the capital city of Yunnan, where General and Madame Chiang were directing operations. According to Edgar Snow, the Chiangs "hastily repaired down the French railway toward Indo-China."[53] Just as quickly and menacingly as the squad appeared at the outskirts of the capital city of Yunnan, the Red Army also disappeared. "It was discovered," Snow writes, "that the drive on Yunnanfu had been only a diversion carried out by a few troops. The main Red forces were moving westward [across] one of the few navigable points of the upper Yangtze."[54]

Stories of Heroism[55]

The Long March contained episodes of heroism, courage, and cunning which could not have been scripted even by the most imaginative of minds. The heroism started from the moment the break-through was completed in October 1934, and as the march continued, the Red Army proved again and again its endurance. No sooner had the Red Army escaped Chiang's bottling strategy along the Yangtze than Red soldiers were called upon to perform feats of courage and were sustained by a fervent sense of purpose. *Crossing the Yangtze.* Edgar Snow has skillfully captured the appearance of the Yangtze River in this part of China.

> Through the wild mountainous country of Yunnan, the Yangtze River flows deeply and swiftly between immense gorges, great peaks in places rising in defiles of a mile or

more, with steep walls of rock lifting almost perpendicularly on either side.[56]

The north bank of the river was occupied by Chiang's forces. Needing boats to cross the river south to north at this point, the Red Army marched eighty-five miles in one night and day to a location where the unsuspecting KMT garrison was caught napping. Without firing a shot, the Red Army captured the KMT position, confiscated boats (which Chiang had ordered burned), and within nine days, ferried the entire Red Army across the Yangtze. The infuriated Chiang, now in hot pursuit, was forced to detour his army seventy-five miles before it could cross the river itself.

The Tatu Heroes. The Red Army continued its northward trek and soon entered the land of the Lolos, warlike aborigines inhabiting the densely forested and mountainous range of Szechwan province. The Lolos, considered to be non-Chinese and a minority tribe in China, were the traditional rivals of the Chinese. The Red Army had treated the tribe well and at one place along the march had freed some Lolo chieftains held captive by local militarists. Fortunately, one Red Army general, Liu Po-ch'eng, was a native of the area and could speak the Lolo tongue. Liu explained to the Lolo chieftains that the Red Army operated on the principle of self-autonomy for all national minorities of China. Liu then drank the blood of a newly killed chicken to cement the alliance between the Red Army and the Lolos.

Shortly after leaving Lololand, the Long Marchers were faced with their most critical obstacle: crossing the Yangtze again at a point where the currents were so strong that even boats were not adequate for crossing. With Chiang's airplanes bombing the marchers along the way, Mao and the Red Army generals realized that they could not afford to stop for even a short period at this point. Some of the soldiers somehow had managed to cross the river, but the raging currents grew worse and worse, until finally, it became impossible for anyone to cross again. The Red Army was split and vulnerable.

In a hurriedly called conference of the Red Army, Mao, Chu Teh, and Chou En-lai were told by Lin Piao of the existence of an iron-chain suspension bridge about one hundred twenty-five miles west of their present location. This bridge was the last possible crossing of the Tatu River (the name of the Yangtze at this point) east of Tibet. The Red Army had three days in which to reach the iron-chain bridge before the KMT would catch up with them. By maintaining a punishing pace, the marchers reached the bridge on schedule.

The bridge was centuries old. It was composed of sixteen heavy iron chains, each strand about one hundred yards long, with the ends of the chains secured to great piles of cemented rocks. The chains had boards strapped to them to form the bridge, but much to the marchers' surprised dismay, the KMT not only had removed most of the boards but had set up a machinegun nest facing the iron chains.

In a burst of courage, one soldier after another began a hand-over-hand journey across the chains, the machineguns cutting some of them down. As more and more Red soldiers got on the chains, supported by their own guns from shore, one finally made it across to the KMT side, "uncapped a grenade, and tossed it with perfect aim into the enemy redoubt."[57] The losses were minimal, and as if to carry the insult even further, Chiang's planes were ineffectual in hitting the iron-chains with bombs, which "only made pretty splashes in the river" below.[58]

The Great Mountains. The Long Marchers had by now covered approximately four thousand miles. The worse was still ahead— the seven high mountain ranges separating Mao's First Front Army and Chang Kuo-t'ao's Fourth Front Army in northern Szechwan. The first mountain range was the Great Snow Mountain. The Communist troops were given about two weeks to rest and prepare for the sixteen-thousand-foot climb over glaciers and snow. From the top of the mountain, the marchers could clearly see Tibet. The climb took its toll as many of the troops who were unused to high altitude and the elements died from exposure. On another mountain range, the Red Army lost two-thirds of its transport animals. "Hundreds," said Mao, "fell down and never got up."[59] Mao came down with malaria during the climb. Diarrhea and upset stomachs were common as were lice. According to Tung

Pi-wu, "It rained, then snowed, and the fierce wind whipped our bodies, and more men died of cold and exhaustion."[60] After it was over, the poet Mao wrote of the mountain range:

> If I could lean on the sky
> I would draw my sword
> and cut you in three pieces. . . .[61]

Reunions and Splits

On June 12, 1935, when the march was nine months old and over four thousand miles long, Mao's First Front Army finally joined Chang Kuo-t'ao's Fourth Front Army in Moukung, Szechwan province. Mao's haggard and tired troops now numbered around forty-five thousand, half the number that had started the march from the Kiangsi Soviet in October 1934. Chang's troops numbered around fifty thousand, and in contrast to the physical and mental condition of Mao's troops, Chang's troops were well rested.[62] Chang was "excited" at the prospects of the reunion. Chang recalled the initial moment:

> As soon as I saw them, I got down from my horse and ran towards them to embrace them and shake hands with them. Words could not describe our rejoicing at this reunion after so many years of tribulation. . . . Mao Tse-tung and I and the others soon walked side by side . . . talking and laughing all the way, telling one another our separate adventures.[63]

The atmosphere soon changed. As Mao told Snow, "There were other factors of intra-Party struggle involved which need not be discussed here."[64] Chang, on the other hand, recalled: "As the wave of warm-hearted rejoicing passed away, there came the internal strife of the Party."[65] Chang's attitude towards Mao's position in the party did not help matters. He refused to acknowledge Mao's chairmanship of the politburo and referred to the men around Mao as "big shots."[66] Chang, however, courted Chu Teh, his former friend and now Mao's loyal commander-in-chief of the Red Army. According to Chang, Chu Teh was highly critical of Mao's First Front Army and had told Chang "not to attach too much significance to the Tsunyi Conference, which elected Mao to take charge."[67] Chu Teh was impressed with Chang's Fourth Front Army, and was "unable to find words to describe his feeling of joy."[68] Since their initial contact as protégés at Peking University, Mao and Chang had grown apart, and the proceedings at Moukung did nothing but magnify the rivalry between the two major contenders for control of the Chinese Communist party and its Red Army.

When the merriment subsided, the rivals sat together in a conference called by the politburo. The animosities of the past fifteen years surfaced now. The major disagreement involved the final destination of the Long March. Briefly, Chang wanted to remain in Szechwan to build up the strength of the party and army, and then to resume activities south of the Yangtze. Mao, and presumably Chu Teh, favored the northwest, where uncontested by Chiang's forces, the CCP could turn its attention toward Japan. Chang, totally frustrated by now by the "malignant growth that had developed throughout the years of erroneous policy and guerrilla warfare,"[69] lost his argument when the politburo voted in favor of Mao's plan.

The aura of distrust between Chang and Mao was intensified when the Red Army was realigned in an effort to neutralize each leader's power. Mao's First Front Army included two columns from Chang's Fourth Front Army while Chang's army contained two from Mao's. Mao and Chang were playing hostage politics with one another. Chu Teh, Mao's loyal commander-in-chief, was assigned to Chang's Fourth Front Army causing speculation about his loyalty to Mao.

The decisions reached at Moukung remained in force for one hundred miles. One hundred miles up the road in the city of Maoerhkai, a second conference was held, and the same tensions and disagreements surfaced again, and once again, Mao's leadership carried the day. After this conference, Mao and Chang went their different ways, Chu Teh accompanying Chang. Shortly after the Second Conference, Chang convened a meeting of senior party and army members accompanying him. At this meeting Chang realized his most elusive of ambitions: his faction passed a resolution refusing to recognize the original Central Committee and founded in its stead a provisional Central Committee with Chang as the party secretary. Chu Teh was not given a post either in the party or the army.[70]

The Grasslands. The heroism of the First Front Army was to continue after the march resumed following the conference at Maoerh-kai. The next critical obstacle was "the Grasslands," a vast swamp where, according to Agnes Smedley, "no tree or shrub grew there, no bird ventured near, no insect sounded. . . . There was nothing, nothing but endless stretches of wild grass swept by torrential rains in summer and fierce winds and snows in winter."[71] The Red Army once again lost men and animals to drowning and other hazards. Stories from some of the participants indicate that the most severe problem was the lack of food. Dead animals became a delicacy, eaten, it seems, even after the carcasses had spoiled. Drinking one's urine and eating one's feces also became commonplace. The Communists survived this ordeal too.

The Journey's End

On October 20, 1935, the First Front Army's ordeal ended. On that day, the army reached its destination and connected with other armies which had already established a soviet in Shensi province. Mao, his wife and child, and a brother arrived in relatively good health. (Mao's wife eventually was sent to the Soviet Union when she became ill following the birth of another daughter. The remaining leaders also arrived in good health.

In recapping the events of the Long March, Edgar Snow tells us that the Red Army fought an average of a battle a day with fifteen whole days devoted to *major* pitched battles. The marchers rested only about forty-four days during the six-thousand-mile trek and averaged nearly twenty-four miles a day, an impressive figure when one realizes that the marchers were loaded down with heavy equipment, and slowed by elderly persons and children. During the trek, the Red Army crossed eighteen mountain ranges, five of which are perennially snow-capped, and twenty-four rivers in twelve different provinces. Altogether, the Red Army occupied sixty-two cities and crossed six aborginal districts.[72]

The poet Mao captured the entire ordeal in his poem "The Long March":

The Red Army does not fear the difficulties of the
  Long March,
the thousand rivers and hundred mountains are but
  routine . . .
We greatly delighted in the thousand li of snow which
  covered Min Mountain,
and as the three armies left it behind,
we all broke into smiles.[73]

Chang Kuo-t'ao's Fate. Chang Kuo-t'ao in the meantime had
headed to his northwest area where he hoped to establish a soviet,
but natural obstacles, warlords, aborigines, the KMT, and lack of
food supplies forced him hither and yon until finally he too turned
toward the Shensi soviet. He arrived on December 2, 1936, more
than a year after Mao. This reunion, unlike the first one in Moukung, was more restrained. "At that time," Chang wrote, "we discussed our future, not our past."[74]

One of the fundamental characteristics of the Chinese Communist Party, then and now, is "to learn from the past," especially
past mistakes. In due time, Chang was to become still another
negative example, from which to learn. In his case, as the four-
month criticism campaign was to show, he was accused of oppor-
tunism, poor judgment in military matters (he had lost the Fourth
Front Army during his peregrinations after the Maoerhkai Conference) and opposition to the party. In one speech, Mao "assumed a light manner, chuckling incessantly . . . and admonished
[me] with a sarcastic grin, saying, 'Confess your sins, then.' "[75]

In April 1937, the Central Committee of the CCP drafted a
resolution condemning Chang's offenses against the revolution.
Thanks to the last-minute interference of the Comintern, Chang
was not expelled as had been expected, but thereafter as he put it:
"Although an actor in name, I was really only a spectator."[76] His
life in Yenan was a lonely one from that point on.

After the struggle, I moved to my new abode. I seemed to
have undergone a great change of mood. I lived like a hermit
there, alone, closing the door to visitors. . . . I wandered
among the mountains and rivers.[77]

Life became unbearable for Chang in the ensuing months.

Finally, on April 4, 1938, he took advantage of an occasion to leave Yenan, and he "left the CCP for good."[78] On May 20, 1938, he issued an open letter to the people of China in which he publicly severed his connections with the CCP. Thereafter he worked for the KMT in Chungking during the war and continued working in China until the Communist victory in 1949. He then moved to Hong Kong, and then Canada, where he now lives.

THE SIAN INCIDENT

By January 1937, the Chinese Communists had finally decided on a permanent base located in the mountains of Shensi province. The headquarters of the party and army from 1937 until 1947, were located in the city of Yenan.

The successful escape to north China by the beleaguered CCP was by no means the end of the extermination campaigns. Before the Long March ended, Chiang was preparing his strategy in the north. He pressed into duty the young Manchurian warlord, Chang Hsueh-liang. Throughout March and April 1936, the Young Marshall's troops engaged the Communists in battle and lost repeatedly. The strength of the Red Army must have surprised Chiang, who believed that "at the end of the long flight there were only some five thousand armed Communists left. From a military standpoint, they no longer constituted a serious threat."[79] Chiang's erroneous assessment was no consolation to the young Manchurian warlord.

During the encounters with the Manchurian-KMT troops, however, one facet of Mao's military strategy became evident: releasing captured troops after they were subjected to Communist propaganda. As early as 1928, while in retreat in the Chingkang Mountains, Mao already believed that:

> The most effective method in propaganda directed at the enemy forces is to release captured soldiers and give the wounded medical treatment. Whenever soldiers . . . of enemy forces are captured, we immediately conduct propaganda among them; they are divided into those wishing to stay and those wishing to leave, and the latter are given travelling expense and set free. This immediately knocks the bottom out

of the enemy's slander that the Communist bandits kill everyone on sight.[80]

The results of this strategy paid off both in the long and short runs. Those captured troops released by the Red Army went back to their units singing the praises of the "patriotic" Communists.[81] And in time the Manchurian troops displayed more willingness to fight Japan than to fight the Communists.

On the diplomatic front, Chou En-lai began a series of moves designed to win over the KMT-coopted Manchurian warlord. Mao, in turn, followed with an order to cease the fighting against the Manchurian troops. By the winter of 1936, Mao's and Chou's efforts were rewarded. The Young Marshall himself admitted that his men were listening to what the Communists were saying: "We are Chinese and you are Chinese.... Your [KMT] officers get rich. They don't pay you your wages. They have their motorcars, their concubines, their silk gowns, and you get nothing."

"Everything they say," the Young Marshall said, "is quite true."[82]

Elsewhere in China, other warlord allies of the KMT had begun to press for a united front against Japan. Thus, the reluctance of the KMT's allies to continue the extermination campaign against the Communists and the advances of Japan in north China finally forced Chiang's hand. He wrote:

> Unless timely measures were taken, the situation could lead to a rebellion. Therefore, I went to Sian (the Young Marshall's headquarters) in the hope that my presence there would constitute a stabilizing factor ... and announce [my policy] on the continued prosecution of the military campaign against the Communists and on the question of armed resistance against Japan.[83]

On October 21, 1936, Chiang flew to Sian, the headquarters of Chang Hsueh-liang, to stabilize the situation. The Young Marshall, however, did not accept Chiang's policy. For Chiang, this was a bitter pill to swallow: he believed that the Japanese were a disease of the body and the Communists a disease of the soul. When the Young Marshall brought up the subject of the united front and resistance to Japan, Chiang exclaimed: "I will never talk about [it] until every Red Soldier in China is exterminated, and every Communist is in prison."[84]

By late November 1936, Chiang had ordered full preparations for what was to be a sixth extermination campaign. Troops, ammunition, tanks, armored cars, and motor transports were assembled at a point outside Yenan. This campaign was provisioned at a time when Japan was bombing Inner Mongolia, a part of China.

Diplomatic exchanges between Tokyo and Nanking restricted Japan's invasion to Inner Mongolia, a condition which was particularly agreeable to Chiang. At this point in his campaign against the Communists, Chiang did not want Japan aroused any further. Indeed, when Japan protested the formation of a "Chinese Anti-Japanese National Salvation Movement" in northern China, Chiang arrested the organization's leaders. Further, Chiang's government openly supported Japan's suppression of strikes occurring against Japanese interests in various parts of China. Chang Hsueh-liang's efforts to persuade Chiang to turn his attention to Japan's aggression in China were met with a stern rebuff from Chiang. Likening Chiang to Yuan Shih-k'ai, the Young Marshall continued to widen the gap between Chiang and himself.[85] Chiang, however, agreed to visit the Young Marshall's headquarters once again to explain his policy further.

In the interval between their initial meeting outside Sian on December 3, and Chiang's kidnapping on December 12, Germany and Japan had entered into an anti-Communist agreement which Chiang greeted cooly.[86] The Young Marshall, on the other hand, was infuriated, for Manchuria (now Manchukuo under Japanese control) had been recognized by Germany and Italy as Japanese territory. The Young Marshall clearly questioned Chiang's attitude toward Japan.

On December 3, 1936, Chiang had received the Young Marshall in Loyang, a city approximately two hundred miles from Sian. The following day, Chiang flew to Sian "to straighten out the complicated situation and . . . to direct the bandit-suppression campaign."[87] According to one newsman in Sian:

Sian welcomed the Generalissimo in the approved New Life Manner. The streets were swept, and all the rickshawmen were given new blue-and-white jackets with a name and a number. . . . The road [to Chiang's quarters] was smoothed for his car by the labour of hundreds of coolies.[88]

Chiang's quarters were protected by forty-five hand-picked Chiang loyalists in addition to fifty other carefully selected local soldiers. He rested in "perfect tranquility" never harboring any suspicions about his safety and welfare.[89]

From the time of his arrival, Chiang spent most of his time putting the "finishing touches to his plan for breaking the power of the Communists once and for all."[90]

The mood in Sian was tense. On December 9, a student demonstration demanded that China unite against Japan. In time, the demonstrators sought out Chiang himself, and to prevent the students from approaching Chiang, the police fired several shots into the mob, wounding several students.[91] On December 11, the tension continued to mount when it was announced that the bandit-suppression campaign, not the anti-Japanese resistance movement, would be given top priority by the general. The decision made, Chiang prepared for his departure scheduled for December 12. He never made it.

Early in the morning of December 12, he was awakened by the sounds of gunfire.[92] Suspecting a "revolt," he scurried outside, and it being still dark, he missed his footing while scaling a wall and fell thirty feet into a moat. In pain, he managed to continue, dodging a hail of bullets; neither his bodyguards nor his nephew were as fortunate.

Chiang was found crouching behind some rocks, fatigued and still in pain, his feet bleeding in the December cold. When finally coaxed to accompany the mutineers to the Young Marshall's quarters, one of Chang Hsueh-liang's men knelt down before Chiang, waiting for Chiang to mount him piggy-back for the trip down the mountain. "He knelt before me," Chiang recalls, "with tears in his eyes and requested me to go down the mountain." Chiang does not say why the soldier knelt before him.

Through the efforts of Chiang's Australian adviser, W. H. Donald, and interestingly, the Young Marshall himself, Chiang's life was spared. Chiang, however, proved to be a stubborn hostage, preferring to die rather than accept the demands presented by his kidnappers on December 14. The demands included the reorganization of the KMT, the cessation of the civil war and the convening of a national conference to review the situation.[93] The principals were stalemated.

Still intent on playing the role of compromiser, Chang Hsueh-liang invited the Communists to Sian. Sometime in mid-December, Chou En-lai, sporting an eighty-thousand-dollar price on his head, arrived in Sian to negotiate a settlement of the mutiny. Contrary to reports thereafter, the Communists neither knew of the mutiny nor helped to plan it.[94] According to Chiang's confidant, W. H. Donald, the Communists "had had no part in Chiang's detention."[95]

From all indications, Chou was instrumental in obtaining Chiang's release, a fact which both Madame and General Chiang fail to include in their respective memoirs of the incident. In discussing the situation with Chou, Madame Chiang said: "We Chinese must stop fighting each other," to which Chou replied: "I know, we Communists have been telling you that for years."[96] Interestingly, Chou acknowledged Chiang as the "Commander-in-Chief."[97] On Christmas Day, Chou finally convinced some recalcitrant generals in the Young Marshall's army that releasing Chiang was in the best interests of the country. On that same day, the principals flew back to Nanking. The mutiny was over, all that is except for Chang Hsueh-liang's fate.

According to the ever-present and ever-recording W. H. Donald, Chiang at first simply admonished the Young Marshall and one other major participant, and ordered them to remain in Sian. "No," said the Young Marshall, "I have been accused of mutiny and of murder [by the press and the KMT]. I'm innocent . . .but I'm going on the plane with you to stand court-martial. . ."[98] On December 31, Chang was tried, convicted and sentenced to ten years imprisonment and deprived of his civil rights for an additional five years. "Donald of China" testified on Chang's behalf, but to no avail. It didn't matter, as it turned out, for the next day, New Years Day, Chang was pardoned—due mainly to Chiang's recommendation. Chang, however, was placed under house arrest by Chiang, and has remained under house arrest to this day in Taiwan, even after Chiang's death on April 5, 1975.

THE SECOND UNITED FRONT

Just what Chiang agreed to or did not agree to during his imprisonment is not known. Despite his reputation for meticulously recording each day's events in a diary, the portions of the diary reproduced in Madame Chiang's book do not make *any* references to the negotiations; indeed, there isn't a single reference to Chou En-lai's presence in Sian. Snow may be correct in assuming that this portion of Chiang's diary was omitted because Chiang steadfastly maintained that during his imprisonment he had at no time entered into a bargain with anyone; not the Young Marshall and certainly not the Communist Chou En-lai.[99] Yet, on December 29, just four days after he had returned to Nanking from Sian, Chiang called an emergency meeting of the standing committee of the Central Committee of the KMT, and, in addition to calling for Chang Hsueh-liang's trial, also "requested" that body to end the extermination campaign against the Communists. Within two months of the incident, negotiations for the establishment of a second united front were underway.

Proposal and Counterproposal

On February 15, 1937, the Central Executive Committee of the KMT convened to discuss, among other things, the CCP's proposal containing four concessions and five demands. The Communists pledged to: (1) discontinue hostilities toward the KMT; (2) give up the soviet name for its government in Shensi, allow the Red Army to be renamed under a KMT designation, and accept direct guidance from the KMT's Military Council; (3) recognize Sun Yat-sen's Three Principles of the People; and (4) abandon all campaigns against the landlords (considered in the next chapter).

The five demands included: (1) a KMT agreement to give up the extermination campaigns; (2) guarantees of freedom of speech, assembly, and association, and the release of all political prisoners; (3) the convening of a national salvation conference; (4) resistance to Japanese aggression; and (5) the improvement of the living conditions of the people.[100]

On February 21, the KMT offered its counterproposal which

included: (1) the abolition of the Red Army and the placement of Communist troops under KMT command; (2) the abolition of the soviet form of government; (3) acceptance of the Three Principles and the rejection of Communism; and (4) the cessation of the class struggle.[101]

Between February and the adoption of the final "Manifesto on KMT-CCP Cooperation" on September 22, both parties negotiated the various points, especially those points relating to the Red Army and the Three Principles. Where the Red Army was concerned, the CCP was willing to abolish its name, but under no circumstances would the CCP agree to place the Communist army under the direct control of the KMT. The only leaders which the Communist army would accept were Communist-appointed ones.

The discussion over accepting the Three Principles again did not involve Sun's original Three Principles (democracy, nationalism, livelihood), but, rather, the three policies which Sun acceded to during the establishment of the first united front: alliance with Russia, cooperation with Communists and assistance for peasants and workers. Mao wrote:

> Without these three cardinal policies, or minus any one of them, they become, in the new period [of the second united front], the false Three People's Principles or the incomplete Three People's Principles.[102]

Japanese actions finally forced both parties to hasten and complete their negotiations. On July 7, 1937, a skirmish outside Peking inaugurated the Second World War in Asia. Shortly after the hostilities broke out, the Communists were included in the National Defense Advisory Council and, in August, the Red Army officially was designated as the KMT's Eighth Route Army. On September 22, the second united front was a reality—at least on paper.[103]

The War of Resistance to Japanese Aggression, 1937–1945

The Second United Front, based as it was on an anti-Japanese policy, afforded the Chinese Communist Party a much-needed immediate respite from the KMT's suppression campaigns. But the expansion of the CCP between 1937 and 1945 was the product of several interrelated factors which for our purposes can be analyzed separately. The eventual success of the party's rise to power was due partly to certain factors beyond its control, such as Japan's invasion of China proper and the inability of the KMT to implement its reform policies after 1928, and also partly to factors over which the party did have some control, such as its successful economic and educational programs and the political and military mobilization of the masses.

ACT I, WORLD WAR II IN ASIA

We already have had occasion to note Japan's interests in China beginning with the First Sino-Japanese war in 1894–95, the Twenty-One Demands of 1915, and the establishment of a puppet-regime, Manchukuo, in north China in 1931. Between the loss of Manchuria in 1931 and the outbreak of hostilities between China and Japan in July 1937, the control of north China and the disposition of the area became the major point of contention between China and Japan.[1] In that same interim period, China, following Chiang's lead, had adopted what amounted to an appeasement policy toward Japan. The extermination of the Communists, we have seen Chiang state, was a precondition to a national effort against Japan. Chiang fought his internal pacification program on borrowed time.

Undoubtedly, the Sian incident forced Japan to act sooner

than it wanted to in north China. The last thing Japan wanted was a united China, ambitious and eager to assume its sovereign place in the community of nations. According to U.S. Ambassador to Japan Joseph C. Grew, "The Japanese nation seemed to be somewhat thunderstruck by the sudden and unexpected determination of China to yield no more to Japanese pressure."[2]

China was, to be sure, important to Japan's grand design for an Asia free from Western influence, a concept which included the elimination of Soviet Communism in East Asia. As we shall see, China's economic wealth and military importance only made it that much more desirable to Japanese expansionist notions in Asia.

By 1936, the Japanese military was convinced that a war with the equally expansionist Soviet Union was inevitable within five years. To prepare for that eventuality, a major reassessment of the Japanese economy was undertaken by the operations division of the general staff. "National economic priorities had to be completely reshaped in order to meet the demands of a modern, mechanized, and mobile army operating far from the Japanese home islands."[3] Japan's reassessment of its economic-military needs led to the adoption of a five-year plan (1937–41) designed to strengthen all its economic weaknesses. On October 16, 1937, a "Tentative Plan for the Economic Development of North China" was adopted that would "place all important industry, economic development, and exploitation of natural resources in occupied China under Japanese control."[4] In October 1937, "occupied" China meant north China, but within a year, it would mean east China from Manchuria to Canton.

The implementation of the tentative plan called for the creation of national companies which would compete directly for China's financial resources with various Western and Chinese companies. In the cities occupied by Japan after the start of the war, Chinese custom revenues, for example, were forced into Japanese banks, while in other areas, tariffs were adjusted downward generally but always with Japanese exports in mind. The reduction of tariffs meant, obviously, the loss of revenues for the Chinese government. In sum, the exploitation of natural resources in occupied areas, the creation of special companies, the diversion of money into Japanese banks, and the reduction of tariffs all helped to realize the tentative plan, and these developments plunged the Chinese economy deeper and deeper into debt.[5]

Strategically, China was important in Japan's overall geomilitary planning. The problem facing the militarists was what kind of China best fitted their plans for Asia generally: a strong China allied with a strong Japan against Soviet expansion or a subjugated China under Japanese control? While the militarists could agree unanimously that the Soviet Union was the primary enemy in Asia, they could not agree on China's part in stymieing Soviet expansion in Asia.

Two views dominated Japanese thinking. One, that of the antiexpansionists, held that Japan should take advantage of China's growing nationalism by helping to strengthen China and then becoming allied to it. The antiexpansionists cautioned against becoming involved in a war on the vast China mainland; Japan simply could not afford a protracted war against a rapidly uniting Chinese people. A strong independent China allied with Japan would stymie Soviet expansion in Asia.

The second view, that of the expansionists, held that it was precisely because of China's growing nationalism that Japan had to act fast. The Chinese, this view continued, were not about to forget Japan's past transgressions against the Chinese people. As Boyle puts it: "Japan dared not risk a war with the Soviet Union with a hostile China to her rear."[6] Eliminating China now, when it was economically weak and militarily unprepared, was the only safe bet open to Japan's military strategists. Tojo, the chief of staff of the Japanese Army in north China, recommended that Japan "should deliver a blow first of all upon the Nanking KMT regime in order to remove this menace at our read."[7] With the KMT and eventually the CCP eliminated, Japan could concentrate fully on the Soviet Union.

The expansionists' views won out.

The "Special Undeclared War"

The spark which started the prairie fire in the Asian war theater was provided by the presence of a contingent of Japanese troops near Peking under the provisions of the Boxer Protocol. On the night of July 7, 1937, an incident occurred close to the famous

Marco Polo Bridge near Peking involving Japanese troops on maneuvers and the Chinese garrison. Shots were fired and deaths were reported.[8] Using this incident as a pretext to insure the safety of its citizens in the area, Japan within a month had increased its troop strength in and around Peking from seven thousand to nearly one hundred sixty thousand men. The month of July was marked by sporadic, violent clashes. By month's end, the Chinese began the evacuation of Peking, but not before three hundred Japanese civilians in the vicinity of Peking were killed by the Chinese.

The Japanese "lightning war" machine struck and it struck decisively. Tientsin fell first on July 30, followed by Peking (August 8), T'aiyuan, Shansi (November 9), Shanghai (November 12), Nanking (December 13),[9] and finally Hankow (December 24). In the five months since the July 7 incident diplomatic efforts had been undertaken to settle the hostilities. The major Japanese proposal of November 5 called for the establishment of an anti-Communist front and the recognition of an autonomous Manchukuo. It was quickly repudiated by Chiang. Only Germany showed any interest in helping to mediate a ceasefire; the other powers kept their respective distances from the Asian war.

Chiang's resolute stand against negotiating with Japan, however, changed proportionally to China's misfortunes on the battlefield. By early December, as the Japanese were nearing Nanking, Chiang resumed talks with Japan. Ironically, Chiang was putting his faith in the success of the negotiations on Hitler, who was caught in the middle, allied to Japan by treaty and at the same time providing military aid to China.[10]

Inspired by the relative ease of its offensive, Japan now made harsher demands to Chiang, including one of Japan's favorite devices from times past, a war indemnity. Chiang hesitated. On January 13, 1938, the Japanese war cabinet issued an ultimatum to Chiang, giving him three days in which to accept the demands or else face total annihilation. Chiang still hesitated. On January 16, Premier Konoe announced that Japan was severing all contacts with Chiang's National government. The position of the antiexpan-

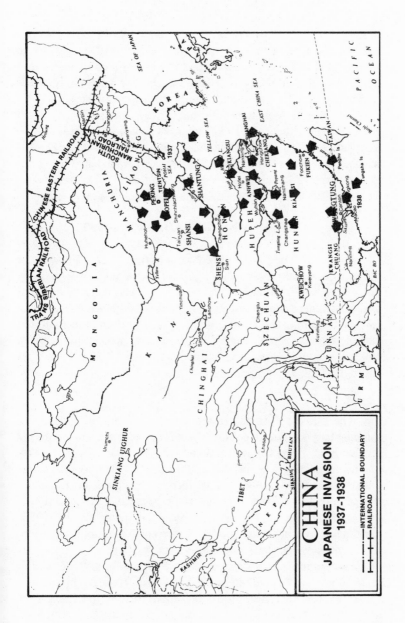

sionists within the Japanese Military Council was irretrievably lost. On March 14, the Japanese offensive was resumed, and with the exception of a bloody, valiant stand by the Nationalist Army in a small town near the city of Hsuchow, the Japanese easily swept southward. In October 1938, Canton was taken by sea.

The war in Asia, now fully under way, was to last for eight years. However, between 1939 and 1944, when a desperate Japan resumed its offensive, the war in China was at a standstill. Incredible as it may sound, during this period, Chiang, acting counter to the advice given by both his American and German advisers, was never to undertake a single major offensive against Japan.[11]

THE NANKING DECADE, 1928–1937

One would be hard pressed to consider Japan's invasion of China as the sole or even the dominant factor leading to the rise of Communism in China. In the period between the establishment of the Nanking government in 1928 and the Japanese invasion of 1937, the claim that the "Kuomintang failed largely by default and that the Chinese Communist Party in a large sense moved into a political vacuum,"[12] needs closer scrutiny. After 1937, the KMT's efforts become a moot point.

The Economy

The Chinese economy in the period between 1928 and 1937 shared many of the characteristics of the economy prior to the revolution of 1911. Chinese national income, for example, increased undramatically but steadily until 1936.[13] One of the major sources of the increasing national income was the average annual rate of growth in the industrial sector between 1928 and 1936. During this period, the growth rate was 8.4 percent.[14] In 1933, consumer goods accounted for 41.6 percent of the total net value added for key industrial goods produced.[15]

Foreign investments also continued to grow from $768 million in 1902 to $3,243 million in 1931. Direct business investment accounted for 78.1 percent of the total foreign investments in 1931. By 1931, Great Britain was the largest contributor with 36.9 percent of all investments, followed by Japan with 35.1 percent,

Russia with 8.4 percent, the United States with 6.1 percent, and France with 5.9 percent. Shanghai and Manchuria accounted for nearly one third of all direct investments in China by 1931.[16]

The traditional sector of the Chinese economy was still dominated in the 1930s by agricultural production. In 1933, for example, agriculture accounted for 65 percent of China's net national product. In the period between 1928 and 1936, this sector of the economy also increased slightly but steadily.[17] In 1933, however, China's population, which was estimated at 500 million, prevented the moderate growth of the Chinese economy from being particularly impressive. Seventy-three percent of the population, or 365 million people, were engaged in agriculture.

As might be expected, the statistics of the moderate growth of the Chinese economy were being influenced mainly by the developments along the major coastal cities, especially Shanghai. The peasant had not yet begun to realize Sun Yat-sen's "land to the tiller" dream. In the period between 1931 and 1936, less than 2 percent of the national budget was allocated for rural reconstruction.[18] Further, the rent-reduction program adopted in 1926, which fixed the rent at 37.5 percent of the annual total produce of the land, was not effectively enforced, with landlords continuing to collect rents as high as 50 to 70 percent. Neither were other land reform measures enforced, such as the abolition of subtenancy and the right of perpetual lease.[19] In short, in the period between 1928 and 1936, the Chinese peasants had not yet benefited from the revolution allegedly being fought in their name. The Communists, we shall see, were to exploit to their advantage the gap between China's prosperity and poverty.

The Government

Like the financial situation in which the early republic found itself, so too did the Kuomintang find itself on the verge of bankruptcy in 1928. In 1928, the government was operating with a 46.4 percent deficit, a condition which only slowly improved by 1935.[20] To remedy the situation, the Kuomintang undertook an overhaul of its financial system, presumably to carry through the reform ideals of Sun Yat-sen. One obvious way of increasing revenues was to increase taxes, which was done and which, as might also be expected, added to the heavy burden of the peasantry.

The second measure which the government undertook was the creation of four government banks to handle its revenues. Of the four banks, the Central Bank of China, headed by Chiang's brother-in-law, T. V. Soong, was the most notable one. The four government banks held 56 percent of the deposits and 40 percent of all capital reserves in China. In 1935, the central government introduced a system of national currency to replace various regional currencies in circulation.[21] By 1937, the financial system of the central government had 164 modern banks with 1,597 branches. The government controlled 61 percent of all bank resources in China.[22]

With the improvement of the financial system one might be inclined to think that the KMT's revenue reform efforts were successful, but whatever gains were realized in public financing, it seems were lost in military and debt service expenditures. Between 1928 and 1937, military spending accounted for nearly one-half of the government's total expenditures, while payments for foreign loans accounted for nearly one-third of the annual expenditures.[23] As one might expect, military spending began to grow concommitantly with the extermination campaigns of 1930.[24] Bianco concludes:

> The regime did introduce modern financial practices, and in general accomplished much more in the financial sphere than its predecessors; we cannot censure it as categorically on this question as on the question of agrarian reform. But censure it we must, if only for misdirecting potentially productive investment capital toward speculation and toward enormous military expenditures.[25]

Chiang

Chiang K'ai-shek was, without a doubt, the dominant figure in Chinese politics and military affairs between 1928 and 1936, and after the Sian incident, he was the undisputed head of the government from 1937 until 1949. Such being the case, it is perhaps appropriate at this time to take a closer look at him as an individual. While no one would for a moment credit Mao solely for the Communist conquest of China, it is not too far-fetched to assume that in Chiang's personality and in his management of state affairs lie part of the explanation for the so-called Kuomintang Debacle.

Fortunately, there were many individuals in a position to observe him and his government first-hand during the critical years following Japan's invasion. These individuals were foreign correspondents, American foreign service officers, military leaders, and senior U.S. government officials. Unfortunately, because most of these individuals were Americans, the sample is somewhat biased. However, there were varying assessments of Chiang within and among the various individuals to indicate that they were dealing with an extremely complicated man.

Foreign Correspondents. Chungking, China's wartime capital, was the center of activity for most of the major news bureaus during the war. The war correspondents in Chungking were an impressive group. Among them were: Edgar Snow (New York *Herald Tribune* and the *Saturday Evening Post*), T. H. White and Annalee Jacoby (*Time–Life*), Jack Belden (UP and INS), A. T. Steele (Chicago *Daily News*), Brooks Atkinson, Hanson Baldwin, and Tillman Durdin (New York *Times*), Spencer Moosa (AP), Agnes Smedley (freelance), Harrison Forman (*Times* of London), and Anna Louise Strong (Moscow *Daily News,* freelance).

Relations between the press and the Nationalist government were never cordial. Because of its allegedly biased news stories of the Chiang-Stilwell controversy, the press was subjected to censorship by Chiang's press relations office, headed by his biographer, Hollington K. Tong.[26] Tong blatantly accused the press of being "pro-Yenan," that is, pro-Communist. In any case, most of the correspondents at one time or another recorded their impressions of the generalissimo.

Brooks Atkinson, the drama critic for the New York *Times* who was to win the Pulitzer Prize for his war correspondence, wrote of Chiang: "Although he is the acknowledged leader of China, he has no record of personal military achievement and his basic ideas of political leadership are those of a warlord."[27] T. H. White and Annalee Jacoby believed that:

> [Chiang's complex character] has been bred of a tempestu-
> ous storm-tossed life and, like his lust for power, his calcu-
> lating ruthlessness, his monumental stubborness, has become
> more than an individual characteristic—it is a force in na-
> tional politics.[28]

Jack Belden rejected the "psychological" approach to the
problems of history and contended that "It was not the personality
of Chiang K'ai-shek that shaped the nature of the despotism, but
the nature of the dictatorship that shaped Chiang K'ai-shek," but
then proceeded to characterize Chiang's personality as

> a little depressing, a little ridiculous, at all times contradic-
> tory, and sometimes tragic . . . an atrocious strategist, a bad
> organizer and a worse administrator . . . [given to] distrust
> of everybody else to a distrust of [himself] . . . unstable
> [and] treacherous . . . vain and touchy to the point of hys-
> teria [and] . . . supercilious.[29]

The Australian correspondent and adviser to Chiang, W. H.
Donald, however, believed that it was precisely Chiang's "hard-
headedness, unyielding, and uncompromising stubborness" that
kept China's resistance and will to fight going in the war against
Japan.[30] As we shall further see, it was not uncommon for one
individual close to Chiang to see in his personality strengths where
others found weaknesses. This, of course, is the mark of a "complex involved character."

Foreign Service Officers. Shortly after General Joseph W. Stilwell
was assigned by the Pentagon to become the U.S. military adviser
to Chiang's staff in January 1942, one of Stilwell's first requests
from the state department was for a staff of political advisers to
help him with diplomatic relations. In time, the state department
assigned four advisers who were to become highly critical of
Chiang: John S. Service, John Paton Davies, Raymond Ludden,
and John Emmerson. It is not our intent here to consider the four
professional officers in light of the "Who Lost China?" controversy, but rather to explore their assessment of Chiang's personality, as they wrote their policy analysis between their arrival in
1942 and their departure in 1944–45.

John S. Service, who was born in China and spoke Chinese

fluently, helped to prepare a highly controversial report in June 1944, on "The Situation in China and Suggestions Regarding American Policy," in which was written:

> The Generalissimo shows a . . . loss of realistic flexibility and a hardening of narrowly conservative views. His growing megalomania and his unfortunate attempts to be "sage" as well as leader, have forfeited the respect of many intellectuals . . . criticism of his dictatorship is becoming more outspoken.[31]

John Paton Davies also was born in China and was fluent in Chinese. His parents were American missionaries in China, "a part of a righteous and consecrated crusade that strove with love to win China to Christ and, in so doing, did much to shatter a civilization that had endured for millennia."[32] Davies recalled the initial mood surrounding Stilwell's appointment to China and Chiang's reception of Stilwell:

> In matters of military science the generalissimo was an eccentric—tea shop aphorisms drained from the classical [fourth and fifth century B.C.] strategist Sun Tzu. He was morbidly defensive-minded. He fretted, vacillated, and indulged in bouts of bad temper. If he had kept this all to himself and his headquarters staff, his vagaries might not have done irreparable damage. Unhappily, he broadcast them in daily bursts of orders, often contradictory, across the chain of command to his bewildered and apprehensive generals in the field, even down to division commanders.[33]

Senior U.S. Officials. With the exception of Stilwell, most high-ranking U.S. civilian and military officials saw what others believed to be personality defects as strong points of character. John Leighton Stuart, who was U.S. ambassador to China between 1946 and 1949, wrote in 1937 that Chiang had a "winning personality," possessed a "highly trained intelligence, a capacity for quick and shrewd decisions, forcefulness, courage and indefatigable energy." Stuart concluded that "China was fortunate to have one with his character and capacity actively leading the nation in this supremely critical period of it rebirth and rebuilding."[34]

General Albert C. Wedemeyer, who succeeded Stilwell in China, was convinced that

> Chiang K'ai-shek was a sincere patriot, preeminently concerned with the interests of his country and his people. He knew very little about modern military strategy, for he had been trained in guerrilla war concepts; but he knew a great deal about the political art of holding his people to the job at hand. He was skillful in playing one person against others.[35]

Again, the measure by which Chiang was scrutinized appears to be one's proximity to him. The nearer one got to the man, the more impressive he appeared. The further one was from this terribly complicated man, the less impressed one was with his personal character.

JAPAN AND THE CHINESE
POLITICAL LEADERSHIP VACUUM

The Japanese invasion had far-reaching implications for the rise of Communism in China. Two developments stand out: the retreat of the KMT into the hinterlands of southwest China and the creation by Japan of Chinese puppet-governments and armies. Both of these developments led to the creation of a leadership vacuum which in the end benefited the growth of the Chinese Communist Party and its Red Army.

Retreat to Chungking

The KMT capital was moved from Nanking shortly before its fall in December 1937, to Hankow and then finally to Chungking in Szechwan province. "Chungking," writes Payne, "is a city made for breaking people's hearts."[36] Floyd Taylor calls Chungking "the city of mud and courage."[37] Located on the confluence of the Yangtze and the Chialing rivers, Chungking was an ancient fortress and with its many rocky hills a natural place to ward off Japan's continual air raids. When the retreating KMT reached Chungking, it found a primitive city of two hundred thousand, which had neither telephones nor electricity until 1934. As late as 1928, water still was carried in buckets, and not until 1928 was the wheelbarrow introduced to the local townspeople.[38] People walked naked around the city, according to Payne, not because they were exhibitionists but because they were too poor to clothe themselves. "There were," wrote White and Jacoby, "only two seasons in Chungking, both bad."[39] It either rained or it was hot, causing dysentery and malaria to run rampant throughout the dirty, primitive city.

Nonetheless, this squalid city saved the KMT from Japanese bombs. Bomb-shelters were carved into the rocky hills, and here, the KMT and the townspeople survived the bombings which began in May 1939. In 1939, the raids were conducted by night; in 1940, by day; and by 1941, both by day and by night.[40] At first, the bombs took their toll, but in time, the KMT installed a siren system to notify the city of Japanese attacks. By 1944, Chungking had almost been bombed into extinction. What few "modern" conveniences were available in the city were inoperable. Again, White and Jacoby tell us:

> Sewage piled up in the gutters and smelled; mosquitoes bred in the stagnant pools of water deep in the ruins, and malaria flourished. Dysentery grew worse; so did cholera, rashes, and a repulsive assortment of internal parasites. . . . Rats . . . grew fat . . . and the press reported that they killed babies in their cribs.[41]

Chungking was also a long distance away from Yenan, where the Communists had established themselves. Like it or not, Chiang was forced under the provisions of the second united front to give the CCP some autonomy in North China. Thus, the KMT not only recognized the CCP's hegemony in Shensi, but as a condition for eschewing the use of the term "soviet," the KMT further extended the CCP's "special area" status to include two other provinces, Kansu and Ninghsia (thus, the area under Communist control is referred to as Shen-Kan-Ning hereafter). When the boundaries of the three provinces were delimited, the Communists controlled twenty-three counties, an increase of seventeen from the six which made up Shensi. The increase in the number of people under Communist control was approximately 2 million, 90 percent of whom were peasants.

The KMT also provided the CCP with a budget for the three-border region. The budget called for a hundred thousand dollar monthly stipend for educational and reconstruction purposes and five hundred thousand dollars for the maintenance of the newly re-designated Red Army, now the KMT Eighth Route Army. The chief political advantage of the stipends was that they "enabled the Communists to mobilize rapidly and keep taxation light as they attempted to consolidate and institutionalize power in the border region."[42]

In sum, from the time of the retreat to Chungking in 1937–38, the KMT had not only isolated itself in southwest China, but had given the Communists in the north a free hand to put into effect a network of programs which would contribute to its growth. Chiang, however, had not totally overlooked the north. By mid-year, 1939, Chiang had seized five districts in Shen-Kan-Ning and set up a blockade designed to keep a closer watch on Communist activities in north China. The blockade, while proving to be a nuisance to Communist expansion in north China, was implemented too late.[43]

The Puppet-Governments

Another far-reaching development which contributed to the rise of Communism in China was the establishment of puppet governments by the Japanese Imperial Army. Between 1938 and 1940, three major puppet governments were established in north China (Peking), central China (Nanking), and Inner Mongolia (Kalgan). Each government controlled its own puppet armies, freeing the Japanese regulars for combat.

The puppet-governments were modeled after the Kuomintang government. Each government had an executive, judicial, and legislative *yuan* and other such institutional ministries as were deemed necessary. Further, each of the main governments had particular jurisdictional boundaries. Organizations also were established to push Japanese propaganda freely among the Chinese people. Finally, the puppet governments were nominally run by Chinese officials who had either become disenchanted with Chiang's rule or else had become dead-weights during the Nanking Decade. In fact, Japanese advisers always were present to direct internal matters. Most of the men selected to head the governments were in their seventies and none was under fifty years of age. Many had exhibited pro-Japanese tendencies in the past.[44] Financially underwritten by Japan, the puppet-governments, nonetheless, were about the only organized administrative units in the Japanese-controlled areas.

By far, the most important of the puppet-governments was the one headed by Wang Ching-wei, the former left-KMT official.[45] After Chiang's ascendancy to power in 1928, Wang spent the next seven years either actively opposing Chiang's growing power (1928–31) or else serving in an uneasy capacity as president of the executive *yuan* under Chiang (1932–1935). In his position as president, Wang found himself in a key role in the negotiations with Japan over Manchuria. Unable to stop the Japanese, Wang gained for himself the reputation of "appeaser," which led to an assassination attempt that left him critically wounded. In 1936, Wang retired from the Kuomintang government and went to Europe to recuperate from his wounds.

When the Sino-Japanese war began in July 1937, Wang returned to China and assumed the position of deputy to Chiang K'ai-shek. Wang accompanied the retreating KMT to Chungking. During his tenure as Chiang's deputy, Wang supported Japan's peace proposals. Chiang flatly refused them. In the environment created by Chiang's staunch antipeace stance, anyone who advocated any kind of rapprochement with Japan was branded a traitor. Wang was not, to be sure, the only high-ranking official who participated in the "peace movement." Indeed, such notables as Hu Shih, later to be the KMT's ambassador to the United States, Chou Fo-hai, one of the twelve founders of the Chinese Communist Party and now one of Chiang's trusted aides, and Ch'en Kung-po, still another founder of the CCP and now a KMT loyalist, all participated in the movement. Perhaps the most influential group in the peace movement was the so-called Low Key Club, which included Hu Shih and Chou Fo-hai. The club was so designated because its peace efforts were intended to be inconspicuous and low keyed. Interestingly, Chiang knew about the various attempts to find a solution to bring the hostilities to an end. When Chiang met with representatives of the peace movement, he never gave any indication of whether he approved or disapproved of the specific proposals to end the war. The advantages of this technique, Boyle tells us, are obvious:

> The generalissimo could easly take credit [for the good proposals] and just as easily shrug off responsibility in the event of failure. After Sian . . . the generalissimo could not afford to be "low-keyed" in public. In private, however, ambivalence had its clear rewards.[46]

In Chungking, Wang was becoming increasingly distressed by certain measures which the Nationalists and Communists were employing to slow down the Japanese invasion. Wang and the members of the Low Key Club particularly were distressed by Chiang's "scorched-earth" policy. For example, in June 1938, the dikes of the Yellow River were dynamited, releasing flood waters over three provinces. Numerous cities and villages were flooded, causing untold damage to the countryside. According to Boyle, "two million people were left homeless, and perhaps a million Chinese died as a result of the floods and their aftermath."[47] This action delayed the Japanese but little.

Another example of the scorched-earth policy was the tragic burning of Ch'angsha on November 13, 1938, when thousands were burned to death. As Boyle has clearly shown, Wang did not object to the scorched-earth policy provided that the earth was scorched as a result of military combat. Such, however, was not the case.

Wang Ching-wei's Defection. Nothing so embittered Wang, however, as Chiang's staunch antipeace stand which dated back to Chiang's famous "Kuling Speech" of July 19, 1937.

One year later, Chiang was just as adamant in his resistance to a peace settlement with Japan as he had ever been, a position which earned him the hatred of the Japanese army and government. What Japan needed and wanted was a Chinese government friendly to it and a person with enough status and prestige to head a new Chinese government. Wang was the perfect choice. "Wang

Ching-wei," wrote Bunker, "since the beginning of the incident and before, had been for peace; his role in Chinese politics was and had been to present the peace-loving and accommodating face of the Kuomintang toward Japan."[48]

Just when Wang decided to defect is difficult to say, but arrangements were being made for his role as the major mediator-collaborator by the fall of 1938. By November, a joint document had been drafted by members of the Low Key Club and Japanese representatives which for all intents and purposes was to serve as Wang's basis for negotiations. While the various items were to be amended or dropped in the negotiations to come, the joint agreement basically recognized Japan's hegemony in north China in exchange for a promise by Japan to withdraw its troops from China immediately once the hostilities ended.

Wang intended to leave Chungking on December 8 while Chiang was out of the city and announce his resignation in either Kunming, Hanoi, or Hong Kong. Chiang, however, returned unexpectedly, forcing Wang to cancel his departure. Between December 9 and 16, Wang met with Chiang presumably to convince him that a peace settlement with Japan was China's only salvation. Chiang refused. In frustration, Wang finally left Chungking on December 18 arriving in Hanoi on December 19.

Wang's role in Chinese politics from his departure from Chungking until he assumed control of the government of Nanking in March 1940, falls into two phases. In the first phase, from December 1938, until the assassination of his closest friend, presumably by KMT agents, on March 21, 1939, Wang was motivated apparently to act as a mediator in a peace settlement between China and Japan. In the second phase, beginning with his friend's assassination, "Wang was no longer content with playing the role of comrade seeking to sway his party to what he considered the better course. Henceforward his aim to bring peace was mixed, not altogether consciously, with a desire to see Chiang's humiliation."[49]

On January 1, 1939, Wang officially was expelled from the Kuomintang, and by October, he was branded a "traitor" by no less than Chiang himself.[50]

The New Central Government. On March 30, 1940, the New Central Government of China at Nanking was inaugurated formally. The inauguration, wrote Boyle, "was a dismal affair" held in a simple hall during a cold and misty morning.[51] The New Central Government ostensibly had absorbed the remaining puppet governments. Not surprisingly, the structure of Wang's government was identical to that of the Kuomintang. Sun Yat-sen's Three Principles were adopted as the ideology of the new government as was the KMT national flag.

Now that Wang's government was legitimized by the Japanese, Japan proceeded to draw up the peace treaty between it and "China." The peace treaty basically recognized Japan's hegemony in north China, including the right to appoint economic and financial advisers to Wang's government. According to Communist historian Ho Kan-chih, Japan increased its "plunder" of China's natural resources markedly: iron ore production increased from 4,502,222 tons in 1939 to 10,654,325 tons in 1943; coal, from 27,451,968 tons in 1938 to 50,075,141 tons in 1943.[52]

Japan, paradoxically, stalled on formally recognizing Wang's government and also stalled signing the peace treaty. The Japanese government continued to hold out the hope that it could negotiate the peace treaty with Chiang's government. For nine months the Japanese government tried to approach Chiang and for nine months no progress was made. Finally, on November 30, 1940, Japan recognized its puppet government in China. On that same day, the peace treaty was signed.

On December 2, at the weekly memorial service of the KMT, Chiang denounced Wang and Japan: "I conceive this action as the perverse and outrageous product of the defeat of their recent peace offensive."[53]

On February 1, 1941, Mao delivered a scathing denunciation of Wang at a mass meeting held in Yenan. Mao said:

> Frightened out of his wits in face of [Japan's ambitions], Wang Ching-wei, political representative of the pro-Japanese faction of the Chinese big bourgeoisie, grovelled before Japan, concluded a treasonable treaty with her and betrayed China to Japanese imperialism.[54]

Finally, there was an attempt to legitimize Wang's government by seeking recognition from foreign powers. The United States denounced the Wang government while pledging its support of Chiang. Indeed, the creation of a new government had an obverse effect on Japanese designs: the United States immediately extended a $20 million loan to Chiang's government. Great Britain hesitated at first, but in the end, sided with Chiang. The only countries to respond positively to Wang's government were Japan's allies, Germany and Italy.

Pearl Harbor made the Wang government a moot question in international politics. After Pearl Harbor, "the Japanese lost interest in Wang and indeed, to a large measure, in China."[55] By October 1942, even Wang expressed his loss of confidence in the peace movement. In March 1944, Wang became fatally ill, a condition caused by an old wound, no doubt exacerbated by the frustrations which he endured during his four years as the head of the new government. "Wang's death," writes Bunker, "was the death of the dream of Sino-Japanese peace for which many in both China and Japan had striven in vain."[56]

Interestingly, Wang was given a hero's burial in Nanking and was buried near Sun Yat-sen's grave. During the war trials of the Chinese collaborators, Wang's wife, herself on trial, declared: "If our actions are condemned as violating the policy of the government, I will gladly be put to death, for what we did was for the people."[57] Ch'en Kung-po, one of the original founders of the CCP, a KMT defector and one of Wang's cohorts, was executed for his collaboration with Japan. Chou Fo-hai was sentenced to life in prison, where he apparently committed suicide. Finally, on January 21, 1946, the KMT symbolically executed Wang Ching-wei when one hundred fifty kilograms of TNT demolished his concrete tomb. His coffin was removed from the ruins and burned in the countryside.[58]

WARTIME EXPANSION OF
THE CHINESE COMMUNIST PARTY

The Japanese, for their part, were equally generous to the CCP—with time. Between 1937 and 1941, with the advent of Japan's reprisal campaign against Communist expansion in north

China, the Japanese virtually ignored the Communist stronghold in Shen-Kan-Ning. With the exception of the puppet-governments in Peking and Kalgan, ostensibly intended to offset the CCP's influence among the populace in north China, the Japanese concentrated their efforts against Chiang's KMT. Wang Ching-wei had cautioned against ignoring the Communists, believing that if the policy of ignoring the CCP continued, the Japanese would find themselves fighting the Communists for control of China rather than the KMT. While the Japanese concentrated on the KMT and believed that to control China they needed only to control key roads, railroads, water routes, and towns ("points and lines"), the CCP gradually came to control everything in between (the "surface").[59]

How the CCP grew behind Japanese lines and how it came to control the "surface" is due mainly to its efforts in (1) introducing an innovative economic reform program, (2) mobilizing and increasing the political consciousness of the peasants, (3) expanding the organization and increasing the sophistication of the Red Army and (4) vigorously promoting an educational-propaganda campaign among the peasants in general, and among the party elites in particular.

Economic Reforms

It would not be far-fetched to claim that the initial program which paved the way for the growth and successes of both the party and the army was the party's economic policies. The land reform program which was introduced in 1935 and refined in the next ten years was not, however, only economic in nature, but also heavily laden with political and social undertones. For our purposes, the economic policies of the CCP may be divided into four slightly overlapping periods: (1) 1935–37, a period of violent agrarian revolution, (2) 1937–39, a period of restrained agrarian reform, (3) 1939–42, a period of inflation, and (4) 1943–45, a period of a well-developed network of economic programs.

1935–1937. In the first period, 1935–37, the party launched its violent agrarian revolution shortly after reassembling its forces after the Long March. The targets of the agrarian revolution were the landlords and rich peasants. To be classified as either could bring death or confiscation of land for redistribution among the poor peasants. The politics of the agrarian revolution foresaw the time when the traditional holders of most of China's private property, the gentry, would lose one of their bases for power, the land, and in their stead, a newly emerging force would rise, the peasant. Politically, the party's violent agrarian revolution succeeded. According to Selden:

> At a single sweep the domination of landlords and rich peasants was destroyed. Everywhere land revolution broke the political monopoly of the rich by striking at its economic roots and creating new leadership and institutions with power centered in revolutionary peasant activists. Not only was the land revolution critical for winning peasant confidence and active support, but in the course of struggle a new village leadership, united in its determination to destroy the old order and by an egalitarian vision of the new, was forged and assumed authority.[60]

That the party succeeded in mobilizing peasant support at this time is clear. The news of the land revolution in Shensi spread throughout north China. In his study of the Shansi warlord, Yen Hsi-shan, Gillin records the attitudes of the villagers: "We know you're the Red Army, the army of us poor people."[61] To be sure, in the first period of the party's expansion in north China, social and economic reforms were given priority over its political and military programs.[62]

1937–1939. It will be recalled that one of the concessions which the party made in establishing the bases for the second united front was to abandon its land confiscation program. In February 1937, Mao agreed to abandon land confiscation, "not because it was undesirable," but because the agreement afforded the party its much needed respite from the KMT's extermination campaigns.[63]

In the period between 1937 and 1939, the party adopted a moderate policy of rent and interest reduction. The party not only abandoned its violence against landlords, but made a complete turnabout and invited exiled landlords to return to the border area to receive their equal share of the land.[64]

The program contained something for both peasants and

landlords. For the peasants, the rent reduction program allowed a reduction of 25 percent; rents could not be collected before a harvest or during periods of natural or man-made disasters; and rents in arrears were negated. The program also insured that the landlords were to receive a certain amount of the yield (40 to 60 percent), thus insuring the continuation of tenancy. In addition, the landlords were guaranteed the collection of their just due by the party.[65]

In 1937, the party also adopted a progressive income tax on agricultural products. Under this system, those with the most wealth, the landlords, paid a higher tax than those with the least wealth, the peasants. In Shansi province, Gillin found that wherever the Red Army was active, "the rich were forced to bear virtually the entire cost of the war against Japan."[66] The Communist historian, Ho Kan-chih, wrote: "The burden of taxation was not laid exclusively on the landlords and the capitalists, but was shared by over 80 percent of the population."[67] Landlords who refused to pay taxes were either denounced by the politically conscious peasant or else were stripped of their belongings.[68]

A system of credit also was introduced in the border region at this time, financed and supported by the monthly stipends which the KMT was providing the CCP under the provisions of the united front.

1939–1942. Between 1939 and 1942, the agrarian policies of the party met their sternest tests. By 1939, the respite offered by the alliance ended. Skirmishes between the KMT and CCP, it will be recalled, had occurred as early as April 1938, and in response to the mutual suspicions which continued between the antagonists, the KMT instituted a loose economic blockade around Shen-Kan-Ning. The blockade, coupled with Japan's new policy of reprisals against the CCP (to be considered later) in late 1940, gravely cut into the rapid progress which the party had made between 1935 and 1939. Between 1939 and 1942, the party was confronted with an economic phenomenon which it was not prepared to deal with: inflation. "In the course of a year," writes Selden, "the value of border currency fell twice as rapidly as that of the National currency."[69] By 1942, prices had risen almost 1,400 percent and the following year another 700 percent.[70] Table 8.1 is, according to

Selden, a representative example of the inflationary spiral which hit Shen-Kan-Ning between 1937 and 1943, noting that a quantum jump in the index is evident between 1941 and 1942.

Table 8.1

Inflation in the Shen-Kan-Ning Border Region, 1937–1943

Year	Cost of one peck of millet (40 pounds) in Yenan (in fa-pi dollars)	Index
1937	2.5	100
1938	2.5–3.8	132
1939	3–4.2	143
1940	4.2–7	214
1941	8.5–15.7	290
1942	63–145	4,038.3
1943	150–2.200	30,683.1

Source: Selden, *The Yenan Way*, p. 181.

As might be expected, taxes were increased to meet the needs of the border region. By 1941, taxes rose about 8 percent above the previous levels, and eventually stabilized around 10 percent.[71]

1942–1945. Inflation, increased taxes, the KMT economic blockade, military skirmishes, and Japan's policy of reprisals, led the Central Committee of the CCP to initiate an extensive production campaign, the goal of which was to be self-sufficiency. From 1943 on, the agrarian policies of the CCP were an amalgamation of rent-reduction, cooperatives, mutual-aid teams, and production campaigns which succeeded in beating the inflationary situation. According to Ho Kan-chih:

> In the rural areas where war was constantly raging and the enemy wrought havoc, the troops and government bodies engaged in productive work, so as to attain gradually complete or partial self-support in foodstuffs and manufactured goods.[72]

The party's first move was to decentralize the management of the economy. Now, the peasant-farmer was given direction and control of his economic activities, with party officials moving to the sidelines. In 1942, the party inaugurated its second major campaign at achieving self-sufficiency behind Japanese lines. By 1943–44, the drive to turn the rural economy over to the small farmers was working. By 1944, fully 50 to 75 percent of the three border regions' rural populace was actively participating in mutual-aid activity such as weeding and spring planting. The area under cultivation increased from (approximately) 1,480,000 acres in 1938 to 2,056,598 acres in 1942. The grain output also increased significantly in the same period, as did homespun cotton and other textiles.[73] By 1945, the party had helped to establish 882 industrial cooperatives with two hundred sixty-five thousand members to process the raw materials available in the area.[74]

Then, in a move to complement the mutual-aid programs, the party launched a production movement designed to insure the participation of all party, army, and governmental personnel. "In 1942," writes Ho Kan-chih, "troops, governmental organizations and schools still had to get all their foodstuffs from the people, but by 1943, they had attained partial self-support."[75]

While the use of troops and civilian cadres was nothing new to the CCP, the impetus provided by the party now became institutionalized. After 1943, party and army personnel adopted a dual role automatically. One spoke now of the "economic role" of such and such an activity, be it political, cultural, or military. In 1943, everyone, including Mao, for example, was asked to work at least one acre of land and was expected to produce enough grain to sustain himself for one season. Clearly, the military had become self-sufficient after 1943, a phenomenon which allowed the party to reduce its budget for the military and use the money for subsidizing rent-reduction guaranties and underwriting the credit system.

During this last period of the CCP's agrarian reform policies, Mao was extraordinarily busy writing the basic guidelines of the party's overall economic program. In "Economic and Financial Problems During the Anti-Japanese War," written in December 1942, Mao stressed the importance of self-sufficiency as well as the economic relationship between the party and the army and the masses.

The further we advance along the line of economic self-support, the lighter will be the tax burden we impose on the people. From 1937 to 1939, we took very little from the people, thus enabling them to recuperate to a very large extent. From 1940 to 1942, the burden on the people was increased.[76]

In "Let Us Get Organized," a speech delivered on November 29, 1943, Mao proudly proclaimed that "our troops depend for their pay neither on the Kuomintang government, nor on the border region government, nor on the people, but can provide for themselves ... [thus] less tax is collected from the people."[77] Mao's persistency is further shown in speeches and articles written on January 10, 1945 ("We Must Learn to Do Economic Work") and January 31, 1945 ("Production Is Also Possible in the Guerrilla Zones"), both of which contained the same message: self-sufficiency. By 1945, he could boast that 90 million people had enthusiastically adopted the party's agrarian policies.[78]

Political Activity

During the first two years of the second united front (1937–39), the CCP enjoyed a much needed respite *militarily* from both the KMT and the Japanese. During this crucial lull in the campaigns against Communism in China, the CCP turned its attention toward political action among the peasantry. Raising the "political consciousness" of the peasants in the three-border region became a key campaign in the growth of the CCP after the alliance had been completed.

What was the level of the peasants' political consciousness immediately prior to the Japanese invasion? One example from Gillin's excellent study of the Shansi warlord, Yen Hsi-shan, may be used to answer the question. According to Gillin:

On one occasion, after a damaged Japanese plane was forced to land behind the Chinese lines, local Chinese farmers stood around watching calmly while the enemy pilot repaired his craft and flew off. The peasants also willingly dug trenches and built defense works for the Japanese, who paid excellent wages for this kind of work ... peasants were unaware of the fundamental difference between Chinese and Japanese.[79]

The success of the economic reform programs notwithstanding, Chalmers Johnson believes that "prior to 1937, the peasants were a passive element in politics. . . . Japan's invasion changed this condition by heightening the peasants' interests in such concepts as national defense, citizenship, treason, legitimacy of government, and the long-range betterment of the Chinese state."[80]

In north China after 1937, the CCP primarily was responsible for the political education of the masses. Moving about freely in the three-border region, the CCP's first call to political action came in May 1937 with the passage of the first election law in Shen-Kan-Ning. Conducted alongside massive education-propaganda campaigns (considered later),

> the ultimate goal was participation of the entire populace in a political program penetrating to every [village] and including party, government, mass organizations, and local military units. The elections, by permitting the peasants to participate in and select a responsible government, helped overcome their fears of the political process. For most peasants this was their first election; indeed, many had probably never before heard of elections.[81]

The election law called for universal suffrage, political campaigns, and a four-step election process beginning with elections at the village level, then the subdistrict level, the district level, and finally the apex of the political system within the base area, the regional level. Election day was a time for festivities—children's games, political reports, bountiful food, and drinks were characteristics of an election meeting at the district level.[82]

The CCP's efforts in raising the political consciousness of the masses were carefully scrutinized by Mao himself. To this end, the party, under Mao's guidance, adopted a "tripartite system" whereby the party intended to broaden its social base by appealing under the rhetoric of a "new democracy" to China's rural middle and upper classes. According to Ho Kan-chih, the "tripartite" or "three-thirds" system was implemented by the CCP to insure that the Communists (representing the working class and the poor peasantry), the progressives (representing the petty bourgeoisie), and the middle-of-the-roaders (representing the middle bourgeoisie and the enlightened gentry) "each occupied one third of the posts in all government organs and people's representative bodies."[83] The CCP also furthered its political objectives by forcing the KMT to open the political process even more to several heretofore excluded groups under the guise of "democracy."

Mao provided the theoretical rationale for the three-thirds system in his major essay "On New Democracy" (January 1940). In this essay, Mao also provided a rationale for opening the seemingly closed proletariat party of Marx and Lenin to other class elements, especially the bourgeoisie. Proving his deft command of Lenin's and Stalin's writings, Mao cited Stalin's revolution thesis that world revolutions were of two kinds: "the first belonging to the bourgeois and capitalist category... [and] the second kind, the proletarian-socialist world revolution."[84] China, Mao declared, was in the "new type of bourgeois-democratic revolution and not yet [in] a proletarian-socialist revolution."[85] Mao continued:

> Since China is a colony as well as semi-colony encroached upon by others, her national bourgeoisie has at certain periods and to a certain degree a revolutionary quality. Here the task of the proletariat is to attach due importance to the revolutionary quality of the national bourgeoisie and establish with it a united front against imperialism and the governments of bureaucrats and warlords.[86]

In this "new democracy," a joint revolutionary-democratic dictatorship of peasants, proletariat, and bourgeoisie was now possible given China's particular historical development. Mao, however, made it clear that the new-democratic republic was the proper form of government for a given historical period, but it was, he emphasized, only a transitional form subject to change as China itself changed.

Ideology being satisfied, the pragmatic Mao then followed with his three-thirds proposal about two months after the appearance of "The New Democracy." The system, however, met with mixed success, being implemented in some places but not others.[87] The importance of this political program was not in its pervasiveness, but in its propaganda value. For example, a KMT report on the effectiveness of the united front in general and the three-thirds system in particular proclaimed:

... gentry who in the past had been dissatisfied with the CCP ... filled the skies with praise, feeling that the CCP government wasn't so bad after all, that it could recognize its own mistakes and could ask for criticism. This was stronger than anything in all Chinese history. ... The [KMT] central government has been away from them too long.[88]

The results of the party's political activities were apparent in the growth of its administrative structure and in the growth of its party membership. By 1945, the party's structure, patterned as it was after the Soviet pyramidical model, was, in descending order, composed of

Central committee (headquarters in Yenan)
Border Region or Provincial Committee
Area Committee
Municipal or County Committee
District Committee
Branch
Sub-Branch.

The principal component of the Central Committee was the politburo which, in turn, oversaw the principal bureaus: propaganda, organization, united front, military affairs, and so forth. In the absence of a central government of its own, the CCP's areas of contact were within the border regions. By April 1945, the Central Committee at Yenan under Mao's control "worked out directives on various important political, military, economic, and cultural problems" for nineteen other liberated areas or red bases, established behind Japanese lines.[89]

Keeping pace with the administrative development of the party between 1937 and 1945, the party's membership also grew by leaps and bounds. Table 8.2 gives the numerical growth of the party between 1937 and 1945.

According to Compton, by 1945, the CCP was the world's second largest Communist party. Peasants constituted the largest percentage of the membership, so "it was anything but a party of the proletariat which emerged from the war bases."[90]

While the party did not claim to be purely a party of the proletariat, thanks to Mao's "New Democracy," the infusion of peas-

Table 8.2

Numerical growth of the
Communist Chinese Party 1937–45

Year	Number
1937	40,000
1938	200,000
1940	800,000
1941	763,447
1942	736,151
1943	800,000
1944	853,420
1945	1,211,128

Sources: J. W. Lewis, *Leadership in Communist China*, p. 110 and
Compton, *Mao's China*, p. XXVIII.

ants was to prove a short-range problem for Mao in 1942. This
problem is considered in some detail in the next chapter.

Military Growth

On August 22, 1937, the KMT announced that in accordance
with the provisions of the Second United Front, the main forces
of the Red Army were to be redesignated as the KMT Eighth
Route Army. Its war zone was to be north China. Shortly there-
after, the KMT announced that the Communist guerrilla units left
behind by the Red Army in the southern provinces during the
Long March were to be reorganized and designated as the New
Fourth Army (the "old" Fourth Army was Chang Kuo-t'ao's disbanded unit). In insisting that the armies' leadership come from
Communist ranks, the Eighth Route Army was commanded by
Chu Teh and ably assisted by such generals in the modern-day
People's Liberation Army as Nieh Jung-chen, Liu Po-Ch'eng, Ho
Lung, Yeh Chien-ying, and other leading military figures (now in
disgrace) as P'eng Teh-huai and Lin Piao. The New Fourth Army
was commanded by Yeh T'ing, Ch'en Yi, Li Hsien-nien, and the
former chairman of the People's Republic of China, now dead and
in disgrace, Liu Shao-ch'i.

In September 1937, the Eighth Route Army invaded Shansi province and engaged the Japanese in battle. Lin Piao's division distinguished itself in this battle, taking the Japanese by surprise and routing three thousand of Japan's crack troops. The Japanese recovered from the initial encounter and in November, captured the capital of Shansi. With the Japanese occupying this part of north China, the Eighth Route Army began its penetration deep behind enemy lines and began establishing its war bases. As has already been mentioned, this strategy permitted the Communists to establish nineteen such war bases by 1945. In the areas designated as war zones, the Communists organized the masses politically and militarily.[91]

By January 1938, the New Fourth Army had established its headquarters in Nanch'ang and its war base in central China. Nanking and Shanghai were in the New Fourth Army's war zone. It too began political activities behind Japanese lines, activities which were to cost the New Fourth Army its life. Before discussing the so-called New Fourth Army incident, however, the political activities of the Communist armies and their growth will be considered first.

The Politics of the Communist Armies. The expansion of the red bases behind Japanese lines can be attributed mainly to the political work of the Communist armies. The responsibility for politicizing both the army regulars and the masses belonged chiefly to the political commissars attached to each company (130 men) in both armies. Two of the most prominent political commissars were Liu Shao-ch'i and Teng Hsiao-p'ing.

The political cadres were expected to infiltrate and carry on their political propagandizing in both the areas occupied (the war areas) and unoccupied (guerrilla areas) by the Japanese. According to Johnson:

> The factor that determined whether or not the Communists' efforts succeeded was the social mobilization of the peasantry. Peasant mobilization in response to the Japanese menace, combined with the Communist readiness to lead the nationalistic upsurge in the countryside, was the essential ingredient of the wartime Communist-peasant Alliance.[92]

That the Communists succeeded generally was due in no small measure to the behavior of the Japanese army. Perhaps the one major event which aided the political work of the Communist armies behind Japanese lines was the inauguration of Japan's infamous "Three-All" policy ("kill all, burn all, destroy all"). This policy was instituted precisely to destroy the CCP's influence among the peasants.[93] In the longest mopping-up campaign of the war, Japanese troops killed forty-five hundred people, burned one hundred fifty thousand houses, and transported about seventeen thousand Chinese to Manchuria for cheap labor. In the 1941–42 campaigns, Japan committed eight hundred thirty-three thousand troops to implement the reprisal policy.[94] The results in north China alone were the reduction of the population in the base areas from 44 million to 25 million.[95]

Military Structure and Growth. If the political cadres were successful in infiltrating an area, and if the populace responded positively (sometimes, but not often, they did not),[96] the next step was to organize the populace into self-defense corps or some mass organization consistent with the area's own demographic characteristics. In time, local organizations were absorbed into the overall structure of the military.

The military structure of the Communist armies was pyramidical as was the party's structure. The three levels were the regular army, the militia, and the guerrillas. The regulars or field forces were usually synonymous to either the Eighth Route or New Fourth Armies. As may be deduced from the personnel involved in the two main armies, the regulars were the better trained and better equipped units.[97] Whereas the regulars were identified with the central level of organization, the militia and the guerrillas were identified with the regional and local levels. The militia, or self-defense corps, consisted of villagers doubling as ready-reserves. By 1941, the militia numbered around two hundred twenty-four thousand persons,[98] and by 1945, the number had grown to about 2 million.[99]

The success of the political propagandizing by both party and army cadres can be seen in the numerical growth of the two principal Communist armies (Table 8.3).

Table 8.3
Numerical growth of the Eighth Route
and New Fourth Armies, 1937–45

Year	8th	4th	Total
1937	80,000	12,000	92,000
1938	156,000	25,000	181,000
1939	270,000	50,000	320,000
1940	400,000	100,000	500,000
1941	305,000	135,000a destroyed	440,000a
1942	340,000a 300,000b	110,960a&b	450,960a 410,960b
1943	339,000a 200,000b	125,892a&b	464,892a 325,892b
1944	320,000a 321,000b	153,767a 154,000b	473,676a 475,000b
1945	600,000b	260,000b	860,000b

Sources: a=Johnson, *Peasant Nationalism*, pp. 214–15 and b=Ch'en, *Mao*, p. 365.

The New Fourth Army Incident. The success of the organizational and political activities of the New Fourth Army south of the Yangtze River was to have a profound implication for the sustained growth of the army and the future of the Second United Front. Table 8.3 shows that in 1941 the New Fourth Army was "destroyed." What the table doesn't show is that the New Fourth Army was destroyed by the KMT on January 4, 1941. Why?

As is the case with most incidents involving the CCP and KMT, it is difficult to determine what really caused the clash between the two rivals. The Communists claim that Chiang turned against them to appease Japan, while Chiang claims that he acted in retaliation to New Fourth Army attacks on KMT troops in central China.[100] As is also the case in such incidents, there was a modicum of truth in each position. Chiang, for example, had not yet undertaken a single offensive against the Japanese and, indeed, he was not to press a single offensive in the eight-year war.[101] The Communists, on the other hand, had been violating the stipulations of the Second United Front with their extensive political and military activities in north and central China.

What is clear is that, by June 1940, both sides had reached a general understanding regarding the territorial responsibilities of each other's armies. The CCP was to concentrate *all* of its military troops north of the Yellow River while the KMT was to assume responsibility for the rest of the country. Between October 19 and December 9, both sides arranged for the evacuation of the New Fourth Army to the north. While some units of the New Fourth did cross the Yangtze according to plan, the headquarters unit remained behind.

The core of the headquarters unit was its medical organization which "was probably the best army medical organization in China."[102] The headquarters unit, however, also included about four thousand troops and three thousand political workers. On December 9, Chiang "personally" ordered Chu Teh, commander-in-chief of all Communist armies, to move his troops to the north before December 30 "and for all units of the New Fourth Army, south of the Yangtze River, to move north before December 31, and to cross the Yellow River northward by January 30, 1941."[103]

According to Johnson, the New Fourth Army headquarters was not north of the Yangtze on December 31, "but was marching instead in a southwesterly direction . . . possibly heading for the old Red areas in south Kiangsi."[104] On January 4, the KMT caught up with the New Fourth, and surrounded it, and a battle ensued with both sides sustaining great losses. Ho Kan-chih estimates that only one thousand of the approximately ten thousand headquarters personnel survived the battle. On January 17, the KMT's National Military Council headed by Chiang ordered the cancellation and dissolution of the New Fourth Army's designation. "Following this date," writes Johnson, "the United Front existed only as a poorly observed truce."[105]

On January 20, however, the Central Committee of the CCP ordered the regrouping of the remaining forces in central China, and in a move to underscore the importance of this army, the party dispatched its most able political commissar to oversee the army's reorganization, Liu Shao-ch'i. Table 8.3 shows that the strength of the New Fourth Army grew to over one hundred thousand men within a year from the incident.

Education Programs

In order to appreciate the task which the CCP faced in educating the masses within the three-border region, one must keep in mind that 90 percent of the people in the region were peasants and the illiteracy rate for the three provinces was close to 99 percent in the 1920s and the early 1930s (nationally the figure was about 90 percent).[106]

The CCP had had some experiences with setting up an educational system in the Kiangsi soviet in the mid–1930s, but the party found it difficult to translate its previous experience into a workable system in the border region even as late as 1942. By 1942, the educational system adopted by the CCP "had barely scratched the surface of the overwhelming illiteracy in the border region."[107] Learning to read and write must have seemed irrelevant to a people conditioned to become passive participants, listening as they did, to "village lecturers" read the emperor's decrees instead of actually studying them.[108] But, the notion and the fact of rural schools in Confucian China was one which was firmly imbedded in the countryside, and the party capitalized on this to introduce its own school system.

In finally establishing a viable educational system, the party adopted the slogan, "develop production, expand the schools," or learn to walk on "two legs." People were encouraged to make every effort to integrate education in whatever they were doing and to every sphere of life touching them. In an effort to place a school within reach of everyone, the party developed a network of schools beginning with primary, and extending to middle and secondary schools. Various twists were added to those traditional levels, including part-time schools, night schools, and winter schools.[109] Curricula were determined by a joint effort on the part of the local people and the teachers. Teachers were local leaders, sometimes almost illiterate themselves, who moved from place to place. Outstanding students were appointed as teachers in their locales.

The results of the education movement in the border region after 1943 are impressive. In one red area (Shansi-Chahar-Hopei),

twenty-three thousand three hundred primary schools were established by 1944. In these schools, the curriculum consisted of Chinese language, math, and "general knowledge." After a short trial
run in Shen-Kan-Ning, compulsory education was abandoned.[110]
According to Lindsay, "this obviously raised very fundamental
questions about the whole basis of education . . . and from this
evolved the principle of 'people manage, public help,' which became the basis for the new development in education."[111]

From 1944 on, the principle of "people manage, public help"
spread over the red bases. The basic idea was that Communist
education officials should encourage villages to set up their own
schools and curricula (people manage) with a minimum of Communist interference, except for finding teachers and meeting part
of the expenses (public help). The flexibility in this approach
proved successful in the long run with 1,404,700 children attend-
ing primary school in one red base.[112]

The success at the lower levels produced a spin-off at the
higher levels also. In time, the educational system was "lock-
stepped," from primary to elementary to middle school. Beginning
in 1941, and spurred by the development of the educational system
at the lower levels, five universities, schools, or institutes existed
as an integral part of the overall educational structure. The three
best known schools of higher education, located in Yenan, included the Anti-Japanese Military and Political University from
which the great majority of China's second-generation leaders
graduated, the Lu Hsun Academy of Literature and Arts where
the political propaganda was prepared for the traveling performing
groups (considered below), and the Marx-Lenin Institute. In
1941, the University of Yenan was founded. Its curriculum included "Economic Reconstruction," "General Theory of Border
Region Reconstruction," "The Revolutionary Spirit," and "Current Affairs." A medical school also was established which, in the
opinion of a United Nations team produced "extremely good"
results.[113]

Propaganda

Propaganda spread by the CCP's propaganda teams was a
central feature of the subject-matter content in the educational system. Propaganda teams were careful to familiarize themselves with

an area's political, economic, and social peculiarities. In addition to assuming the dress habits of the local areas, the propaganda teams also were expected to learn the language dialect of that region.[114]

By 1940, there were at least fifty-one newspapers and journals being published in the border regions.[115] The main propaganda organs of the CCP were *The New China Daily* (Yenan branch), *The Masses,* and *Liberation Daily,* which was the most important daily in the border regions.

The main themes stressed in the literature included resistance to Japan, the general mobilization of the people, the reform of the KMT government, the CCP's economic reform program and its benefits and the improvement of the people's living conditions. For example, on August 25, 1937, the propaganda department of the CCP disseminated "an outline for propaganda and agitation" prepared by Chairman Mao which included a Ten-Point National Salvation Program for defeating Japan. The outline read:

> Our task will henceforth be "to mobilize all forces for winning victory in the Armed Resistance," and the pivot here lies in a total and thorough change of the Kuomintang's policies. The progress shown by the Kuomintang on the question of resistance is commendable; to such a progress, which has been long expected by the Chinese Communist Party and the people of the whole country, we tender our welcome. But the Kuomintang has not changed its policies at all in matters like arousing the masses into action and making political reforms; basically the Kuomintang is still unwilling to unleash the people's anti-Japanese movement, is still unwilling to make fundamental changes in the government apparatus, still has no plans for improving the people's living conditions, and is still not sincere enough in its cooperation with the Communist Party. If, at this critical moment when our nation is threatened with destruction, the Kuomintang still procrastinates, sticks to these policies and refuses to change them quickly, it will cause a great disaster to the Armed Resistance.[116]

The Ten Points included:

1. Down with Japanese imperialism
2. General military mobilization throughout the country

3. General mobilization of the people
4. Reform the [KMT] government structure
5. Anti-Japanese foreign policy
6. Wartime financial and economic policy
7. Improvement of the people's living conditions
8. Anti-Japanese educational policy
9. Elimination of collaborators, traitors, and pro-Japanese elements in order to consolidate the rear
10. National solidarity for resisting Japan.

Finally, because of the extremely high illiteracy rates in the border regions, the propaganda teams relied on techniques other than reading materials to convey the party's message. For example, in 1942, the party used the most popular cultural form of propaganda, native folk dances, and songs, to get the message across to the people. The party's "native folk teams" traveled throughout the border regions, tying in the new culture with the new democratic politics. The theater became one of the most potent weapons in the party's propaganda efforts, a technique still in use today in the People's Republic of China.

Chiang Ch'ing, Madame Mao Tse-tung, arrived in Yenan in the mid–1930s, and with her acting background, assisted the party in training the traveling folk teams.

9

The Sinification of Marxism

The formative period of Mao's maturity as a Marxist-Leninist thinker coincided with his ascendancy to power within the party. We have so far examined some of his writings prior to the appearance of his two major philosophical works in 1936–37,[1] particularly those works concerned with the characteristics of the Chinese revolution and the question of the peasants' involvement in the revolution. The major concern of this chapter is with presenting the basis of Mao's epistemology, his conception of the origins of knowledge. The first part of the chapter presents Mao's theoretical writings; in the second part, we see an attempt by Mao to "test theory in light of practice" during the ambitious rectification program of 1942. The thrust of this chapter is Mao's thinking processes in the context of the formative years (1936–42).

THEORY

Life in Yenan

Mao's thirst for knowledge continued after the Long March with much the same consummate drive which characterized his period of self-education while a youth in the Ch'angsha library. In Yenan, he lived in a cave, which was "sparsely furnished with a rickety chair, a low sofa with bad springs, and a shaky miniature table, and was surrounded by an orchard of date trees."[2] It was not unusual for him to work thirteen or fourteen hours a day, beginning generally around 3 P.M. and working into the early morning hours. Once he began writing a major essay, he would work himself into fatigue, usually requiring a physician's attention. By this time he had become a chain-smoker, and his teeth were blackened because of the habit. By now Mao had met and was living with his future fourth wife, the present-day Madame Mao (Chiang Ch'ing).

Here in all likelihood Mao wrote his two major Marxist-Leninist works, "On Practice" and "On Contradictions." To understand these two works requires some knowledge, however basic, of at least four key concepts in Marxist-Leninist literature, the so-called "universal truths."

The Universal Truths of Marxism-Leninism

Class Struggle. Class struggle is the central idea of Marxism. The opening sentence of the *Communist Manifesto* reads: "The history of all hitherto existing society is the history of class struggles." Class struggles are the real secret of historical development and progress—the "stuff" which moves people and makes history.

What causes the class struggle? According to Marxist dogma, private property. The ownership of private property, goes this line of reasoning, gives power to certain individuals who use this power against the nonpropertied class. Private property is an instrument of oppression, since the propertied class controls all aspects of a society, including government, and the "state" which in turn becomes the instrument for oppressing people. Capital, in the form of property, is equated with social power. The abolition of ownership of private property, then, sums up the theory of Communism.

The major figure in the development of this theory was Karl Marx. Because Marx's analysis of society and the class struggle used economics as the base, the analysis is generally considered an economic interpretation of history. This analysis began with the premise that the production of the goods and services that support human life, and the exchange of those goods and services, are the basis of all social processes and institutions. Economics, it is held, may not be the only factor in human history, but it is the most important one.

Economics becomes the foundation upon which is erected the "superstructure" of culture, law, and government. Where one stands in relationship to his material condition of life determines how one thinks. In an agrarian society such as China's, ownership of land provided the first clue as to who controlled the political, social, legal, and cultural institutions of the society. In agrarian societies, the landowners were the real rulers of the state, and it was they who determined the predominant social standards and values. During the cultural revolution (1966–68), one of the favorite quotations from Mao was one which dated back to 1926–27:

> In China, culture has always been the exclusive possession of the landlords, and the peasants had no access to it. But the culture of the landlords is created by the peasants, for its source is nothing else than the peasants' sweat and blood. In China, 90 percent of the people have no culture or education, and of those the majority are peasants.[3]

In modern industrial societies, the owners of the means of industrial production are the real rulers of the state. Thus, a rule of thumb to follow is: whoever controls the economy controls man and man's institutions. In such an environment, *revolution is the only way out,* but one should fully expect the ruling class to mobilize all of its legal, political, and military superstructures to prevent such social revolutions. Again, the *Communist Manifesto* declares: "their [the revolutionists] ends can be attained only by the forcible overthrow of all existing social conditions."

Believing that class struggle was the primary tool of historical change, Marx and Engels then claimed to have discovered a basic "law" of historical development which spanned five stages:

> fifth stage: Communist society
> fourth stage: capitalist society
> third stage: feudal society
> second stage: slave society
> first stage: primitive communal society.

According to this basic law of historical development, history had seen the development of society beginning with the primitive communal stage, a time during which there were no ideas of private property and thus no class struggle. However, as history moved on to the second stage of development, the slave period, the notion of ownership of property evolved, and with that notion, two classes developed: the slaveholders and the slaves. In the third period, the feudal, class distinctions continued to sharpen between the feudal lords (the owners of the means of production) and the serfs. In the fourth stage, the capitalist period, the two classes which formed the class struggle were the capitalist owners and the proletariat (the working class). It was during the fourth stage that predictions were made of the proletarian revolution, which was to be the act of salvation for the liberation of mankind. The proletarian revolution was to become the impetus for pushing history into the final stage, Communism, in which all class distinctions would disappear. However, this development was to be a gradual one, necessitating a substage entitled *socialism,* a lower stage of Communism. It was during the socialist substage that the "dictatorship of the proletariat" was needed to liberate the people from ways of capitalist society. While capitalist remnants would eventually disappear, the dictatorship of the proletariat had to be on its guard to prevent the reemergence of capitalist thinking.

The final stage of historical development would be characterized by two slogans: (1) "from each according to his work; to each according to his needs" and (2) the "withering away of the state." In the first instance, the assumption was that man had adopted and inculcated an entirely new value-system devoid of the need or desire to acquire private property. Common property owned jointly by all the people would assure the equal and just distribution of the goods and services produced by the society. In the second instance, the assumption was made that while the idea of "government" would remain, the "state" as an instrument of oppression would disappear. Since the legal, political, and cultural institutions were now the product of a "new man," then these institutions would reflect new orientations. A small elite presumably would not exist.

Historical Materialism. This universal truth holds that the explanation for everything that man does, says, thinks, and feels can be found only in man's material environment and not in the productive power of the brain. According to this principle, the world exists independent of our knowing it, and it is material, not mental or spiritual in origin and nature (thus, God is dead). Matter produces the mind, thought, and consciousness. While the mind is considered to be the highest product of matter, it is matter (economics) which determines ultimately how man thinks. Man's entire existence and thinking are determined by external factors, not spiritual ones, the most important being the economic bases of society. The diagram below illustrates the effects of the economic base on such matters as superstructure number 1 (law, government, culture) and superstructure number 2 (human consciousness).

Superstructure 2:   Human Consciousness
                               ↑
Superstructure 1:   Law, Government, Culture
                               ↑
                       Economic Base

Thus, if the goal is to change man's thinking or consciousness, the means to that end is the attainment of the control of the economic base through revolution. Control the economic base and one controls man's mind, or, to change consciousness, change the economic base. If the economic base is changed, then man's knowledge will reflect that change.

Dialectical Materialism. This principle had its origins in Hegel, who adopted a procedure for explaining his view of the development of history. Hegel reasoned that history basically was a conflict of ideas and that opposing ideas eventually became locked in struggle. For Hegel, all change in history occurred because of the conflict of ideas, which always produced new ideas. He developed a three-step procedure to explain the role of conflicting ideas in the development of history.

$$\begin{aligned} \text{first idea} &= \text{thesis} \\ \text{opposing idea} &= \text{antithesis} \\ \text{out of conflict} &= \text{synthesis} \end{aligned}$$

The "dialectic," or the examination of ideas or doctrines in light of our own experiences and knowledge, became the chief method for viewing the objective world and the study of thought processes.

Marx disagreed with Hegel's conception of what causes change in history. For Marx, it was a matter of "matter over mind." Granted, Marx did not reject Hegel's three-step dialectic, but claimed that Hegel's philosophy was "upside down" and that he, Marx, would put it "rightside up" by substituting matter for mind. Marx then proceeded to combine the dialectic with his concept of historical materialism to arrive at his revolutionary theory of the historical development of society. By adopting Hegel's dialectic to his own needs, Marx could explain what the element was which made one stage of development dissolve and the next emerge. For example, in the capitalist stage, feudal lords were viewed as the "thesis" and serfs as the "antithesis." The ensuing class struggle gave rise to the revolution which dissolved the feudal stage and which saw the emergence of the next stage, capitalism. During the fourth stage, the dialectic would repeat itself until the final stage was reached. The dialectic then would no longer be needed.

Imperialism. This fourth universal truth was Lenin's contribution to Communist doctrine. By the end of the nineteenth century, it was clear that Marx's analysis and predictions of the destruction of capitalism had not come true. As conditions of the working class improved and as wages rose, the theory of class struggle and the remaining universal truths lost their appeal. To this, Lenin asked: "What is delaying the fall of capitalism?" In 1916, one year before the Russian revolution, he published his answer, *Imperialism: The Highest Stage of Capitalism.* Lenin's thesis was that capitalism had managed to survive by extending its system throughout the world through imperialism. Worse yet, Lenin believed that imperialism had particularly rooted itself in the underdeveloped areas of the world. Imperialism, he reasoned, was the force preventing the world proletarian revolution. It is Lenin who made imperialism relevant for China, as we have seen. For Lenin, the destruction of capitalism in the industrially advanced countries first required the destruction of capitalism where it was the weakest, in the economically backward areas such as Russia, Asia, and Africa. Lenin's strategy was to send professional revolutionaries into the underdeveloped areas to push for the permanent revolution. Mao accepted Lenin's thesis on imperialism.

The Philosophical Thought of Mao Tse-tung

In 1937, Mao wrote what turned out to be his most important two philosophical works, "On Practice" and "On Contradictions."

In each work, Mao's concern is with understanding the universal truths of Marxism-Leninism *in a Chinese context*. The "Sinification of Marxism," we shall see, becomes one of Mao's major contributions to Communist doctrine.

On Practice. This essay bears the subtitle, "On the Relation between Knowledge and Practice—Between Knowing and Doing." Here Mao concerns himself with the epistemology (the branch of philosophy which investigates the origins, nature, methods, and limits of human knowing—of knowledge) of *dialectical materialism,* written, according to Chinese sources, "to expose from the viewpoint of Marxist theory of knowledge such subjectivist mistakes in the Party as doctrinairism and empiricism."[4] The essay rests on three major premises: (1) dialectical materialism, (2) the role of practical experience in knowledge, and (3) practice underlies thought.

In the first major premise—the affirmation of dialectical materialism as a universal truth—Mao establishes his orthodoxy as a Marxist thinker. "To begin with," he writes, "the Marxist regards man's productive activity as the most fundamental practical activity, as the determinant of all other activities." Just as man's social behavior develops step by step from a lower to a higher level given man's material surrounding, so man's knowledge also develops from a lower to higher level. In this conception of the stages of human knowing, Mao is affirming the Marxist-Leninist process of knowledge, a process conceived to be totally dependent on "objective reality," which at base is material. Knowledge is, therefore, a reflection of the material base.

From this initial affirmation of dialectical materialism, Mao develops his second major premise: knowledge starts from experience. If one wants to know something, one must come into contact with that something in practice. All knowledge originates in man's perceptions of the external and material world through man's sensory organs. To deny perception is to deny materialism.

> The theory of knowledge of dialectical materialism raises practice to the first place, holds that human knowledge cannot be separated from the least bit from practice, and repudiates all incorrect theories which deny the importance of practice or separate knowledge from practice.[5]

Using this reasoning process, Mao explains why Marx himself "could not have known specifically beforehand some of the special laws pertaining to . . . imperialism, because imperialism—the last stage of capitalism—had not yet emerged and the corresponding practice did not exist."[6] Imperialism was a phenomenon which only Lenin and Stalin could have known and experienced and thus built their practice on it. Indeed, even the Chinese themselves did not acquire the knowledge of the special laws of imperialism until the 1920s. The reason for this late understanding of imperialism lies in the step-by-step development of man's knowledge.

Man's knowledge generally proceeds through two steps of development, the perceptual and the rational. Perceptual knowledge is characterized by the first understanding of a given phenomenon. For example, the first stage in China's awareness of imperialism came in the 1850s during the foreign encroachments into China. This was the perceptual stage in the knowledge of imperialism. However, during the next fifty years, as China experienced firsthand the special laws of imperialism, knowledge of imperialism became more sophisticated; it had become rational. "Such knowledge," writes Mao, "began only about the time of the May Fourth movement of 1919."[7]

> The dialectical-materialistic theory of knowledge is that rational knowledge depends upon perceptual knowledge and perceptual knowledge has yet to be developed into rational knowledge.[8]

The third major premise—practice underlies thought—establishes Mao's Marxism. Reaching theoretical conclusions is not enough; theories must be checked and modified in the light of practice. "Social practice alone is the criterion of truth." If a person wants to know something firsthand, it can be accomplished only through taking part personally in the practical struggle to change reality. "If you want to know the theory and methods of revolution, you must join the revolution."[9] (During the recent cultural revolution, Mao conceived of the upheaval as a "laboratory" in which those who had never experienced revolution could come into firsthand contact with the continuing Chinese revolution). Mao concludes:

> To discover truth through practice, and through practice to verify and develop truth. To start from perceptual knowledge and actively develop it into rational knowledge, and then, starting from rational knowledge, actively direct revolutionary practice so as to remould the subjective and the objective world. . . . Such is the whole of the dialectical materialist theory of knowledge, and such is the dialectical materialist theory of the unity of knowing and doing.[10]

On Contradictions. One of the major ideas in the thought of Mao Tse-tung is his conception of the theory of contradictions. This concept is formally called "the law of the unity of opposites (thesis-antithesis, life-death, plus-minus, positive-negative, class struggle, war-peace, defense-offense). According to Lenin, "In its proper meaning, dialectics is the study of the contradiction within the very essence of things."[11] The law of the unity of opposites (contradictions) is the most basic law in materialist dialectics. In this essay, Mao identified several problem areas in which one finds the law of contradictions operating: (1) two kinds of world outlooks, (2) the universality of contradictions, (3) the particularity of contradictions, (4) the principal contradiction and the principal aspect of a contradiction, and (5) the role of antagonisms in contradictions.

In discussing the two contradictory world views, the metaphysical versus the dialectical, Mao of course rejects the metaphysical (or idealist) world view in favor of the dialectical materialist world view. Here Mao simply reaffirms Marx's repudiation of the "upside down view" which held that the stuff which moved history was ideas, not matter.

> Changes in society are chiefly due to the development of the internal contradictions in society, namely, the contradiction between the productive forces and the relations of production, the contradiction between the classes, and the contradiction between the old and the new; it is the development of these contradictions that impels society forward and starts the process of the supersession of the old society by a new one.[12]

In conceptualizing the "universality" or absoluteness of contradictions, Mao posits that contradictions exist in the process of the development of all things. "The interdependence of the contradictory aspects of a thing and the struggle between them determine the life and impel the development of that thing. . . . There is nothing that does not contain contradiction; without contradiction there would be no world."[13] According to Mao, Lenin explained the universality of contradiction through the following formula:

> In mathematics: + and −; differential and integral
> In mechanics: action and reaction
> In physics: positive and negative electricity
> In chemistry: the combination and dissociation of atoms
> In social science: the class struggle.[14]

Universal contradictions, however, all have their own particular contradictions, for it is the particular contradiction which distinguishes one thing from another. For example, the class struggle is a universal and absolute contradiction, but the particular contradiction of the class struggle depends on time, place, and the concrete problems of world history. Thus, during the feudal period, the particular contradiction in the class struggle was between the serfs and the landlords; in the capitalist period, the particular contradiction of the class struggle was between the proletariat and the capitalists. If imperialism is the universal contradiction, then one particular contradiction within the universal one might be: China versus the foreign nations.

The universality and particularity of contradictions supports the view, says Mao, that everything must be analyzed from two angles: the whole and the part; the general and the particular.

> These are the two processes of knowing: one is from the particular to the general, and the other is from the general to the particular. Man's knowledge always proceeds in this cyclical, recurrent manner.[15]

Each different contradiction must be solved by different methods. If the nature of the universal and particular contradictions is understood qualitatively, then the solution will also be qualitatively different. Thus, the contradiction between the proletariat and the bourgeoisie is solved by the method of socialist revolution; the contradictions of the feudal period by democratic revolution and the working class and the peasantry in socialist society is solved by the method of collectivization and mechanization of agriculture. Contradictions which arise within the party are solved by the method of criticism and self-criticism.

Analyzing the particularity of contradictions further requires taking into consideration the principal contradiction and the principal aspect of a contradiction. These two considerations will differentiate between primary and secondary contradictions, since one cannot treat all contradictions in a process as being equal. For example, in a capitalist society, the principal contradiction is the proletariat and the bourgeoisie, but the appearance of this contradiction does not prevent others from also arising. The problem then is to consider all possible contradictions and then rank them in order of importance. In the war of resistance to Japanese aggression, the various contradictions apparently included the CCP v. KMT, Japan v. China, China v. all foreign nations, proletariat v. bourgeoisie and the remnant feudal classes and the bourgeoisie. Obviously, not all of the contradictions were of equal importance given the time, place, and concrete problems of world history. China's survival at this point was of paramount importance, thus the principal contradiction at this time was Japan and China. Lesser or secondary contradictions, such as the CCP v. KMT, had to be put aside for the time being. Under such circumstances, an alliance with an enemy was permissible.

> When imperialism wages a war of aggression on such a country, the various classes in that country, apart from a small bunch of traitors, can temporarily unite to wage a national war against imperialism.[16]

Finally, the one important component of understanding the development of contradictions is their "antagonistic" or "non-antagonistic" nature. Contradictions contain this dual nature and thus antagonistic or non-antagnostic is to contradictions what the atom is to the atom bomb, an important and essential component of the thing itself. In this essay, Mao attempts to differentiate between antagonistic contradictions and non-antagonistic ones. Obviously, Mao felt that not all contradictions were necessarily bad, since the effect of a contradiction was the result of its manifestation in time and place. Within Chinese society, some contradictions, such as the one between the working class and the peasantry, could be nonantagonistic and so the method of solving it did not involve conflict (solved by the method of collectivization and mechanization of agriculture). Other contradictions, such as that between China and Japan, were considered to be antagonistic, and the only method for solving them was through struggle. While this concept is the least developed one, it is nonetheless important, for it allowed for some struggle which was constructive in the long run.

PRACTICE

In the absence of its own central government, the Central Committee of the CCP located in Yenan was faced with two particular problems brought about by the increasing growth of both the party and the army. On the one hand, a need arose for an administrative structure to coordinate the activities of the party at the border region level with the various party, army, and mass organizations. In 1943, the party created the Unified Leadership Committees to communicate effectively to the lower-level branches of the party organization.

The second problem, however, required a massive educational program in the border region among the party and nonparty cadres since the peasantry formed the greater part of the numerical strength of both the party and the army. In the spring of 1942, Mao inaugurated a major educational campaign with the goal of fixing the party line according to the thought of Mao Tse-tung.

Cheng Feng

On February 1, 1942, over one thousand party members jammed a Yenan lecture hall to hear Mao inaugurate a rectification (*cheng feng*) campaign against subjectivism (emphasis on theoretical Marxism-Leninism without practical application), sectarianism (remaining aloof from the masses), and formalism (art and literature for an elite audience only).

Subjectivism. In Mao's essay "On Practice," we have noted Mao's emphasis on the relationship between theory and practice. In his inaugural speech, Mao made it clear what the relationship of Marxism-Leninism was to the actual Chinese situation. He said:

What type of theoretician do we need? We need theoreticians who base their thinking on the standpoints, concepts and methods of Marx, Engels, Lenin and Stalin, who are able to explain correctly the actual problems issuing from history and revolution, who are able to give a scientific interpretation and theoretical explanation of the various problems of Chinese economics, politics, military affairs, and culture. . . . Our Party School should not be content merely to read the doctrines of Marxism-Leninism but should be able first to master, and then to apply them. Application is the sole object of this mastery.[17]

Writing four years earlier, Mao had already begun advancing the notion of the "Sinification of Marxism." In his report to the Sixth Plenum of the Central Committee of the CCP in 1938, he said:

There is no such thing as abstract Marxism, but only concrete Marxism. . . . Consequently, the Sinification of Marxism—that is to say, making certain that in all of its manifestations it is imbued with Chinese peculiarities, using it according to the peculiarities—becomes a problem that must be understood and solved by the whole party without delay. . . .[18]

According to Schram, while Mao's own conception of the "Sinification of Marxism" was complex and even ambiguous, still Mao's intent was clear: each nation had to solve its own problems in its own way.[19] "The arrow of Marxism-Leninism," Mao told the cadres in his inaugural address, "must be used to hit the target of the Chinese Revolution."[20]

Beginning with Mao's formal speech, the party went to school to study the methods by which to avoid subjectivism. In the first part of the rectification campaign, party cadres were expected to read twenty-two documents, seven of which were the "thoughts" of Mao. The remaining documents were the works of Stalin, Lenin, Dimitrov, the then ideologically correct Liu Shao-ch'i, and Ch'en Yun. A general examination was conducted on the twenty-two documents to determine how well the cadres understood their theoretical content. Thereafter, the cadres were expected to conduct a period of actual investigation, applying theory to some concrete problem of the Chinese situation.

Sectarianism. According to Mao, by 1942, there were some remnants within the CCP who continued to work against the interests
of the party. Uppermost in Mao's thinking were those individuals
who "clamored for independence" and who did not accept the
party's organizational principle, democratic centralism. Evidence
that such "individual-firstism" existed in intraparty matters included wrong relations "between parts and the whole, individuals
and the party, outside and local cadres, army and local cadres,
army unit and army unit, locality and locality."[21]

In the party's external relations, Mao noted that "many comrades delight in speaking to non-party men with an exaggerated
air of self-importance, look down on others, belittle them, and are
unwilling to respect others or understand their merits."[22] There
was, Mao reminded the party cadres, "no basis whatsoever for any
action leading to separation from the masses."[23] To insure that
the party rectified its tendency toward subjectivism and sectarianism, the party introduced two solutions: criticism campaigns and
the mass line.

The method by which the party resolved its internal disputes,
and by which the cadres could assess correctly any given situation,
is summed up in the phrase "unity-criticism-unity." In one of the
required reading documents of the rectification campaign, entitled
"On the Intra-Party Struggle," the then ideologically correct Liu
Shao-ch'i suggested that "the purpose of our self-criticism and the
intra-party struggle is not the weakening of party discipline and authority . . . on the contrary, the purpose is the strengthening of
party organization and solidarity, an increase in party discipline
and authority. . . ."[24] Reflecting on the method fifteen years later
(1957), Mao wrote:

> In 1942 we worked out the formula "unity-criticism-unity"
> to describe this democratic method of resolving contradic-
> tions among the people. To elaborate, this means to start off
> with a desire so as to achieve a new unity on a new basis. . . .
> In 1942 we used this method to resolve contradictions in-
> side the Communist party, namely contradictions between
> the doctrinairism and Marxism.[25]

Because of this feature, the rectification campaign has at
times been characterized as a purge, but as Compton tells us,

"it was not called a purge" and no one was specifically mentioned as negative examples in the *Reform Documents*.[26] While the CCP's leading comintern-appointed representative, Wang Ming, was a target, he was not named. Further, no CCP leaders were directly criticized, although some, such as Chou En-lai, criticized themselves. Indeed, during the campaign, the party's overall membership *increased* significantly.

The second effective method by which the party fought against the tendency toward sectarianism was through the concept of the "mass line." One could go a step further and suggest that all of the reforms associated with the rectification program culminated in the concept of the mass line. For Mao, the concept of the mass line was a methodology by which to elevate Marxist theory to the practical problem of linking the party to the masses. How was this to be accomplished?

In a directive of the Central Committee published in June 1943, the party set the guidelines for implementing the mass-line policy. The following excerpt represents the classic statement of Mao's conception of the methodology by which to link the Marxist theory of knowledge to the party's political, economic, educational, and military self-sufficiency movements in the troubled countryside:

> In all practical work of our Party, correct leadership can only be developed on the principle of "from the masses, to the masses." This means summing up (i.e., coordinating and systematizing after careful study) the views of the masses (i.e., views scattered and unsystematic), then taking the resulting ideas back to the masses, explaining and popularizing them until the masses embrace the ideas as their own, stand up for them and translate them into action by way of testing their correctness. Then it is necessary once more to sum up the views of the masses, and once again take the resulting ideas back to the masses so that the masses give them their wholehearted support.... And so on, over and over again, so that each time these ideas emerge with greater correctness and become more vital and meaningful. This is what the Marxist theory of knowledge teaches us.[27]

John Wilson Lewis has summed up Mao's conception of the mass line by noting that the concept is made up of four progressive stages: perception, summarization, authorization, and imple-

mentation.[28] The progressive stages correspond to Mao's understanding of how knowledge develops from the perceptual to the
rational and the assumption that practice underlies thought. The
mass line is a continuous methodology, with party cadres diligently
analyzing their contacts with the masses, writing their experiences
in light of Marxist theory, attempting to solve problems, and doing
it all over again as necessary until the best possible (although not
the final) solution is found. In a sense, under the mass-line concept, everyone in China is a leader, a development hitherto not experienced by the everyday citizen. However, the continuous inter-
action encouraged by the mass line did require defining certain
relationships, such as that which theoretically posited all power in
the people, and the redelegation of that power to the vanguard, the
CCP. That the CCP succeeded in forging a new and effective
relationship with the workers-peasants as a result of the mass line
is what the Yenan period is all about. For above all, the mass line
concept was a methodology intended to provide both the party's
cadres and the masses with a new vision of man in the future. For
both the cadres and the masses, the rectification program meant
the creation of a new vision of life by a new kind of person based
on a working consensus and a shared value system in which everyone played a key role.

Formalism. Because the third corrupting influence within the party
was considered by Mao to be important, he addressed himself to
the problem of party formalism in a speech dedicated solely to this
topic. In doing so, however, he made it clear that the three wrong
tendencies (subjectivism, sectarianism, and formalism) were all
related and that indeed "subjectivism and sectarianism [were us-
ing] party formalism as their propaganda tool and form of expression."[29]

Party formalism was the term given to a method of writing
or speaking which could not be understood by the masses. In his
speech, "In Opposition to Party Formalism," Mao outlined the
eight components of party formalism:

1. writing long essays or reports which say nothing,
2. hiding behind authority to make a point rather than
   allowing the free play of facts,
3. not considering one's audience,

4. not learning the language of the masses,
5. improper and confusing classification schemes,
6. irresponsible writing or speaking,
7. "Polluting the Party, Harming the Revolution,"
8. spreading propaganda harmful to the Party and country.[30]

Mao then cautioned the cadres to consider his speech "carefully" and adopt the proper method of relating to one another within the party and to the masses in general.

The attack against party formalism also had a profound spin-off in the party's attempt to fix the party line among the intellectuals. In the environment created by the second united front and Japan's aggression in China, a great many intellectuals followed the Communists to Yenan. The intellectuals, referred to as "revolutionary writers" when the party line was followed, were drawn to Yenan by the CCP's vision of a new China. They had been disillusioned with the KMT's performance during the so-called Nanking Decade, and were attracted by the party's supposed commitment to free speech and the free expression of ideas.

During the initial stages of the rectification program, and in keeping with the "unity-criticism-unity" method of resolving problems, the revolutionary writers wrote essays critical not only of Chiang K'ai-shek's government but also of the CCP's leadership style. As Merle Goldman so aptly puts it:

> [The revolutionary writers] etched the apathy, hypocrisy, and bureaucratism of the cadres with the same sharp pen they had used against KMT officials earlier.[31]

Underlying the revolutionary writers' bitter criticisms of the CCP was the realization that the party's vision of a new China was not a practicing reality in Yenan. Yenan did not concretely reflect the new China heralded by party ideals. Further, once in Yenan, it became apparent that the free expression and exchange of ideas was determined by party line and not by a commitment to individual freedoms and creative energies. The most prominent critics of the party's lack of adherence to theory and practice included Ting Ling, a woman novelist and editor of the party's official organ, *Liberation Daily*. Most of the prominent writers in China present in Yenan followed Ting Ling's bitter criticisms.[32] One poet wrote:

> How many times I have left my everyday life. . . . And have
> gone to a place where there are no human faces.[33]

On May 2, 1942, the rectification program was expanded to include nonparty people. On this date, Chairman Mao invited the cadres to the Yenan Forum on Literature and Arts "to exchange ideas and examine the relationship between work in the literary and artistic fields and revolutionary work in general."[34] This lecture at Yenan was to become the guiding principle for the rectification of the revolutionary writers' style and content. The revolutionary writers, Mao pointed out, suffered from the same shortcomings as the party cadres who had recently joined the party or the army. Said Mao:

> It is very good that since the outbreak of the War of Resistance Against Japan, more and more revolutionary writers and artists have been coming to Yenan and our other anti-Japanese base areas. But it does not necessarily follow that, having come to the base areas, they have already integrated themselves completely with the masses of the people here. The two must be completely integrated if we are to push ahead with our revolutionary work.[35]

The revolutionary writers needed, Mao cautioned, a better understanding of the party's class stand (that of the proletariat and the masses), a better attitude toward the revolution and the War of Resistance, an awareness of the audience they were writing for (workers, peasants, soldiers), a proper understanding of the mass line, and a better knowledge of Marxism-Leninism.

In his concluding remarks delivered on May 23, Mao focused on specifics, and here he made it clear that:

> There is in fact no such thing as art for art's sake, art that stands above classes or art that is detached from or independent of politics.[36]

Not only did Mao "demand" the unity of politics and arts,

but he made it clear that just as some party members had joined the party organizationally but not ideologically, so it was with the revolutionary writers also. Mao also made it clear that "opposition to this arrangement" was tantamount to the politics of Trotsky. The message could not have been clearer: art and literature was political and the party determined what was politically correct. Using Marxist philosophical argumentation, he reminded the writers that the criterion for judging the "subjective" worth of a piece was its value in social practice and effect. If there were any doubts about the value of a piece of art and literature, then the revolutionary writers were to adopt literary and art criticism as the principal method of struggle. Mao was aware that the process of becoming integrated with the masses would "involve much pain and friction," but he was likewise confident that during the rectification movement the intellectuals would bring about the desired "transformation" in themselves and in their work.

Mao's "Talks at the Yenan Forum on Literature and Art" went a long way toward fixing the purpose of art and literature in Chinese politics, but as Merle Goldman tells us, "The underlying conflicts between the Party and its intellectuals remained."[37] Nonetheless, in the critical years of Mao's attempt to fix his system of thinking, the CCP was successful in implementing its policy on the politicization of art and literature.

The *cheng feng* campaign played an important role in the consolidation of Mao's power over the Chinese Communist Party. First, the movement led to the increasing independence of the Chinese Communists from Stalin's control. As Compton tells us: "Wartime Moscow was too far away"[38]; thus, the party was forced to look to its own resources to survive. The most valuable resource at this time was Mao.

Second, the rectification movement allowed the party to translate its wartime guerrilla policies into concrete policies culminating in the mass line. Third, because of mass-line politics, the party was able to construct a new conception of the ideal Communist man, one who worked unselfishly for the good of all people without regard for ego. Fourth, the rectification movement decisively made Mao's conception of the relationship between Marxism-Leninism and the Chinese situation the basis on which to develop the revolution Chinese style. While Mao's power over the party was to be challenged sporadically after the rectification program, he had by now consolidated his position to the extent that by 1945 the *Reform Documents* had "become Party dogma and the reform process had become a continuing organizational mechanism."[39]

Epilogue:
China After Mao:
The First Thirty Days

An Extraordinary Year

"Comrades," announced the new chairman of the Chinese Communist Party at the Second National Learn-from-Tachai in Agriculture Conference, "nineteen seventy-six has been a most extraordinary year in the history of our Party. . . ."[1] In what may rank as one of history's great understatements, he proceeded to list several "rigorous tests" met in 1976. The arrest of the "gang of four" headed the list, followed by the deaths of Chairman Mao Tse-tung, Premier Chou En-lai, Chu Teh (the People's Liberation Army's Commander-in-Chief), K'ang Sheng (fifty year veteran in intelligence matters) and Tung Pi-wu (one of the twelve original founders of the Chinese Communist Party along with Mao), and such natural disasters as droughts, waterlogging, low temperatures, early frost and the violent earthquake which destroyed the city of T'angshan, Hopei province. The gang of four, however, dominated the agenda at the Second Tachai Conference so it was not surprising that the criticism of the four headed the "central tasks" for 1977.

Never have so many criticized so few for so much. There is simply no other way to characterize the torrential outpour of criticism directed against the four by China's leaders and its 800 million people. Even if one allows for exaggeration, one still cannot help but be bewildered at the thought that four people could have instilled such fear in 800 million people, cowed 30 million party members, nearly destroyed an economy, threatened civil war, committed national betrayal, hampered foreign trade, ruined the educational system, and prevented a single poem or play from being printed, much less published without their approval.[2]

223

They must have done something wrong, however, be it the alleged coup d'etat they are charged with, or something less dramatic, such as seeking votes in the Politburo. There is no denying their *motives* (succeed to Mao's position); it is the *method* (coup or votes) which has confused the issue of their arrest. Whatever the truth is there are still some interesting questions which cannot be ignored. What caused their arrest? How could four prominent party leaders be arrested without so much as a clue until four days later? What was Hua Kuo-feng's role in the arrest? If Shanghai was their stronghold, how can one explain the frenzy and the festive mood there once the news of the arrest became known? How does one explain the release of the pent-up feelings, emotions and frustrations of 800 million people which suddenly erupted in a volcanic fury?

Kuo Mo-jo, the venerable President of the Chinese Academy of Sciences and one intellectual with whom Mao enjoyed exchanging poems, let out his joyful burst in a poem entitled, "Smashing the Gang of Four":

> An event most gratifying to the people,
> Is the pulling out of the 'gang of four.'
> The political rogue, the literary rascal,
> The damned tactician Chang,
> And the white-boned demon
> Who compared herself to the Empress Wu,
> Have all been wiped out by the iron broom....
> Their ambition was big,
> Their plots vicious,
> And their intrigues wild.
> They are guilty of a crime deserving ten
>   thousand deaths,
> For persecuting the Red Sun (Mao).[3]

This was the same Kuo Mo-jo who at the heighth of the cultural revolution dedicated another poem to Chiang Ch'ing:

> Dear Comrade Chiang Ch'ing, you are the fine
>   example for us to follow,
> You are good at creatively studying and applying
>   the invincible thought of Mao Tse-tung,

Fearlessly, you charge forward on the literary
  and art front.
Thus, the heroic images of the workers, peasants,
  and soldiers now dominate the Chinese stage;
And we must do the same for the stage the world over.[4]

Nineteen seventy-six was, to be sure, an extraordinary year, but one could not fault Hua if for a moment his thoughts went back to 1975. In particular, he must have reviewed in his mind the events beginning with the second plenum of the Tenth Party Congress (January 8–10) and the first session of the Fourth National People's Congress (January 13–17). These two congresses had much to do with making him what he became—acting premier (February 7, 1976), premier (April 7) and party chairman (October 7)—and the four what they became, inmates (October 6).

One of the most significant events that occurred at both congresses was the appointment of Teng Hsiao-p'ing to two key party and government positions. At the party congress he was elected vice-chairman of the Standing Committee of the Politburo, replacing Li Teh-sheng (for reasons unknown).[5] The NPC elected him first vice-premier, placing him second only to Chou En-lai on the State Council. He also headed the list of twelve vice-premiers of the State Council, followed by Chang Ch'un-ch'iao, Li Hsien-nien and Hua Kuo-feng, among others. On January 29, he was named chief-of-staff of the PLA while Chang was named chairman of the PLA's General Political Department. By the end of 1975 he was, perhaps, the most powerful man in China with the exception of Mao, who sacked him.

Teng was the most prominent name among those purged during the cultural revolution who slowly were filtering back into both the party and the government between 1972 and 1973, but he was not the only one rehabilitated and appointed to key positions by the NPC. At least thirty-one members of the congress, including Teng, had been purged, accused, or had dropped out-of-sight during the cultural revolution and were now assigned key positions in the government. The most notable among them were Ku Mu (chairman of the State Capital Construction Commission), Su

Chen-hua (who figures prominently in the arrest of the four, and is now Mayor of Shanghai), T'an Chen-lin (vice-chairman of the Standing Committee of the NPC), Ulanfu (long-time power in Inner Mongolia), Wan Li (Minister of Railways), Chou Jung-hsin (Minister of Education), Yeh Fei (Minister of Communications), Yu Ch'iu-li (chairman of the State Planning Commission) and Wang Chen (vice-premier of the State Council). Chou En-lai has generally been credited with paving the way for the rehabilitation of Teng. Teng, thereafter, also played a key role, and he paid the price for it.

One of the outstanding characteristics of the twelve vice-premiers selected to assist Chou in the State Council is the predominance of men with an economic background. Five of the twelve members, Yu Ch'iu-li, Ku Mu, Ch'en Yung-kuei, Wang Chen and Li Hsien-nien, all had previous backgrounds in economic work. This coupled with Chou En-lai's "Report on the Work of the Government," which he delivered to the Fourth People's Congress, set a target-date for building "an independent and relatively comprehensive industrial and economic system in fifteen years," or, by 1980.[6] In this report, Chou served notice that the economy would receive top priority in the coming years and not, if one reads between the lines, revolution (which is what the four and Mao, a "gang of five," considered to be top priority). Chou credited Mao with the economic plan.

The Fourth National People's Congress was also Hua Kuo-feng's congress. He was appointed a vice-premier of the State Council and concurrently Minister of Public Security, China's top police job. In 1975, after his appointments, he made at least fifty-seven public appearances in Peking in everything ranging from greeting ping-pong teams to heads-of-state.

Teng Hsiao-p'ing's presence at the NPC was as conspicuous as was Mao's absence. Why Mao did not attend either the Party or People's congresses is open to conjecture, but his absence may have been more political than medical. We do know that while the two congresses were in session he met with at least two foreign officials at an undisclosed location outside of Peking. So why did he stay away? Was it Teng's re-emergence or perhaps Chou En-lai's emphasis on the economy at the expense of the revolution? Or was it a little of both?

"Without struggle," Mao has said, "there can be no progress." Less than a month after the Fourth Congress adjourned, the first clue to Mao's state-of-mind appeared in the press. On February 9, the *People's Daily* published an editorial announcing his latest "important instruction on the question of theory: 'Why did Lenin speak of exercising dictatorship over the bourgeoisie.' "[7] This, to be sure, signalled the start of a new campaign, and the phrase, "people like Lin Piao," which appeared for the first time, was an indication that someone other than Lin Piao was the target. To make Mao's case even clearer (or confusing), the party unleashed the vitrolic pens of Yao Wen-yuan and Chang Ch'un-ch'iao. Yao's article was his first since 1968, and must have caused some uneasy moments among those who remembered vividly that it was his article in 1965 which signalled the start of the cultural revolution. Chang's article was just as significant, for it was the first such article written by a high-ranking Party official since Lin Piao's "People's War" article appeared in 1965. Both articles, therefore, merit a close look.

"It would be easy," Yao began his article, "for people like Lin Piao to push the capitalist system if they come to power."[8] As if to dispel doubt about whom he was referring to he continued, "as long as the overthrown reactionary classes still exist, the possibility remains for the emergence within the Party (and society as well) of representatives of the bourgeoisie who will try to turn their hope for restoration into attempt at restoration."[9]

Invoking still another Mao quotation, he criticized China's eight-grade wage system which be believed "consolidated, extended, and strengthened bourgeois rights and that part of inequality which it entailed."[10] Yao feared that if such rights were allowed to continue they could only lead to "polarization," whereby some people would use any and all legal or illegal means to get ahead of others. Material incentives, he also feared, would follow thus turning "public property into private property."[11]

It is possible that Yao had at least one target in mind—Chou En-lai. In the article there is one oblique reference which could be

construed as an attack on Chou, whom it is believed was responsible for the "restoration" of the cadres purged during the cultural
revolution. "Chiang K'ai-shek," wrote Yao, "took advantage of
Sun Yat-sen's trust, and in running the Whampoa Academy, he
gathered a bunch of reactionaries around him."[12] Chou En-lai,
we know, was Chiang K'ai-shek's political commissar at Whampoa
during the period of the first united front (1923–1927). Was Yao
comparing Chiang to Chou and Sun to Mao? Did Chou violate
Mao's "trust" at the Fourth National Congress? Did Mao now
have second thoughts about the massive "restoration" of the cadres
purged during the cultural revolution?

Chang's article took off where Yao's left off, but there is a
fundamental difference between the two. While both address themselves to the theme, "restricting bourgeois rights," Chang's is certainly better organized and more authorative than Yao's.[13] For
Chang, the subject of "bourgeois rights" was like a homecoming,
having written an article on the same subject in 1958, when Mao
first introduced the theme. In 1958, Mao was sufficiently impressed with Chang's article to have written, anonymously, a letter
to the *People's Daily* urging that it be published and that party
cadres read it.[14]

"We must," Chang wrote, "be soberly aware that there is still
the danger for China to turn revisionist."[15] The "new" bourgeoisie is, as Lenin once said, "being engendered daily and
hourly."[16] Chang's main emphasis, however, was on Mao's analysis that the system of ownership in China had changed.

Chang offers a wide-range of statistics to support Mao's view.
In industry, the state owns 97 percent of all fixed assets, 63 percent of the employees and 86 percent of the total output. The collective owns 3 percent of all fixed assets, 36 percent of all employees and 14 percent of the total output. Individuals make up
only 0.8 percent of the employees in industry. In agriculture, the
collective owns 90 percent of workable land and irrigation-
drainage machinery, 80 percent of the tractors and draught animals. The state, on the other hand, owns a negligible amount of
land and machinery. Individuals also account for "small plots" and
limited sideline production, an apparent slap at the constitutional

provision (Chapter One, Section 7) which allows the people to engage in limited sideline production.

In commerce, the state owns 92 percent of the total volume of retail sales, the collective 7 percent and individuals only 0.2 percent.[17]

Industry and commerce, then, are primarily stateowned while agriculture is collectively owned. This situation is both good and bad. It is good in that the state, or "socialist ownership by the whole people," owns industry and commerce, but the situation in agriculture must change. In agriculture there is a system of dual ownership (the state and the collective), but the state is "rather weak in agriculture, the foundation of the national economy."[18] If bourgeois rights are to be eliminated, then it is imperative that the state own all three sectors. This, Chang admits, will take some time. It is equally imperative to eliminate the private ownership in each of the three sectors, for it is this capitalist remnant (including material incentives, bonuses, profits and money) which serves to engender the bourgeoisie. Apparently the cultural revolution, Chang quotes Mao, "remained unfinished."[19] He makes it clear that the existence of bourgeois rights will not be tolerated either within the party or within the masses, and that includes China's eight-grade wage system.

All we know for certain about China's wage system is that workers, officials, and technicians are paid according to very complicated grade scales. The worker's are paid according to an eight-grade system, officials by a twenty-four grade system and technicians by an eighteen-grade system. Cost of living adjustments are also made depending on where one lives. What this essentially means is that the PRC is far from realizing the ultimate goal of Communism, a classless society. As in capitalist countries, some are more equal than others. Thus, Party and government officials not only make more money than the common worker, peasant, and soldier, but in China rank also has its privileges. High-ranking cadres and their spouses are known to have limousines at their disposal, entertainment expense accounts, State-paid medical expenses, privileges on trains and airplanes (usually first-class travel), comfortable homes with servants and other help, and are entitled to use the State-owned retreats.[20] The privileges enjoyed by the adults are also enjoyed by their children, who in turn rank themselves according to their parents' position in the hierarchy.[21]

The campaign to restrict bourgeois rights continued throughout 1975 and in September, ran headlong into the first national conference on learning from Tachai in agriculture. On September 15, the First Tachai Conference convened at the Tachai brigade in Hsiyang county, Shansi province. That this conference was held to promote more than agriculture was evident by the thirteen Politburo members, twenty-five high-ranking government officials, sixteen provincial first Party secretarys, and numerous county officials in attendance. Overall, the participants numbered 3,700, making this conference the largest of its kind since the cultural revolution.

Undoubtedly, all eyes were on Teng Hsiao-p'ing and Chiang Ch'ing, both of whom delivered speeches which, for some reason were not published. Ch'en Yung-kuei, Tachai's model peasant who rose to positions in the Central Committee and the State Council, also attracted considerable attention, appearing in five of the six photographs published in the *People's Daily* on September 16 and 17. By contrast, Teng, Chiang Ch'ing, and Hua Kuo-feng appeared in only one photograph each.

Hua, however, delivered the summing-up report.[22] Following Chou En-lai's speech at the Fourth Congress, Hua reiterated China's determination to push its economy to the front ranks of the world before the end of the century. This could only be accomplished, he said, on the basis of stability and unity (not class struggle). Learning from Tachai would further help the country realize the goal to achieve the four modernizations in agriculture, industry, national defense, science and technology. The key to modernization lay with the county Party committees. In those county committees where cadres were "soft, lax and lazy," a general rectification program would be instituted, "to insure success in the county Party's committee's rectification, the stress should be on ideological rectification, with organizational adjustment where really necessary."[23]

"Organizational adjustment" was a euphemism for "purge," for those unwilling to correct their mistakes despite repeated edu-

cation should be resolutely cleared out of the party. For someone
who had just recently been thrust into the national limelight, these
were rather harsh and threatening words. The significance of the
speech, however, was as much in its harsh tone as in the substance
of his speech—economic modernization. This speech clearly identified him with the Chou-Teng policy of economic development.

Nineteen seventy-five still had one more campaign to see
through, the criticism of *Water Margin,* once one of Mao's favorite
novels of Chinese literature. This was the same novel from which
he had quoted so often in building up the case against P'eng Teh-
huai, who was purged in 1958. But now he had changed his mind,
and more than one repentant literatist quickly joined the chorus
of those who saw the genius of Mao's new interpretation.

Briefly, *Water Margin* is a story of bandits who eventually
join the emperor's service. Sung Chiang, one of the bandit heroes
of the novel, is singled out for his role in first accepting the emperor's amnesty and then for offering his services to the imperial
forces. On August 14, Mao issued his reassessment of the novel:
"The merit of the book *Water Margin* lies precisely in the por-
trayal of capitulationism."[24] Who was the 1975-version of Sung
Chiang? In looking back at this period it is not hard to conclude
that Sung Chiang was none other than Teng Hsiao-p'ing.

Nineteen seventy-six, the extraordinary year, began on a
revolutionary note. The 1976 joint editorial, China's state-of-the
union message, declared first that "class struggle was the key link"
and second drew attention to the "right deviationist wind to re-
verse previous verdicts" (mostly of the cultural revolution). On
January 8, Chou En-lai died. His death, among other things,
brought China a much needed respite to the revolutionary tone of
the January 1 editorial. The respite was shortlived.

On February 24, the *People's Daily* quoted Mao once more:

What 'taking the three directives as the key link.' Stability
and unity do not mean writing off the class struggle. Class
struggle is the key link and everything else depends on it.[25]

Who had advocated taking the three directives as the key
link? As was noted before, at the First Tachai Conference Teng
Hsiao-p'ing's and Chiang Ch'ing's speeches were not published.

Shortly after the conference, however, a provincial secretary quoted a part of Teng's speech, including three directives linked with him:

1. study theory and combat and prevent revisionism.
2. promote stability and unity.
3. boost the national economy.[26]

On February 25, Hua delivered a speech (not published to my knowledge) which apparently outlined the campaign to criticize Teng and which had Mao's approval.[27] On February 26, posters appeared at Peking University attacking Teng by name. On February 28, *People's Daily* anonymously attacked him by referring to the "one leader" in the party still taking the capitalist road. On February 29, "Liang Hsiao" criticized the slogan, "white cat, black cat, what difference does color make if the cat can catch mice," a reference associated with Teng during the cultural revolution.

The campaign progressed without Teng. He had disappeared once more from public view shortly after he delivered the euology at Chou's memorial rally on January 15. Then, on February 7, the announcement was made that Hua Kuo-feng had been named acting premier of the State Council to succeed Chou. Within a month of Hua's promotion, the press continued the criticism campaign against Teng, only this time the phrase, "Teng Hsiao-p'ing and his ilk," appeared, indicating that someone other than Teng was the target. In Hunan, Chang P'ing-hua, the second party provincial secretary, was attacked in a wall poster, leading some to speculate that the attack was really on Chang's boss, Hua Kuo-feng, who still retained the position of first secretary.

In the first week of April, the Ch'ing Ming Festival started. This is the time when the graves of the dead are swept and also a time to commemorate the dead. On April 4, wreaths commemorating Chou En-lai's death were placed at T'ienanmen Square in Peking, but sometime during the night the wreaths were removed. The following day, as some students attempted to replace the wreaths, they were prevented from doing so, touching off a riot which caused much damage and led to the arrest of hundreds of demonstrators. On April 7, the Politburo announced that Hua had been unanimously appointed first vice-chairman of the Central Committee and premier of the State Council. Teng Hsiao-p'ing was officially dismissed from all of his positions, but was allowed to retain his party membership so as to see how he would behave in the future. It is yet not clear who provoked the April 5 incident, but now we are told that the gang of four was responsible for it and not, presumably Teng. The only thing that is known for sure was that Teng's second purge did not improve matters at all.

On May 29, the *People's Daily* reprinted an article due to appear in the June issue of *Red Flag* (no. 6) denouncing the "capitalist roaders who were precisely the bourgeoisie within the Party."[28] While the author could not identify the capitalist roaders within the party, he did know that they "appear unanimously in the capacity of leading personnel, and certain person's positions are very high."[29] Hua, it should be recalled, was elected unanimously to his two high posts on April 7. On July 20, the *People's Daily* published an article resurrecting the message of the novel, *Water Margin,* only this time the emphasis shifted slightly. Sung Chiang, the capitulator in the novel and Teng by allusion, actually wanted to give up his post as leader of the rebels to another rebel because he thought the other rebel was better suited for the position.[30] Here, too, one could read between the lines, but nothing in the article could be interpreted as collusion between Hua and Teng. It is overwhelmingly tempting to interpret the several articles which appeared after Hua's promotion on April 7 as veiled criticisms of him. With the exception of Mao, he was the highest ranking official in both the party and the government. The articles could have hardly been referring to Mao.

This campaign was beginning to gather momentum, and it seemed for a moment that the country was in for another Teng Hsiao-p'ing re-run. It took an earthquake this time, not the death of an individual, to give the country another badly needed respite from internal politics. While the four have not been held personally responsible for earthquake (surprisingly), they are charged with attempting to push the anti-Teng campaign at the expense of the earthquake relief work.

During 1976, the PRC was rocked by seven severe earthquakes, hitting such provinces as Hopei, Yunnan, Szechwan,

Kansu and the major cities of Peking and Tientsin. The T'angshan (Hopei) earthquake occurred on July 28, and measured 8.2 on the Richter scale. According to statistics contained in a classified document released by the Hopei Provincial Party Committee on August 6 to an emergency conference on earthquake relief work, the quake claimed 655,237 lives, seriously injured another 79,000 and another 700,000 required treatment for lesser injuries. This was China's second worst earthquake. In 1556, an earthquake in Shensi claimed over 800,000 lives.[31]

The extent of the relief effort for the combined areas of T'angshan, Fengnan, Peking and Tientsin, can be gauged by a sample of the provinces and cities which responded immediately. Shensi province sent 630 tons of materials, pork, cotton cloth and three million pounds of wheat flour. Kwangtung province sent fourteen tons of medicine, medical equipment, food, clothes, and 300 tons of roofing materials. Chekiang, Inner Mongolia, Shantung and Kiangsi sent around 2,200 medical personnel, while Liaoning sent "over 3,000" medical workers, a 470-person rescue team, and a 87-person medical team.[32]

The effects of the earthquake on the economy nationally are not known, but regionally the effects must have been devastating. For example, the earthquake seriously damaged the K'ailuan coal mines in T'angshan, the principal source of coking coal for the steel plants in Peking, Tientsin and Shanghai, one of China's most important regional industrial areas. According to the *People's Daily* (March 14, 1977), eight months after the quake, six of K'ailuan's seven pits were nearly restored to pre-earthquake levels. The serious coal shortage which struck the northern industrial area forced the steel plants to revert to alternative fuel usage. On March 11, *People's Daily* also reported that a campaign was under way to offset the "temporary" difficulties in industrial production and coal supply. There was also apparently a loss of generating capacity in the Peking-Tientsin-T'angshan area, and it was not until November (1976) that the T'angshan power plant had restored its ten damaged generating units to pre-earthquake levels.[33]

Droughts, which have plagued China historically, also hurt the economy in 1976 and 1977. While Hua did not elaborate on this "test" in his second Tachai speech, subsequent news from the mainland made it clear that the country was experiencing the worst drought since 1949. The drought extended from the north China plains to Kwangtung province in the South.[34] The provinces of Chekiang, Kiangsi, Fukien, Szechwan, Yunnan and Kweichow were particularly hardhit. Grain was rationed in some areas, and the newly harvested grain was eaten instead of being stored in granaries. In Shanghai, wall posters appeared asking for more grain and cooking oil. "This is not a small problem," one wall poster noted, "the masses are eating bitterness."[35] Disease brought about by the drought also developed into epidemic proportions, affecting in particular the pig industry.[36] The black market flourished at this time,[37] and some people were reportedly executed for stealing grain from the state's granaries.[38] To counter the effects of the drought on agriculture and the earthquake on industry, the *People's Daily* suggested on several occasions that for the country to get back on its feet, it might be necessary to make "profits," that foul practice associated with decadent capitalist countries. Overall, the GNP rose by only 3.5 percent in 1976, the smallest increase since before the cultural revolution.

One of the main reasons for focusing on the effects of the earthquake and the drought is that the gang of four has been blamed for China's recent economic problems. While the four did in fact support a policy of self-reliance in economic development and their revolutionary rhetoric may have impeded the economic program announced by Chou En-lai at the Fourth People's Congress and by Hua at the First Tachai Conference, it must be kept in mind that in doing so they did it with Mao's blessing. The four enjoyed quoting Mao's: "without class struggle, there can be no progress." Mao's blessings and protection, however, ran out on them shortly after September 9, 1976.

The Politics of Mourning

On September 9, at 3:19 P.M. (Peking time), Radio Peking alerted foreign correspondents in the capital and Hong Kong that there would be an "important announcement" at 4:00 P.M., at which time it was announced that Chairman Mao Tse-tung had died early that morning at 12:10 A.M., at the age of eighty-two.[39] It was generally believed that he died of advanced Parkinson's disease or cerebral arteriosclerosis.

Chairman Mao's death was officially announced nearly sixteen hours after in a joint "Message to the Whole Party, Whole Army and People of all Nationalities Throughout the Country" by the Central Committee, the Standing Committee of the National People's Congress, the State Council of the PRC and the Military Commission of the Central Committee.[40] The sixteen hour delay was caused undoubtedly by last minute alterations to the contingency plan prepared before Mao's death. We do know that the four took part in the discussions on the "Message" as well as the memorial speech delivered by Hua on September 18, but there is no evidence that any problems occurred at this time.[41]

The "Message" was, fittingly, a testimonial to Chairman Mao. It proclaimed him the "founder and wise leader" of the Communist Party, the People's Republic of China, the People's Liberation Army and, predictably, the "greatest Marxist of the contemporary era." For anyone looking for even the slightest clue or hint of a will left by him or some such startling announcement on the succession question, the message was, in this sense, a keen disappointment. The September 9 message was but the first opportunity during the first week after Mao's death to assess the impact of his death on the party's leadership. In the next few days, the composition of the funeral committee, the messages of condolence from the provinces and military regions to the Central Committee and the official photographs of the receiving lines during the memorial period all revealed nothing out of the ordinary.

At 10:00 A.M. on September 11, the solemn mourning services began inside the crepe-draped Great Hall of the People. Inside a huge portrait of Chairman Mao greeted the incoming mourners. Above the portrait, a streamer read, "We mourn with deepest grief over the great leader and teacher, Chairman Mao Tse-tung." The hall was filled with the scent of wreaths, layers of pine, cypresses and other evergreens. Chairman Mao's body, "his face firm and serene," eyes closed, rested beneath a glass case. The bier was surrounded with flowers which added to the heavy scent in the hall. His body was partially covered with the party flag, the hammer and sickle prominently displayed. The top of the grey "Mao suit" was visibly contrasted against the red flag. Standing guard on both sides of the bier were the soldiers of the PLA. Hua, Wang Hung-wen, Yeh Chien-ying, Chang Ch'un-ch'iao, Chiang Ch'ing, Yao Wen-yuan, Li Hsien-nien and other high-ranking Party, government and military officials stood before the bier, bowed three times, and observed a three minute period of silent mourning. They stood as honor guards at the sides of the bier.

Chiang Ch'ing placed a wreath before Chairman Mao's bier "made of sunflowers, green corn, ears of wheat, maize and fruit of yellow corn." The inscription on the wreath read: "deeply mourn the esteemed great teacher, Chairman Mao Tse-tung, from your student and comrade-in-arms, Chiang Ch'ing and Mao An-ch'ing, Li Min, Li Na, Mao Yuan-chih and Mao Yuan-hsin."[42] Her choice of words may on the surface appear rather cold and distant and at the memorial services she certainly did not play the role of the grieving widow. She did not appear at the receiving lines during the mourning period. However, it would be terribly unfair to even hint that she felt nothing for Mao. It is quite possible that nearly forty years of marriage, founded, nurtured and matured by revolution, had taken its toll on the kind of behavior normally expected from the surviving spouse.

There was a time, nonetheless, when the relationship had all the makings of a classic (revolutionary) love story. When Mao first met her as Lan P'ing, her stage name, in 1937, he was still married to Ho Tzu-chen. Mao was forty-five; Chiang Ch'ing twenty-four. Dramatics aside, it was love at first sight. "Without Lan P'ing," he once said, "I cannot go on with the revolution."[43] This may or may not have been an idle threat, but we do know that he defied the party when he and Lan P'ing began to live as man and wife. The party objected to this arrangement because Mao had not formally divorced Ho Tzu-chen at this time. Say what one will, Mao and Chiang Ch'ing's marriage did last through four decades of revolution, nation-building, tragic illnesses (she nearly died of cancer in the mid–1950s), internal conflict, external threats and little or no peace. Marriages today are known to fall apart for less compelling reasons.

The revolutionary environment in which their marriage was

founded did change their relationship. During the cultural revolution she described it once again on teacher-student terms:

> Chairman Mao is very strict with me. Most of all, he is a strict teacher to me. Naturally he does not take my hands and make them do things the way he wishes others to do. . . . We have lived together, but he is the silent type; he does not talk much.[44]

It should be kept in mind that Mao was seventy-four at this time.

The arrest of Chiang Ch'ing has also revealed other facets of their relationship which portray deterioration of their marriage. We are told that they were not living together since 1973, shortly after he presumably read the transcription of the interview Chiang Ch'ing gave to an American professor in preparation for her biography.[45] Chiang Ch'ing is also portrayed as a nagging wife, constantly badgering Mao for more money and ignoring him while his health got progressively worse. In the end, she had to make appointments to see him, and even then, he allegedly told her:

> Nothing is gained by seeing me. Books by Marx and Lenin, my books, are all there, and yet you read none of them. There is no point in seeing me. . . . I really envy the Chou En-lai's marriage.[46]

Responding to still another letter requesting an appointment, Mao replied:

> Even when you see me we have nothing to talk about. We have seen each other several times, but you still have not carried out my instructions. You always talk about petty things, but you never discuss important matters with me. . . . You must know your own ability. Don't you realize that people are dissatisfied with you.[47]

Mao presumably kept this correspondence stored in the general office of the Central Committee, where it was safeguarded by Wang Tung-hsing, his personal body-guard and the director of the general office. Mao and Chiang Ch'ing's correspondence was entered as evidence of her alienation from the chairman by Hua Kuo-feng at a Politburo meeting held on October 7, the day after the arrest of the four.

Publicly, during the first five days of the mourning period (September 11–15) there were no indications of any party (or family) squabbles. The peace, however, was over even before Chairman Mao's body was cold. But, as things are wont to happen in China, only the Chinese leadership knew that the struggle of contending wills had begun in earnest on September 16.

The Struggle of Contending Wills

On September 16, the *People's Daily, Red Flag* and *Liberation Army Daily* published a joint article in the form of a eulogy for the late chairman. This article contained the first reference to a so-called "adjuration," which in the following days was to become identified as Mao's deathbed will.

> There are worthy successors to the proleterian revolutionary cause which he pioneered in China. Chairman Mao adjured us: 'Act according to the principles laid down,' which mean 'to act according to Chairman Mao's proleterian revolutionary line and policies.'[48]

It did not take the adjuration very long to find its way to the masses. The New China News Agency, for example, reported a pledge made to Chairman Mao by the worker's militia of Peking *on the same day* on which the editorial appeared. On the seventeenth, the adjuration was prominently headlined in the *People's Daily,* while on page five, the newspaper carried five photographs, one which showed peasants, workers and soldiers standing solemnly in front of Chairman Mao's bier vowing to "carry out Chairman Mao's behest 'act according to the principles laid down.' "

The adjuration thus appeared two days before the mass memorial rally scheduled in Peking. On the afternoon of the eighteenth, over one million people jammed T'ienanmen Square to attend the solemn mass memorial. Wang Hung-wen presided over the rally. Hua Kuo-feng delivered the memorial speech.

There are several important features in this speech, not the least being the prominence given to the historical importance of the PLA. Two Mao quotations, in retrospect, were given special mention by Hua. The first was: "Chairman Mao drew the scientific conclusion: you are making the socialist revolution, and yet don't know where the bourgeoisie is. It is right in the Communist party—those in power taking the capitalist road."[49] Since this slogan had been used several years before, in and of itself, it provided no clue to Hua's thinking at that time. The slogan which was to achieve a measure of importance in the days ahead, however, was the "Three Do's and Don'ts:"

1. practice Marxism, and not revisionism.
2. unite, and don't split.
3. be open and aboveboard, and don't intrigue and conspire.[50]

Hua's speech was as significant for what it did include as what it did not include: any mention of the deathbed adjuration. His omission must not have been any comfort to him when the *People's Daily* featured another long article on September 18, the same day he was delivering the memorial speech, entitled, "Conscientiously study Chairman Mao's important adjuration, 'Act according to the principles laid down.'" Further, all twenty-nine provinces, autonomous regions and municipalities included the adjuration in their memorial rallies.

In Peking, on the surface, it was business as usual. On the morning of the twenty-third, Chang Ch'un-ch'iao accompanied by Ch'en Hsi-lien, commander of the Peking Military Region, Wu Teh, mayor of Peking, and Ch'iao Kuan-hua, China's Foreign Minister, among others, led a delegation to the embassy of the Democratic People's Republic of Korea in Peking to express mourning over the death of a member of the Korean Communist Party Central Committee. Hua Kuo-feng sent a wreath. That afternoon, Chang welcomed a Jamaican government delegation led by Mr. David Coore, Deputy Prime Minister, at the airport, and shortly thereafter, held talks with Mr. Coore. On the evening of the twenty-fourth, Hua met Mr. Coore, and in his welcome speech reiterated China's determination to "carry out Chairman Mao's behests," but did not mention a specific one. On the twenty-sixth, Chang and Mr. Coore signed an agreement and some protocols concerning trade and economic cooperation between the PRC and

Jamaica. On September 27, Yeh Chien-ying, vice-chairman of the Military Commission and Minister of Defense, met with former U.S. Secretary of Defense, James R. Schlesinger. On the twenty-eighth, Mr. Schlesinger met with Hua.

Seven Days in October

Toward the end of September, perhaps on the twenty-ninth, the Politburo met and pointed out to the gang of four "that their propaganda policy" concerning the adjuration "was wrong."[51] At this meeting, Chiang Ch'ing "formally proposed" to Hua that he support her bid to become the head of the Central Committee.[52] Hua's response is not known, but it is safe to assume that he rejected her proposal. The meeting was adjourned with nothing settled.

At seven o'clock on the evening of September 30, Wu Teh opened a "grand meeting" held at T'ienanmen Tower by four hundred representatives of workers, peasants and soldiers to celebrate the 27th anniversary of the founding of the country. Hua gave the closing talk, a rather short one, devoid of any political import. Present at that meeting in addition to Hua and Wu Teh were Wang Hung-wen, Yeh Chien-ying, Chang Ch'un-ch'iao, Yao Wen-yuan and Chiang Ch'ing. They all appeared for the photographing session. This photograph has been entered into evidence as part of the plot of the four to usurp party and state power. According to the media, Chiang Ch'ing and Yao Wen-yuan arranged to have the picture taken from such an angle that it would show her more prominently than Hua. Depending on how one looks at it, this is true. The official photograph which appeared in *People's Daily* was taken in such a manner that Hua, who had led the procession of the Politburo members to the session, is actually at the far right of the photograph. Chiang Ch'ing, who came in fifth, is in the middle of the photograph, one step in front of the line. However, had the picture been taken so as to show Hua first, then it would have obscured those behind him. Further, there is no particular reason why Hua's position required that he be the focal point of the photograph. While he held the top two positions in the party and government any photograph which explicitly focused on him in such a leading position could have been interpreted out of context also—no one was ready to make such a deliberate move just yet.

This was Chiang Ch'ing's last public appearance before her arrest, and with the possible exception of Wang Hung-wen, it was the last public appearance of Yao and Chang.

The war of words continued throughout the October 1 celebrations. Two more articles appeared in *Red Flag* (October issue) which escalated the militancy behind the adjuration. Hua must have become particularly alarmed at the militant tone of the articles, for after October 1, he began to "resolutely hit back" at the intrigues of the four. On October 2, he reviewed a document which apparently contained the adjuration and he crossed it out. "I've checked it up," he wrote on the back of the document, "three of the characters are wrong compared with the original in Chairman Mao's own handwriting."[53] From available evidence it is apparent that the document Hua reviewed was a draft of a speech Ch'iao Kuan-hua was about to deliver to the United Nations General Assembly.[54] Although Ch'iao was already in New York on October 2 (he left Peking on September 30), Hua in all probability reviewed the draft routinely and discovered that the adjuration was included. He was certainly not anxious to give the adjuration world-wide coverage. According to Kyodo news agency, Peking then wired Huang Hua in New York to delete it from the speech.[55] Since the adjuration did not appear in Ch'iao's speech of October 5, it is safe to assume that it was crossed out in New York. We do know that Ch'iao was implicated with the four for both he and his wife disappeared from public view after November 11, the day when he met in Peking with the new ambassador from Outer Mongolia. Shortly thereafter, he was replaced as foreign minister by Huang Hua.

The October 2 incident must have been the first direct confrontation between Hua and the four over the adjuration's validity. It was certainly the first time, to the knowledge of the outside world, that he had decided to reveal that the adjuration was a forgery. According to the media, on April 30, 1976, after he and Mao had met with New Zealand's Premier Robert Muldoon, he (Hua) reported to Mao on the progress of the anti-Teng criticism campaign. After the report was delivered, Mao personally wrote a directive containing three instructions:

1. Take your time, don't be anxious.
2. Act according to past principles.
3. With you in charge, I am at ease.[56]

The four knew that these were the original instructions conveyed by Mao to Hua because Hua revealed them to ·a meeting of the Politburo shortly thereafter. Chiang Ch'ing, Wang Hung-wen, Yao Wen-yuan and Chang Ch'un-ch'iao were at that meeting. Yao had seen the original copy of the directive.[57] The instruction which was forged was the second one, "act according to past principles." The second instruction is comprised of six Chinese characters (chao kuo-ch'u fang-chen pan) and the alleged forgery was accomplished by exchanging the first three (chao kuo-ch'u) with another three (an chi-ting), which effectively changed the meaning from "act according to past principles" to "act according to the principles laid down." The latter was the slogan which first appeared on September 16. We are not told, however, how anyone could have possibly forged Mao's calligraphy, which even Chiang Ch'ing had acknowledged was unique.[58] But we are told, unwittingly, that the three instructions were specifically related to the *anti-Teng* campaign, in which case the third directive, "with you in charge, I am at ease," should not be interpreted, as the party obviously has, as Hua's mandate to succeed Mao.[59]

The four are portrayed at this time as stepping up their pace to overthrow Hua. Chiang Ch'ing was allegedly "running up and down and traveling around to sell her ideas . . . feasted and had photographs taken."[60] On October 2, Wang had a portrait "taken secretly," presumably in anticipation of becoming chairman of the Standing Committee of the National People's Congress.[61] Then, on October 3, he went to P'ingku county, a suburb of Peking, and delivered an anti-party and anti-Hua speech.[62]

On October 4, an article appeared in *Kuangming Daily* written by "Liang Hsiao," the pseudonym for the radical theoretic group from Peking and Tsinghua Universities.[63] This article, as it turns out, was the swan-song for both the four and the adjuration. Going against the adjuration, Liang Hsiao wrote, meant meeting with setbacks and defeats. "All chieftains of the revisionist line who attempt to tamper with this principle laid down necessarily have to tamper with Marxist-Leninist-Mao Tse-tung Thought, emasculate its revolutionary soul and blunt its revolutionary edge." The only "chieftain," revisionist or otherwise, still around was, of course, Hua Kuo-feng. Finally, just as the "Communist Manifesto" sounded the death knell of capitalism and the rise of Communism, so the principles laid down by Chairman Mao would sound the death knell of its opponents and witness the rise of a "revolutionary army of hundreds of millions."

This article we are now told was the "mobilization order" for the four and their followers. It is not clear just when the coup was to have taken place, but of greater importance is not when the coup was to occur but with what. According to the charges, Chiang Ch'ing attempted to enlist the support of two prominent Politburo members and PLA officials, Ch'en Hsi-lien[64] and Su Chen-hua,[65] the political commissar of the PLA's navy. Both immediately reported the incidents to Hua Kuo-feng. For someone planning a coup, she could not have made her intentions more public if she had planned it that way. But, were the four planning a coup? It is conceivable that while the *motive* was the take-over of the leadership of the party and government (as charged) the *methods* might not have been quite as devious as one is led to believe. It is probable that Chiang Ch'ing did in fact approach Ch'en and Su with nothing more in mind than seeking additional support, and votes, within the Politburo. Of what remained of the Politburo before the arrest, but after Mao's death, a simple majority would have been nine votes (sixteen full members). The four could count on four votes and needed five more. Ch'en Hsi-lien could help, but Su Ch'en-hua, an alternate, is doubtful. Whether or not they could have received the additional support is also doubtful, but that they tried is very probable.

The October 4 article was the last article to carry the adjuration. In the period between October 1 and October 4, the adjuration appeared at least forty-two times in both *People's Daily* and *Kuangming Daily* to only eleven times for the "Three Do's and

Don'ts," the only slogan with which Hua had ever associated. Further, the "Three Do's and Don'ts," *never* appeared by itself uncontested by the adjuration. In *most* cases, the adjuration appeared in the same paragraph as the "Three Do's and Don'ts."

The October 4 article, we are told, alerted Hua. In the early hours of October 6, the four were arrested and placed in solitary confinement.[66] The "issue was settled without firing a single shot or shedding a drop of blood," Hua told the participants at the Second Tachai Conference. Indeed, he might have added that the entire episode was accomplished with the utmost swiftness and secrecy. It is difficult to tell whether or not the average person knew about the arrests when they occurred or even up to four days later (October 10).[67] Correspondents in Peking reported that the capital was calm on the sixth and subsequent days, and if some people did know, the occasion was used to go to tea houses, canteens and restaurants to discuss the event calmly and to toast a few "bottoms up."[68] "The amazing thing right now in the capital," wrote one correspondent "is precisely this total calm and the way that life seems to be going on perfectly normal."[69]

On the morning of October 7, a meeting of the Politburo was held at which time Hua read two reports on the arrest, Yeh Chien-ying one and Wang Tung-hsing two. The Politburo unanimously supported Hua's decision to arrest the four, an indication that Hua must have acted without the knowledge of the Politburo or Central Committee. On that same day, the Politburo voted to name Hua Kuo-feng chairman of the Central Committee. The major problem facing the Politburo now was the handling of the announcement that the four and their accomplices (about thirty others were arrested on the sixth) had been arrested and announcing at the same time that Hua had just been elected chairman of the party, succeeding Mao. The problems were solved when the Politburo decided to announce on October 8 two historic decisions: first, to establish a memorial hall in Peking for Chairman Mao and second, to publish volume five of the *Selected Works of Mao Tse-tung*. Anticipating that the masses would greet both decisions amid great fanfare the two decisions, important as they were, would also serve as the perfect cover for the Politburo report prepared by Hua, Yeh, and Wang which was to be secretly circulated nationwide to middle and high-ranking cadres.[70] On the surface the party, army, and masses would be hailing the two decisions while covertly they were also learning of the arrest of the four and Hua's promotion.

But for the shouting, it was all over.

Notes

Chapter 1
Introduction

1. Edgar Snow, *Red Star over China* (New York: Random House, 1938), p. 131.
2. "The People's Middle Kingdom," *Foreign Affairs* (July 1966): 580.
3. Snow, *Red Star,* pp. 127, 134.
4. *Peking Review,* no. 27 (July 5, 1974): 15.
5. *Peking Review,* no. 29 (July 19, 1974): 6.
6. Wing-tsit Chan, *A Source Book in Chinese Philosophy* (Princeton: Princeton University Press, 1963), p. 36.
7. Ibid., p. 39.
8. James Legge, *The Chinese Classics,* vol. 1 (Oxford: Clarendon Press, 1893), p. 266.
9. Chan, *Source Book,* p. 44.
10. Ibid., p. 69.
11. "Report of an Investigation into the Peasant Movement in Hunan," *Selected Works of Mao Tse-tung,* vol. 1 (New York: International Publishers, 1954), p. 47.
12. Chan, *Source Book,* p. 34.
13. See James R. Townsend, *Political Participation in Communist China* (Berkeley: University of California Press, 1967).
14. Chan, *Source Book,* p. 40.
15. Ibid., p. 32.
16. Ibid.
17. Joseph Needham, *Science and Civilization in China, History of Scientific Thought,* Vol. 2, (Cambridge: University Press, 1956), pp. 30–32.
18. Snow, *Red Star,* p. 143.
19. Jerome Ch'en, *Mao and the Chinese Revolution* (New York: Oxford University Press, 1967), p. 44.
20. Quoted in Stuart Schram, *The Political Thought of Mao Tse-tung,* rev. and enlarged ed. (New York: Frederick A. Praeger, 1969), p. 13.

21. Cited in Ch'en, *Mao,* pp. 44–45.
22. *Peking Review,* no. 47 (November 22, 1974): 8–13.
23. Fairbank, "The People's Middle Kingdom," *Foreign Affairs* (July 1966): 586.
24. A. T. Steele, *The American People and China* (New York: McGraw-Hill Co., 1966), pp. 8–9.
25. Ssu-yu Teng and John K. Fairbank, *China's Response to the West: A Documentary Survey, 1893–1923* (Cambridge: Harvard University Press, 1961), p. 19.
26. Owen Lattimore, "China: The American Mystique," *The Listener* (October 1, 1964): 493.
27. Kwang-ching Liu, *Americans and Chinese* (Cambridge: Harvard University Press, 1963), p. 7, cited in Steele, *The American People,* p. 14.
28. Steele, *The American People,* p. 22.
29. Quoted in Foster Rhea Dulles, *American Policy toward Communist China, 1949–1969* (New York: Thomas Y. Crowell Co., 1972). p. 44.
30. Ibid., p. 78.
31. Ibid., pp. 75–76.
32. Quoted in E. J. Kahn, Jr., *The China Hands* (New York: Viking Press, 1975), p. 295.
33. Quoted in Arthur M. Schlesinger, Jr., *A Thousand Days* (Boston: Houghton Mifflin Co., 1965), p. 479, and Dulles, *American Policy,* p. 193.
34. Schlesinger, *Thousand Days,* p. 479 and Dulles, *American Policy,* p. 194–95.
35. Dulles, *American Policy,* pp. 238–39.
36. Jane Hamilton-Merritt, "A Case of Cavalier Neglect," *Saturday Review* (October 19, 1974): 50.
37. Ibid.
38. Quoted in Dulles, *American Policy,* p. 121.
39. Ibid.
40. For the dispute in its early stages, see Donald S. Zagoria, *The Sino-Soviet Dispute, 1956–1961* (Princeton: Princeton University Press, 1962).
41. This account follows Stanley Karnow, *Mao and China* (New York: Viking Press, 1972).
42. Ibid., p. 503.
43. Ibid., p. 505.
44. *Peking Review,* no. 3 (January 17, 1975): 6–8.
45. *Peking Review,* no. 8 (February 29, 1975): 17–19.
46. *Peking Review,* no. 3, p. 8.
47. *Arizona Daily Star,* October 23, 1975.

Chapter 2
The Revolutionary Environment in
Nineteenth–Twentieth Century China

1. Richard M. Nixon, *U.S. Foreign Policy for the 1970s, Building for Peace* (Washington, D.C.: U.S. Government Printing Office, 1971), p. 106.

2. A. T. Steele, *The American People and China* (New York: McGraw-Hill Book Co., 1966), p. 7.

3. John K. Fairbank, Edwin O. Reischauer, and Albert M. Craig, *East Asia: The Modern Transformation*, vol. 2 (Boston: Houghton Mifflin Co., 1965), p. 3.

4. Chiang K'ai-shek, *China's Destiny*, trans. Philip Jaffe (New York: Roy, 1947), p. 44.

5. Mao Tse-tung, *Chinese Revolution and the Chinese Communist Party* (Peking: Foreign Languages Press, 1954), p. 13.

6. Ping-ti Ho, *Studies on the Population of China, 1368–1953* (Cambridge: Harvard University Press, 1959), pp. 246–470, 282. Ho believes that this widely accepted figure is still low. Using his established population figures for 1850 and the next reliable census in 1953, he concludes that the area where the T'ai-p'ing rebellion was largely confined was down 19,200,000 in 1953, or 14 percent less than in 1850. He further believes that his figures "reflect the permanent wounds that the population of the lower Yangtze provinces received" during the T'ai-p'ing rebellion, 1850–64 (p. 246).

7. Ibid.

8. Andrew J. Nathan, *A History of the China International Famine Relief Commission*, Harvard East Asian Monographs (Cambridge: Harvard University Press, 1965), pp. 2–3.

9. This account follows John L. Buck, *Land Utilization in China* (N.Y.: Paragon Book Reprint Corporation, 1964), pp. 9, 194–96 and Lucien Bianco, *Origins of the Chinese Revolution, 1915–1949* (Stanford: University Press, 1971), Ch. 4, pp. 82–107.

10. Bianco, *Origins*, p. 99.

11. Treaty ports were places where foreigners were allowed to live, carry on business, and acquire land. They were established either by treaty or by permission of the Chinese government. By the time of the revolution, there were approximately ninety such treaty ports opened to foreigners in China (Fairbank, Reischauer, and Craig, *East Asia*, p. 342).

12. Chi-ming Hou, *Foreign Investments and Economic Development in China, 1840–1937* (Cambridge: Harvard University Press, 1965), p. 91.

13. Ibid., p. 16.

14. Ibid., p. 126.
15. Ibid., p. 134.
16. Fairbank, Reischauer, and Craig, *East Asia,* p. 96.
17. *Foreign Investments and Economic Development,* pp. 183–84.
18. Zenone Volpicelli, *The China-Japan War* (London: 1896), p. 414, quoted in C. F. Remer, *Foreign Investments in China* (New York: Howard Fertig, 1968), p. 121.
19. Hou, *Foreign Investments and Economic Development,* p. 29.
20. Ibid., p. 35.
21. Remer, *Foreign Investments in China,* p. 161.
22. *Ibid.,* p. 220. Remer cannot account for the unexplained difference.
23. Fairbank, Reischauer, and Craig, *East Asia,* p. 132.
24. H. B. Morse, *The Trade and Administration of China.* Rev. ed. (Shanghai: Kelly and Walsh, Limited, 1913), pp. 360–61.
25. Ibid., pp. 352–53.
26. Fairbank, Reischauer, and Craig, *East Asia,* p. 132.
27. Ibid.
28. Ibid., p. 470. Also, W. L. Langer, *The Diplomacy of Imperialism, 1890–1902,* 2 vols. (New York: Knopf, 1935: reprint, 1950).
29. Great Britain, United States, France, Germany, Denmark, Norway, Sweden, Russia, Netherlands, Spain, Belgium, Italy, Austria-Hungary, Japan, Peru, Brazil, Portugal, Congo Free-State, and Mexico (Hou, *Foreign Investments and Economic Development,* p. 248).
30. For a full discussion on extraterritoriality, see: Wesley R. Fishel, *The End of Extraterritoriality in China* (Berkeley: University of California Press, 1952).
31. H. B. Morse, *The International Relations of the Chinese Empire,* 3 vols. (London: Longmans, Green, 1910–1918). Vol. 3: "Subjection of China."
32. Li Chien-nung, *The Political History of China,* 1840–1928, trans. and ed. Ssu-yu Teng and Jeremy Ingalls (New York: D. Van Nostrand Co., 1956), p. 88.
33. Ibid., p. 95.
34. Quoted in Li Chien-nung, *Political History.* p. 160, from Chien Po-tsan's *Collected Source Materials on the Reform Movement of 1898* [Wu-hsu pien-fu], 4 vols. (Shanghai, 1953), vol. 1, p. 476.
35. Fairbank, Reischauer, and Craig, *East Asia,* p. 614.
36. Crane Brinton, *The Anatomy of Revolution* (New York: Vantage Books, 1965), p. 49.
37. K'ang yu-wei and Liang Ch'i-Ch'ao pose great difficulties in being characterized as revolutionaries. They were reformers out to preserve the dynasty under a constitutional monarchy. But these ideas in a traditional imperial system were revolutionary in themselves and no doubt provided the impetus for others to cast themselves as revolutionary intellectuals. Li Chien-nung would agree (*Political History,* p. 190).

38. Y. C. Wang, *Chinese Intellectuals and the West, 1872–1949* (Chapel Hill: University of North Carolina, 1966), p. 74.
39. Ibid., p. 56.
40. Howard L. Boorman (ed.), *Biographical Dictionary of Republican China*, 4 vols. (New York: Columbia University Press, 1967–1971), II, 412. The reasons for the student's change of mind are not known.
41. Wang, *Chinese Intellectuals and the West*, pp. 90–91.
42. H. Chalmers Johnson, *Revolutionary Change* (Boston: Little, Brown and Co., 1966), p. 125.
43. Li Chien-nung, *Political History*, p. 194.
44. Michael Gasster, *Chinese Intellectuals and the Revolution of 1911* (Seattle: University of Washington Press, 1969), p. 35.
45. Quoted in Ibid., p. 38.
46. Ibid., p. 39.
47. Joseph Levenson, *Liang Ch'i-ch'ao and the Mind of Modern China* (Cambridge: Harvard University Press, 1965), p. 19.
48. Ibid., p. 206.
49. Wang, *Chinese Intellectuals and the West*, p. 225.
50. Li Chien-nung, *Political History*, p. 217.
51. George T. Yu, *Party Politics in Republican China: The Kuomintang, 1912–1924* (Berkeley: University of California Press, 1966), p. 7. There are many books of doubtful and uneven quality written about Sun. One book, however, stands out: Lyon Sharman, *Sun Yat-sen: His Life and Meaning* (Hamden: Archon Books, 1965 [1934].
52. Sharman, *Sun Yat-sen*, p. 39.
53. Yu, *Party Politics*, p. 28.
54. Ssu-yu Teng and John K. Fairbank, *China's Response to the West: A Documentary Survey, 1893–1923* (Cambridge: Harvard University Press, 1961), Document 56, pp. 227–29.
55. Yu, *Party Politics*, p. 43.
56. Li Chien-nung, *Political History*, pp. 221–36.
57. Sharman, *Sun Yat-sen*, p. 101.
58. Ibid., p. 271 and Boorman, *Biographical Dictionary*, III, 186.
59. They were not published in their final form until 1924, after he had presented them as a series of lectures in Canton.
60. Boorman, *Biographical Dictionary*, III, 187.
61. Ibid., I, 94.
62. Ibid., III, 176.
63. In 1648, as the Manchus swept through Wang's native province in Hunan, he raised an army to fight them, and thus restore the truly Chinese Ming dynasty. He was defeated, however, and at the age of thirty-three, he returned to the mountains where he spent the next forty years writing.
64. Sharman, *Sun Yat-sen*, p. 116.
65. T. C. Woo, *The Kuomintang and the Future of the Chinese Revo-*

lution (London, 1928), p. 51, quoted in Sharman, *Sun Yat-sen* pp. 116–17.

66. Quoted in Li Chien-nung, *Political History,* p. 212.

67. The quotation is Wang's, as printed in the alliance's *The People,* and quoted in Gasster, *Chinese Intellectuals and the Revolution,* pp. 86–87.

68. Li Chien-nung, *Political History,* p. 234.

69. Hsieh Pao-chao, *Government of China, 1644–1911* (London: Frank Cass and Co., 1966), p. 52.

70. Ibid., pp. 45–46.

71. Edict quoted in Hsieh, *Government,* pp. 53–54.

72. Fairbank, Reischauer, and Craig, *East Asia,* pp. 394–95, and Victor Purcell, *The Boxer Uprising,* (Cambridge: University Press, 1963), ch. 11.

73. Purcell, *Boxer Uprising,* p. 252.

74. Chester C. Tan, *The Boxer Catastrophe* (New York: Columbia University Press, 1955), pp. 93–94 and Purcell, *Boxer Uprising,* p. 253.

75. Fairbank, Reischauer, and Craig, *East Asia,* p. 403.

76. Ibid., pp. 403–4.

Chapter 3
Republican and Warlord Interregnums

1. According to Sun Yat-sen's appraisal after the uprising: "The success at Wuch'ang was accidental and was mainly due to the flight of (the Manchu official Jui-Ch'eng" (quoted in Li Chien-nung, *The Political History of China, 1840–1928,* trans. and ed. Ssu-yu Teng and Jeremy Ingalls (New York: D. Van Nostrand Co., 1956), p. 247.

2. George T. Yu, *Party Politics in Republican China: The Kuomintang, 1912–1924* (Berkeley: University of California Press, 1966), p. 62. Sun read about the revolt while traveling between Denver and Kansas City.

3. Ibid., p. 63.

4. Jerome Ch'en, *Yuan Shih-k'ai,* 2nd ed. (Stanford: Stanford University Press, 1972), p. 28.

5. Quoted in Ibid., p. 36.

6. Ibid., p. 214.

7. Quotes from Ibid., p. 75.

8. Ibid., p. 85.

9. Li Chien-nung, *Political History,* pp. 266–67.

10. Ch'en, *Yuan Shih-k'ai,* p. 97.

11. Quoted in Li Chien-nung, *Political History,* p. 260.

12. Quoted in Ibid., p. 27.

13. Quoted in Ch'en, *Yuan Shih-k'ai,* 2nd ed. p. 110.

14. Quoted in Yu, *Party Politics*, p. 95.
15. Quoted in Ch'en, *Yuan Shih-k'ai*, 2nd ed., p. 114.
16. Ch'en, *Yuan Shih-k'ai*, p. 114, Yu, *Party Politics*, p. 103, and Li Chien-nung, *Political History*, p. 286.
17. Yu, *Party Politics*, p. 107.
18. Ch'en, *Yuan Shih-k'ai*, 2nd ed., p. 117.
19. Ibid., p. 129.
20. Quoted in Ch'en, *Yuan Shih-k'ai*, 2nd ed., p. 130.
21. Ibid., pp. 130–31.
22. Ibid., pp. 162–63.
23. Quoted in Li Chien-nung, *Political History*, pp. 316–17.
24. Ibid., p. 317 and Ch'en, *Yuan Shih-k'ai*, 2nd ed., p. 175.
25. Jerome Ch'en, *Yuan Shih-k'ai: Brutus Assumes the Purple*, 1st ed. (Stanford: University Press, 1961). Ch'en has subsequently revised his work, dropping the "Brutus" identification and suggesting that Yuan's actions were caused by the circumstances of the Chinese situation in the late nineteenth and early twentieth centuries, and of Yuan's own traditional upbringing (see Ch'en's second edition, 1972).
26. John K. Fairbank, Edwin O. Reischauer, and Albert M. Craig, *East Asia: The Modern Transformation*, vol. 2 (Boston: Houghton Mifflin Co., 1965), p. 651.
27. Li Chien-nung, *Political History*, p. 288.
28. O. Edmund Clubb, *Twentieth Century China* (New York: Columbia University Press, 1964, paperback), p. 59.
29. Ch'en, *Yuan Shih-k'ai*, 2nd ed., pp. 214–15.
30. Stephen R. MacKinnon, "The Peiyang Army, Yuan Shih-k'ai, and the Origins of Modern Chinese Warlordism," *Journal of Asian Studies*, vol. 43, no. 3 (May 1973): 423. For a basic definition of a warlord, see Jerome Ch'en, "Defining Chinese Warlords and Their Factions," *Bulletin of the School of Oriental and African Studies*, vol. 31, no. 3 (1968), pp. 563–600.
31. MacKinnon, "The Peiyang Army," p. 422.
32. For reasons behind the division between north and south, see Ch'en, "Defining Chinese Warlords," pp. 581–86, and MacKinnon, "The Peiyang Army," p. 420, and below.
33. Lucien W. Pye, *Warlord Politics* (New York: Praeger Publishers, 1971), p. 3.
34. James E. Sheridan, *Chinese Warlord: The Career of Feng Yu-hsiang* (Stanford: Stanford University Press, 1966), p. 1.
35. Ch'en, "Defining Chinese Warlords," p. 563.
36. Sheridan, *Chinese Warlord*, p. 18.
37. Ch'en, "Defining Chinese Warlords," p. 563.
38. Ch'en, "Defining Chinese Warlords," pp. 568–69 and Sheridan, *Chinese Warlord*, p. 18.
39. Sheridan, *Chinese Warlord*, p. 17.
40. Ibid., pp. 24–25.

41. Pye, *Warlord Politics*, p. 58.
42. Sheridan, *Chinese Warlord*, p. 22.
43. Ch'en, "Defining Chinese Warlords," p. 582.
44. MacKinnon, "The Peiyang Army," p. 420.
45. Fairbank, *East Asia*, p. 654.
46. Ch'en, "Defining Chinese Warlords," pp. 583–85.
47. See Sheridan, *Chinese Warlord*; Donald Gillin, *Warlord: Yen Hsi-shan in Shansi, 1911–1949* (Princeton: Princeton University Press, 1967); and MacKinnon, "The Peiyang Army," p. 423.
48. Pye, *Warlord Politics*, p. 170.

Chapter 4
The May Fourth Movement

1. The authoritative source on the May Fourth Movement is Chow Tse-tsung's, *The May Fourth Movement: Intellectual Revolution in Modern China* (Cambridge: Harvard University Press, 1960; re-issued by Stanford University Press, 1967, paperback). The paperback edition is used here. Chow lists other great movements in China's history dating back to the time of Confucius but reaffirms the primacy of the May Fourth Movement (pp. 11–15).
2. Mao Tse-tung, *The Chinese Revolution and the Chinese Communist Party* (Peking: Foreign Languages Press, 1954), pp. 47–52, esp. p. 49.
3. Chang Kuo-t'ao, *The Rise of the Chinese Communist Party, 1921–1938: Autobiography;* vol. 2, 1928–1938 (Lawrence: University of Kansas, 1971–1972), I, 63.
4. Chiang K'ai-shek, *China's Destiny and Chinese Economic Theory,* trans. Philip Jaffe (New York: Roy, 1947), p. 71.
5. Werner Levi, *Modern China's Foreign Policy* (Minneapolis: University of Minnesota Press, 1953), ch. 11. For a good discussion of Japanese political maneuvering leading to its declaration of war on Germany, see Russell H. Fifield, *Woodrow Wilson and the Far East* (New York: Thomas Y. Crowell Co., 1952), pp. 3–48, esp. pp. 14–24.
6. Paul S. Reinsch, *An American Diplomat in China* (New York: 1922), cited in Fifield, *Woodrow Wilson,* p. 25.
7. John V. A. McMurray, *Treaties and Agreements With and Concerning China, 1894–1919* (Washington, D.C.: Carnegie Endowment for International Peace, 1921), pp. 1231–34.
8. Ibid., p. 1235.
9. Chow, *May Fourth,* pp. 21–23.
10. Roy Watson Curry, *Woodrow Wilson and Far Eastern Policy, 1913–1921* (New York: Octagon Books, 1968), p. 128.
11. Ibid.
12. For an excellent discussion of the problem of immigration in the

U.S. Asian foreign policy, see A. Whitney Griswold, *The Far Eastern Policy of the United States* (New York: Harcourt, Brace and Co., 1938), ch. 9, pp. 333–379. For U.S. attitudes toward the Chinese prior to the passage of the Exclusion law of 1882 see Stuart C. Miller, *The Unwelcomed Immigrant: The American Image of the Chinese, 1785–1882* (Berkeley: University of California Press, 1969).

13. Griswold, *Far Eastern Policy*, p. 365.
14. Curry, *Woodrow Wilson . . . 1913–1921* p. 140.
15. Ibid., p. 30.
16. Fifield, *Woodrow Wilson*, p. 10.
17. Ibid., pp. 119, 125.
18. Ibid., p. 148.
19. Curry, *Woodrow Wilson . . . 1913–1921* p. 264.
20. Ibid., and Fifield, *Woodrow Wilson*, pp. 198–205.
21. Quoted in Fifield, *Woodrow Wilson*, p. 285.
22. Chow, *May Fourth*, p. 104.
23. Chang Kuo-t'ao, *Rise of the Chinese Communists* vol. I, pp. 55–56.
24. Chow, *May Fourth*, pp. 358–59.
25. Ibid., p. 123.
26. Ibid., p. 150.
27. Ibid., p. 157.
28. Ibid., p. 166.
29. Ibid., p. 359.

Chapter 5
The Origins of Marxism-Leninism in China

1. Benjamin I. Schwartz, *Chinese Communism and the Rise of Mao* (New York: Harper and Row, 1967, paperback), p. 7.
2. For a good discussion of the origin of Marxism-Leninism in China, and for the respective roles of Li Ta-chao and Ch'en Tu-hsiu in this movement see Schwartz, *Chinese Communism and the Rise of Mao*; Maurice Meisner, *Li Ta-chao and the Rise of Chinese Marxism* (Harvard: University Press, 1967); and Huang Sung-k'ang, *Li Ta-chao and the Impact of Marxism on Modern Chinese Thinking* (The Hague: Mouton, 1965).
3. There are several biographies of varying quality on Mao tse-tung. Among Western sources, Edgar Snow's *Red Star over China* (New York: Random House, 1938) is acknowledged to be the authoritative source. Two outstanding biographies have recently appeared: Jerome Ch'en, *Mao and the Chinese Revolution* (New York: Oxford University Press, 1967, paperback) and Stuart Schram, *Mao Tse-tung* (New York: Simon and Schuster, 1966). Other biographies in English, but of a lesser and uneven quality include: Robert Payne, *Portrait of a*

Revolutionary: Mao Tse-tung, rev. ed. (New York: Abelard-Schul-mann, 1961); George Paloczi-Horvath, *Mao Tse-tung: Emperor of the Blue Ants* (London: Secke and Warburg, 1962); and Roy Mac-Gregor-Hastie, *The Red Barbarians: The Life and Times of Mao Tse-tung* (London: T. V. Boardman and Co., 1961).

Chinese sources include: Li Jui, *Mao Tse-tung t'ung-chih ti ch'u-ch'i ke-ming huo-tung* (The Early Revolutionary Activities of Com-rade Mao Tse-tung) (Peking: China Youth Press, 1957); Siao Yu, *Mao Tse-tung and I Were Beggars* (New York: Syracuse University Press, 1959); and Hsiao San (Emile Hsiao), *Mao Tse-tung t'ung-chih ti ch'ing-shao-nien shih-tai* (Comrade Mao Tse-tung's Boyhood and Youth) (Peking: Foreign Languages Press, 1949; Bombay People's Publishing House, 1953).

The Chinese accounts are not as authoritative as the Snow account. That biography was the only one to have been authorized and checked by Mao himself. In fact, the Chinese sources frequently rely on Snow for their information for events before 1937.

Hsiao San and Siao Yu were brothers who befriended Mao in 1912–13. Hsiao San became a Communist and Siao Yu a Nationalist. Accordingly, their accounts are biased by their political preferences. Unfortunately, Hsiao San's book was unavailable to me. Jerome Ch'en, however, cites from it extensively.

Edgar Snow has recently made available his story concerning *Red Star over China* and the unauthorized accounts of Mao's life pirated from him, in his *The Other Side of the River: Red China Today* (New York: Random House, 1962), pp. 773–74. See also, Schram, *Mao Tse-tung,* p. 9 and Ch'en, *Mao,* p. 410.

4. A. Doak Barnett, Foreword in Chang Kuo-t'ao, *The Rise of the Chinese Communist Party, 1921–1927: Autobiography,* I, vii.

5. Ibid., p. 22.

6. Snow, *Red Star,* p. 139.

7. Ibid., p. 140.

8. Chang Kuo-t'ao, *Rise of the Chinese Communist Party,* I., 31.

9. Ibid., p. 123.

10. Snow, *Red Star,* p. 150.

11. Chang Kuo-t'ao, *Rise of the Chinese Communist Party,* I, 87.

12. Ibid., p. 98.

Chapter 6
Russia, the Founding of the
Party and the First Revolutionary Civil War, 1921–1927

1. Ch'en Kung-po, *The Communist Movement in China,* an essay written in 1924, edited with an introduction by C. Martin Wilbur (New York: Octagon Books, 1966), pp. 103–5. Ch'en was one of the

original founders of the party. The generalized account of the political history of the Chinese Communist Party which follows relies heavily on several excellent works, including Jerome Ch'en, *Mao and the Chinese Revolution* (New York: Oxford University Press, 1967); Stuart Schramm, *Mao Tse-tung* (New York: Simon and Schuster, 1966); James P. Harrison, *The Long March to Power* (New York: Praeger Publishers, 1972); Jacques Guillermaz, *A History of the Chinese Communist Party, 1921–1949* (New York: Random House, 1972); Ho Kan-chih, *A History of the Modern Chinese Revolution* (Peking: 1960); and, Hu Ch'iao-mu, *Thirty Years of the Communist Party of China* (Peking: 1954). The Ho and Hu accounts are the official histories of the Chinese Communist Party.

2. Shao Chuan-leng and Norman D. Palmer, *Sun Yat-sen and Communism* (New York: Praeger Publishers, 1960), pp. 92–93.

3. Ibid., pp. 62–65.

4. Most of the account of the Chinese Labor movement follows Jean Chesneaux's powerful book, *The Chinese Labor Movement, 1919–1927*, translated from the French by H. M. Wright (Stanford: Stanford University Press, 1968).

5. Ibid., p. 187.

6. Conrad Brandt, *Stalin's Failure in China* (Cambridge: Harvard University Press, 1958), p. 24. See also, Allen S. Whiting, *Soviet Policies in China, 1917–1924* (Stanford: Stanford University Press, 1953).

7. Chesneaux, *Chinese Labor Movement,* p. 207.

8. Ibid., p. 208.

9. Chesneaux, *Chinese Labor Movement,* says 35 (p. 209) and Brandt, *Stalin's Failure,* says 60 (p. 25).

10. Chesneaux, *Chinese Labor Movement,* p. 218.

11. Quoted in Schwartz, *Chinese Communism,* p. 48.

12. Ibid.

13. Ibid.

14. Ch'ien Tuan-sheng, *The Government and Politics of China* (Cambridge: Harvard University Press, 1967), p. 152. See also, Sun Yat-sen, *Fundamentals of National Reconstruction* (Taipei: China Cultural Service, 1953) and *San Min Chu I: The Three Principles of the People* (Taipei: China Publishing Co., n.d.).

15. Ch'ien, *Government and Politics,* p. 123.

16. Statement by Communist party member, Liu Jen-ching, to the Fourth Congress of the Comintern in Moscow, cited in Shao and Palmer, *Sun Yat-sen,* p. 72.

17. Chesneaux, *Chinese Labor Movement,* p. 263.

18. Brandt, *Stalin's Failure,* p. 50.

19. Chesneaux, *Chinese Labor Movement,* p. 263.

20. Ibid.

21. Brandt, *Stalin's Failure,* p. 54.

22. John Wilson Lewis, *Leadership in Communist China* (Ithaca: Cornell University Press, 1963), pp. 110–11 and Ch'en, *Mao*, p. 100.

23. Edgar Snow, *Red Star over China* (New York: Random House, 1938), pp. 159–60.

24. Chiang K'ai-shek, *Soviet Russia in China* (New York: Farrar, Straus, and Cudahy, 1957), p. 42.

25. Ibid., p. 43.

26. The following brief biographical sketch is a composite from the following sources: Howard L. Boorman, ed. *Biographical Dictionary of Republican China* (New York: Columbia University Press, 1915–1949) I, 319–38; S. I. Hsiung, *The Life of Chiang K'ai-shek* (London: Peter Davies, 1948); Paul M. A. Linebarger, *The China of Chiang K'ai-shek* (Boston: World Peace Foundation, 1943), and Hollingon K. Tong, *Chiang K'ai-shek: Soldier and Statesman*, 2 vols. (London: Hurst and Blackett, 1938). The quote from Linbarger appears on pp. 260–61.

27. Chiang, *Soviet Russia,* pp. 43–47.

28. Ibid., p. 45.

29. Ibid., pp. 38–39.

30. Ibid., p. 39.

31. Ibid.

32. C. Martin Wilbur and Julie L. Y. How, *Documents on Communism, Nationalism, and Soviet Advisers in China, 1918–1927* (New York: Columbia University Press, 1956), p. 3.

33. Tong, *Chiang K'ai-shek,* I, 148.

34. Chesneaux, *Chinese Labor Movement,* p. 360.

35. Tong, *Chiang K'ai-shek,* I, 137–38.

36. O. Edmund Clubb, *Twentieth Century China* (New York: Columbia University Press, 1964, paperback), p. 137.

37. Chesneaux, p. 370, and James P. Harrison, *The Long March to Power* (New York: Praeger Publishers, 1972), p. 96.

Chapter 7
The Period of the Second Revolutionary War, 1927–1937

1. For Trotsky's point-of-view, see his *Problems of the Chinese Revolution,* 2nd ed. (New York: Paragon Book Gallery, 1962 [1932]).

2. Ibid., p. 103.

3. Lyon Sharman, *Sun Yat-sen: His Life and Meaning* (Hamden: Archon Books, 1965 [1934]), p. 304.

4. Jerome Ch'en, *Mao and the Chinese Revolution* (New York: Oxford University Press, 1967, paperback), p. 121.

5. M. N. Roy, *Revolution and Counter-Revolution in China* (Calcutta: Renaissance Publishers, 1946), p. 520 note.

6. Ibid. Roy claims that Wang had been told of the policy during a visit to Moscow one month before May 30, 1927.

7. O. Edmund Clubb, *Twentieth Century China* (New York: Columbia University Press, 1964, paperback), p. 138.

8. Quoted in Ch'en, *Mao*, p. 124.

9. Clubb, *Twentieth Century China*, p. 185.

10. Ch'en, *Mao*, p. 125.

11. Stalin apparently sent a telegram allowing the uprising if there was some assurance that it would succeed. There were no assurances forthcoming, and thus all of the participants, including Stalin, Lominadze, the Comintern representative, and Chang Kuo-t'ao, who was supposed to act as an intermediary, have absolved themselves of any responsibility for the ensuing defeats. See Chang Kuo't'ao, *The Rise of the Chinese Communist Party, 1921–1938: Autobiography,* 2 vol. (Lawrence: University Press of Kansas, 1971–72) II, 3–9; Conrad Brandt, *Stalin's Failure* (Cambridge: Harvard University Press, 1958), pp. 142–43, and Stuart Schram, *Mao Tse-tung,* pp. 104–7.

12. Chang, *Chinese Communist Party,* II, 6.

13. My translation from the Chinese of Mao Tse-tung, *The Poetry of Mao: Thirty-seven Poems* (Peking: n.d.), p. 1. Poems used hereafter are from this particular edition. Other translations of Mao's poetry include Jerome Ch'en and Michael Bullock in Ch'en's *Mao*, pp. 313–60, and Hua-ling Nieh Engle and Paul Engle, *Poems of Mao Tse-tung* (New York: Dell Publishing Co., 1972).

14. Snow, *Red Star over China,* pp. 167–68.

15. Ibid., p. 169.

16. Ch'en, *Mao*, p. 137.

17. *The Essential Stalin: Major Theoretical Writings, 1905–1952* ed. Bruce Franklin (New York: Anchor Books, 1972), p. 217.

18. Ibid., pp. 208–19.

19. Snow, *Red Star,* p. 169.

20. Ibid., pp. 169–70.

21. Ibid., p. 170.

22. John Rue, *Mao Tse-tung in Opposition, 1927–1935* (Stanford: Stanford University Press, 1966), pp. 110–15, 250.

23. Benjamin I. Schwartz, *Chinese Communism and the Rise of Mao* (New York: Harper and Row, 1967, paperback), p. 194.

24. Ch'en, *Mao*, p. 140.

25. Snow, *Red Star,* p. 176. It is safe to assume that Chu Teh, the CIC of the Red Army, had as much to do with the development of the Red Army's strategy as Mao did.

26. Ibid.

27. Ibid.

28. Ibid., p. 177.

29. Mao Tse-tung, "The Struggle in the Chingkang Mountains,"

Selected Works of Mao Tse-tung, 1st Eng. ed. of 2nd Chinese ed. (Peking: Foreign Languages Press, 1960 , 1965), I, 73–104; citation on p. 99.

30. Mao Tse-tung, "A Single Spark Can Start a Prairie Fire," *Selected Works,* I, 116–28, esp. p. 117.

31. Ch'en, *Mao,* p. 156.

32. Snow, *Red Star,* p. 167.

33. Ch'en, *Mao,* p. 54.

34. This poem is dedicated to Li Shu-yi, the widow of the "willow" in the poem, Liu Chih-hsun. Liu joined the Communist party in 1923, served with Mao in the Hunan branch, took part in the Nanch'ang uprising in August 1927, and died in still another uprising in Hunghu, Hupeh Province, in 1932. In 1933, Liu's wife wrote a poem in memory of her dead husband, which she in turn sent to Mao. Mao wrote his "Reply to Li Shu-yi" (the fore-title of the poem) in 1957. Yang, Mao's second wife's surname, means "poplar," while Liu means "willow." Wu Kang is the Chinese equivalent of Sisyphus. Wu Kang is a legendary figure who committed a crime in his search for immortality, was exiled to the moon, and condemned to cut down the cinnamon tree. Each time he cut it down, it grew again. Ch'ang O stole the elixer of immortality and fled to the moon to become a moon goddess. The "tiger" is Chiang K'ai-shek (Ch'en, pp. 347–48, and *Ta Kung Pao,* January 6, 1977). While first secretary of the Hunan branch of the CCP Hua Kuo-feng was responsible for constructing a tomb in the memory of Yang K'ai-hui. Mao was of course appreciative (*Ta Kung Pao,* January 6, 1976).

35. Ch'en, *Mao,* p. 159.

36. Howard L. Boorman (ed.), *Biographical Dictionary of Republican China* (New York: Columbia University Press, 1967–1971), I, 328.

37. Chiang K'ai-shek, *Soviet Russia in China* (New York: Farrar, Straus, and Cudahy, 1967), p. 63.

38. My translation from *The Poetry of Mao Tse-tung,* p. 20.

39. Ch'en, *Mao,* p. 175.

40. Snow, *Red Star,* p. 186.

41. Chiang, *Soviet Russia,* p. 64.

42. Dick Wilson, *The Long March, 1935* (New York: Viking Press, 1971), p. 53.

43. Ibid., p. 56.

44. Snow, *Red Star,* Part V, chs, 1–4, pp. 195–218.

45. Ch'en, *Mao,* p. 185.

46. Robert Payne, *Portrait of a Revolutionary: Mao Tse-tung,* rev. ed. (New York: Abelard-Schulmann, 1961), pp. 140–41.

47. Ch'en, *Mao,* p. 187.

48. Wilson, *Long March,* p. 74.

49. Chang Kuo-t'ao, *Chinese Communist Party,* II, 360–65.

50. The following account follows Jerome Ch'en's article, "Resolutions of the Tsunyi Conference," *The China Quarterly,* no. 40 (October-December 1969), pp. 1–38. Ch'en apparently came across what was believed to have been the lost or edited versions of the resolutions.

51. Chang Kuo-t'ao, *Chinese Communist Party,* II, 364–65.

52. Quoted in Snow, *Red Star,* p. 198.

53. Ibid., p. 199.

54. Ibid.

55. The following stories are taken from Snow, *Red Star over China,* Jerome Ch'en, *Mao and the Chinese Revolution,* Dick Wilson, *The Long March* and *Stories of the Long March* (Peking: Foreign Languages Press, 1958).

56. Snow, *Red Star,* p. 199.

57. Ibid., p. 208.

58. Ibid., p. 209.

59. Ibid., p. 210.

60. Quoted in Wilson, *Long March,* p. 178.

61. Ch'en, *Mao,* pp. 338–39.

62. Ibid., p. 193.

63. Chang Kuo-t'ao, *Chinese Communist Party,* II, 374–77.

64. Snow, *Red Star,* p. 213.

65. Chang Kuo-t'ao, *Chinese Communist Party,* II, 378.

66. Ibid., pp. 378–80.

67. Ibid., p. 380.

68. Ibid., p. 381.

69. Ibid., p. 403.

70. Chang mentions all the important posts in the party and army and makes no mention of Chu Teh (Ibid., pp. 427–28).

71. Agnes Smedley, *The Great Road: The Life and Times of Chu Teh* (New York: Monthly Review Press, 1956), p. 337.

72. Snow, *Red Star,* pp. 215–18.

73. My translation of *The Poetry of Mao Tse-tung,* p. 37.

74. Chang Kuo-t'ao, *Chinese Communist Party,* II, 474.

75. Ibid., p. 514.

76. Ibid., p. 516.

77. Ibid., pp. 516–17.

78. Ibid., p. 579.

79. Chiang, *Soviet Russia,* p. 65.

80. Mao, *Selected Works,* I, 73–104.

81. Ch'en, *Mao,* p. 202.

82. Quoted in Earl Albert Selle, *Donald of China* (New York: Harper and Brothers, 1948), p. 319. The quotations used here and elsewhere are actual quotations written down by the Australian reporter, William H. Donald, advisor to Chiang K'ai-shek, who was present dur-

ing the Sian incident. He interviewed the principals involved, taking copious notes. He also was on good terms with Chang Hsueh-liang.

83. Chiang, *Soviet Russia*, p. 74.

84. Quoted in Snow, *Red Star*, p. 435.

85. Selle, *Donald*, p. 323.

86. Hollington K. Tong (ed.), *Chiang K'ai-shek: Soldier and Statesman* (London: Hurst and Blackett, 1958), II, 454–55.

87. Ibid., p. 456.

88. James M. Bertram, *First Act in China: The Story of the Sian Mutiny* (New York: Viking Press, 1938), p. 111.

89. Tong, *Chiang K'ai-shek*, II, 457.

90. Ibid., p. 458.

91. Snow, *Red Star*, p. 441 and Bertram, *First Act*, pp. 114–15. Tong makes no mention of this incident.

92. The following account is taken from Tong, *Chiang K'ai-shek*, II, 24; Bertram, *First Act, passim;* Selle, *Donald*, ch. 23; but especially, Chiang's diary excerpted in Chiang Mayling Soong (Madame Chiang K'ai-shek), *Sian: A Coup de'Etat* (Shanghai: Kelly and Walsh, 1937), "A Fortnight in Sian: Extracts from a Diary," pp. 53–108, and "The Admonition of Chang Hsueh-liang," pp. 109–15.

93. Snow adds to this demand "and adopt the policy of armed resistance against Japan" (*Red Star*, p. 445). None of the other sources corroborate Snow's addition. None was probably needed since the goal behind the entire incident was to unite against Japan.

94. Bertram, *First Act*, p. 133; Snow, *Red Star*, p. 456, and Selle, *Donald*, p. 333 and Lyman P. Van Slyke, *Enemies and Friends: The United Front in Chinese Communist History* (Stanford: Stanford University Press, 1967), pp. 77–80.

95. Selle, *Donald*, p. 333.

96. Donald's quotes in Selle, *Donald*, p. 333.

97. Snow, *Red Star*, p. 457.

98. Quotes in Selle, *Donald*, p. 334 and corroborated in Madame Chiang, *Sian*, p. 107.

99. (Madame) Chiang, *Sian*, p. 102; Snow, *Red Star*, p. 468; and Chiang, *Soviet Russia*, pp. 74–75.

100. The full text of the proposals is located in several sources including: Tong, *Chiang K'ai-shek* II, 508–9; Ch'en, *Mao*, pp. 231–32; Chiang, *Soviet Russia*, pp. 79–81; *China Handbook, 1937–1945* (New York: MacMillan, 1947), pp. 66–67; and Conrad Brandt, Benjamin Schwartz, and John K. Fairbank, *A Documentary History of Chinese Communism* (Cambridge: Harvard University Press, 1952).

101. Chiang, *Soviet Russia*, p. 80.

102. Mao, *Selected Works*, III, 134–35; and Ch'en, *Mao*, p. 232.

103. For an excellent analysis of the concept of the united front, see Van Slyke, *Enemies and Friends*.

Chapter 8
The War of Resistance to Japanese Aggression, 1937–1945

1. Unless otherwise noted, this account follows George E. Taylor, *The Struggle for North China* (New York: Institute of Pacific Relations, 1940) and especially John Hunter Boyle, *China and Japan at War, 1937–1945* (Stanford: Stanford University Press, 1972).
2. Cited in Boyle, *China and Japan*, p. 43.
3. Ibid., p. 46.
4. Ibid., p. 63, and see pp. 63–66.
5. Ibid.
6. Ibid., p. 48.
7. Ibid., p. 46.
8. The causes of the clash are many and varied as is the charge that the clash was premediated. For varying accounts see, Guillermaz, *A History of the CCP, 1921–1945* (New York: Random House, 1976), pp. 287–88; O. Edmund Clubb, *Twentieth Century China* (New York: Columbia Press, 1964, paperback), p. 213; Sven Hedin, *Chiang K'ai-shek; Marshal of China* (New York: John Day Co., 1940), pp. 166–67; Robert Payne, *Chiang K'ai-shek* (New York: Weybright and Talley, 1969), pp. 223–25; F. F. Liu, *A Military History of Modern China, 1924–1949* (Princeton: Princeton University Press, 1956), p. 197; and, for a good eyewitness account see Edgar Snow, *The Battle for Asia* (New York: World Publishing Company, 1944), pp. 15–21.
9. For a personal account of the historic "rape" of Nanking see H. J. Timperley, *Japanese Terror in China* (New York: Modern Age Books, 1938).
10. For an overview of German military aid to China see Liu, *Military History*, ch. 10, pp. 90–102.
11. Jerome Ch'en, *Mao and the Chinese Revolution* (New York: Oxford University Press, 1967, paperback), pp. 238–39.
12. Pichon P. Y. Loh, *The Kuomintang Debacle of 1949: Conquest or Collapse?* (Boston: D. C. Heath and Co., 1965), p. vii. Unless otherwise noted, the following account follows the several excerpts in Loh; Tang Tsou, *America's Failure in China, 1941–50* (Chicago: University of Chicago Press, 1963); Ch'ien Tuan-sheng, *The Government and Politics of China* (Cambridge: Harvard University Press, 1967); Tien Hung-mao, *Government and Politics in Kuomintang China, 1927–37* (Stanford: Stanford University Press, 1972).
13. D. K. Lieu, *China's Economic Stabilization and Reconstruction* (New Brunswick; Rutgers University Press, 1948), p. 147.
14. John K. Chang, *Industrial Development in Pre-Communist China* (Chicago: Aldine Publishing Co., 1969), p. 71.
15. Ibid., p. 76.
16. C. F. Remer, *Foreign Investments in China* (New York:

Howard Fertig, 1968), and Hou Chi-ming, *Foreign Investments and Economic Development in China* (Cambridge: Harvard University Press, 1965).

17. See Chang, *Industrial Development,* pp. 85–88.

18. Lucien Bianco, *Origins of the Chinese Revolution, 1915–1949* Stanford: Stanford University Press, 1971), p. 110.

19. Ping-chia Kuo in Loh, *Kuomintang Debacle,* p. 50.

20. Tien, *Government and Politics,* pp. 76–77.

21. Bianco, *Origins,* p. 114.

22. John K. Fairbank, *The United States and China* (Cambridge: Harvard University Press, 1948), p. 236.

23. Tien, *Government and Politics,* pp. 83–84.

24. Ibid.

25. Bianco, *Origins,* p. 115.

26. For a short overview of the press in China and Asia, see John Hohenberg, *Foreign Correspondence: The Great Reporters and Their Times* (New York: Columbia University Press, 1964), pp. 369–72 and *passim.*

27. Quoted in Ch'en, *Mao and the Chinese Revolution,* p. 241.

28. T. H. White and Annalee Jacoby, *Thunder Out of China* (New York: William Sloane Associates, 1946), p. 119.

29. Jack Belden, *China Shakes the World* (New York: Harper and Brothers, 1949), ch. 56, pp. 432–36.

30. Earle Albert Selle, *Donald of China* (New York: Harper and Brothers, 1948), p. 343.

31. John S. Service, *The Amerasia Papers: Some Problems in the History of U.S.–China Relations* (Berkeley: Center for Chinese Studies, University of California, 1971), p. 201. The entire report is appended in *Amerasia Papers,* with portions reproduced in the Department of State, *United States Relations with China (The White Paper),* (Washington, D.C.: GPO, 1949), pp. 657–70.

32. John Paton Davies, Jr., *Dragon by the Tail* (New York: W. W. Norton and Co., 1972), p. 9.

33. Ibid., pp. 225–26.

34. John Leighton Stuart, *Fifty Years in China: Memoirs* (New York: Random House, 1954), pp. 118–21.

35. General Albert C. Wedemeyer, *Wedemeyer Reports* (New York: Henry Holt and Co., 1958), p. 301.

36. Payne, *Chiang K'ai-shek,* p. 233.

37. Floyd Taylor, "Chungking: City of Mud and Courage," in Hollington K. Tong (ed.), *China: After Seven Years of War* (New York: MacMillan Co., 1945), pp. 31–55.

38. Ibid., pp. 50–51.

39. White and Jacoby, *Thunder Out of China,* p. 9.

40. Ibid., p. 15.

41. Ibid., p. 16.

42. Mark Selden, *The Yenan Way in Revolutionary China* (Cambridge: Harvard University Press, 1971), pp. 139–40.
43. For a good discussion of relations between the KMT and CCP during the critical first years of the war, see Guillermaz, *History of the Chinese Communist Party,* ch. 26, pp. 344–60.
44. Boyle, *China and Japan,* chs. 5, 6, 7, pp. 83–133.
45. For a sympathetic but good account of Wang's complictiy in this affair, see Gerald Bunker, *The Peace Conspiracy: Wang Ching-wei and the China War, 1937–1941* (Cambridge: Harvard University Press, 1972) and Boyle, *China and Japan, passim.,* especially pp. 194–305.
46. Boyle, *China and Japan,* p. 172.
47. Ibid., p. 187.
48. Bunker, *Peace Conspiracy,* p. 87.
49. Ibid., p. 132.
50. See Chiang's interview with the foreign press in Chungking in *The Collected Wartime Messages of Generalissimo Chiang K'ai-shek,* 2 vol. (New York: John Day Co., 1946), vol. 1, pp. 336–40.
51. Boyle, *China and Japan,* p. 293.
52. Ho Kan-chih, *A History of the Modern Chinese Revolution,* (Peking: 1960) pp. 408–9.
53. *Collected Wartime Messages,* vol. II, pp. 524–33.
54. Mao Tse-tung, *Selected Works of Mao Tse-tung* (New York: International Publishers, 1954–56), vol. 3, pp. 161–66.
55. Bunker, *Peace Conspiracy,* p. 270.
56. Ibid., p. 280.
57. Quoted in Ibid., p. 284.
58. Ibid., pp. 284–85.
59. Ibid., p. 272.
60. Selden, *Yenan Way,* p. 88.
61. Gillin, *Warlord,* p. 265.
62. Ibid.
63. Chao Kuo-chun, *Agrarian Policy of the Chinese Communist Party, 1921–1959* (New Delhi: Asia Publishing House, 1960), p. 39.
64. Ibid., p. 41.
65. Ibid., pp. 43–44 and Ho Kan-chih, *Modern Chinese Revolution,* pp. 376–77.
66. Gillin, *Warlord,* p. 267.
67. Ho Kan-chih, *Modern Chinese Revolution,* p. 377.
68. Gillin, *Warlord,* p. 267.
69. Selden, *Yenan Way,* p. 180.
70. James P. Harrison, *Long March to Power* (New York: Praeger Publishers, 1972), p. 316.
71. Ibid.
72. Ho Kan-chih, *Modern Chinese Revolution,* pp. 338–39.
73. Ibid., p. 390.

74. Guillermaz, *History of the Chinese Communist Party*, p. 341 and Edgar Snow, *Red Star over China* (New York: Random House, 1938), pp. 265–270.

75. Ho Kan-chih, *Modern Chinese Revolution*, p. 390.

76. Mao, *Selected Works*, vol. IV, pp. 105–10.

77. Ibid., pp. 148–56.

78. Ibid., pp. 230–31.

79. Gillin, *Warlord*, pp. 260–61.

80. H. Chalmers Johnson, *Peasant Nationalism and Communist Power* (Stanford: Stanford University Press, 1962), p. 69.

81. Selden, *Yenan Way*, p. 131.

82. Ibid., p. 132.

83. Ho Kan-chih, *Modern Chinese Revolution*, p. 376.

84. Mao Tse-tung, "On New Democracy," *Selected Works*, vol. III, p. 114.

85. Ibid., p. 115.

86. Ibid., p. 117.

87. Lyman P. Van Slyke, *Enemies and Friends: The United Front in Chinese Communist History* (Stanford: Stanford University Press, 1967), pp. 146–50.

88. Quoted in Ibid., p. 153.

89. Ho Kan-chih, *Modern Chinese Revolution*, pp. 427–30.

90. Boyd Compton, *Mao's China: Party Reform Documents, 1942–1944* (Seattle: University of Washington Press, 1966), pp. xxvii–xxix. Paperback edition.

91. For a thorough discussion of the criteria for the establishment of bases behind Japanese lines, see Mao's essay, "Strategic Problems in the Anti-Japanese Guerilla War," *Selected Works*, vol. II, pp. 119–56.

92. Johnson, *Peasant Nationalism*, p. 84.

93. Ibid., p. 56.

94. Ho Kan-chih, *Modern Chinese Revolution*, p. 373.

95. Selden, *Yenan Way*, p. 179.

96. Johnson, *Peasant Nationalism*, p. 91.

97. Ibid., p. 77.

98. Selden, *Yenan Way*, p. 143.

99. Compton, *Mao's China*, p. xxii.

100. Chiang K'ai-shek, *Soviet Russia in China* (New York: Farrar, Strauss, and Cudahy, 1957), p. 65.

101. Ch'en, *Mao and the Chinese Revolution*, pp. 238–39.

102. Snow, *Battle for Asia*, p. 140.

103. Chiang, *Soviet Russia*, p. 65.

104. Johnson, *Peasant Nationalism*, p. 138.

105. Ibid.

106. Harrison, *Long March*, p. 320 and F. W. Mote, "China's Past in the Study of China Today," *The Journal of Asian Studies*, vol. 32,

no. 1 (November 1972), pp. 107–20. As Mote has so clearly shown, literacy rates in China pose a difficult question, and very little research actually has been done on the subject. I am here following his estimate that in late Ch'ing China, the level of literacy was "close to ten percent of the total population . . ." (p. 110).

107. Selden, *Yenan Way*, p. 269.

108. Hsiao Kung-ch'uan, *Rural China: Imperial Control in the Nineteenth Century* (Seattle: University of Washington Press, 1960).

109. Selden, *Yenan Way*, p. 271.

110. Michael Lindsay, *Notes on Educational Problems in Communist China, 1941–1947* (New York: Institute of Pacific Relations, 1950), pp. 36–37.

111. Ibid., p. 37.

112. Ibid., p. 39.

113. Ibid., p. 41.

114. Johnson, *Peasant Nationalism*, p. 87.

115. Van Slyke, *Enemies and Friends*, p. 155 and Harrison, *Long March*, p. 318.

116. Mao, *Selected Works*, II, 67–73.

Chapter 9
The Sinification of Marxism

1. The debate on the dating of Mao's works, their originality, and their contributions to Marxism-Leninism are covered extensively by Stuart Schram in *The Political Thought of Mao Tse-tung*, rev. and enlarged ed. (New York: Frederick A. Praeger, 1969 [1963]), pp. 84–110.

2. Jerome Ch'en, *Mao and the Chinese Revolution* (New York: Oxford University Press, 1967, paperback), p. 210.

3. Mao Tse-tung, "Report on an Investigation into the Peasant Movement in Hunan," *Selected Works of Mao Tse-tung* (New York: International Publishers, 1954), I, 56.

4. Mao, Tse-tung, *Selected Works*, I, 282. References to "On Practice" are from the International Publishers Edition, 1954.

5. Ibid., I, 284.

6. Ibid., I, 287.

7. Ibid., I, 289.

8. Ibid., I, 292.

9. Ibid., I, 288.

10. Ibid., I, 297.

11. Ibid., II, 13.

12. Ibid., II, 16.

13. Ibid., II, 19.

14. Ibid., II, 20.

15. Ibid., II, 24.
16. Ibid., II, 36.
17. Boyd Compton, *Mao's China: Party Reform Documents, 1942–1944* (Seattle: University of Washington Press, 1966, paperback), pp. 13–14.
18. Schram, *Political Thought of Mao Tse-tung,* rev. ed., p. 112.
19. Ibid., pp. 112–117.
20. Compton, *Mao's China,* p. 21.
21. Ibid., p. 28.
22. Ibid., p. 29.
23. Ibid., p. 30.
24. Ibid., p. 228.
25. Mao Tse-tung, "On the Correct Handling of Contradictions among the People." in *Four Essays on Philosophy* (Peking: Foreign Languages Press, 1968), p. 87.
26. Compton, *Mao's China,* p. xxxvii.
27. Mao Tse-tung, "On Methods of Leadership," *Selected Works,* IV, 111–17, excerpt on p. 113.
28. John Wilson Lewis, *Leadership in Communist China* (Ithaca: Cornell University Press, 1963), p. 72. This work is by far the best analysis of the mass line.
29. Compton, *Mao's China,* p. 33.
30. Ibid., pp. 38–47.
31. Merle Goldman, *Literary Dissent in Communist China* (Cambridge: Harvard University Press, 1967), p. 21.
32. See Ibid., pp. 22–32.
33. Quoted in Ibid., p. 31.
34. *Mao Tse-tung on Literature and Art* (Peking: Foreign Languages Press, 1967), p. 1.
35. Ibid., p. 2.
36. Ibid., p. 25.
37. Goldman, *Literary Dissent,* p. 50.
38. Compton, *Mao's China,* p. xliv.
39. Ibid. xlvi.

Epilogue
China After Mao: The First Thirty Days

1. "Speech at the Second National Conference on Learning from Tachai in Agriculture," (hereafter, Second Tachai Conference), *Peking Review,* No. 1, January 1, 1977, p. 32.
2. Chiang Ch'ing is accused of "distorting" Mao's famous poem, "Reply to Li Shu-yi," in which Mao immortalizes his second wife, Yang K'ai-hui. The September 1976 publication of Mao's poetry does leave

out the footnote explaining the circumstances under which Mao wrote the poem. The remaining poems include the footnotes.

3. *People's Daily*, November 7, 1976, trans. in *Survey of People's Republic of China Press*, No. 6220, November 16, 1976, p. 71.

4. *Peking Review*, No. 24, June 9, 1967, pp. 23–24.

5. *People's Daily*, January 18, 1975.

6. *Peking Review*, No. 4, January 24, 1975, pp. 21–25.

7. Trans. in *Peking Review* No. 7, February 14, 1975, pp. 4–5.

8. "On the Social Basis of the Lin Piao Anti-Party Clique," *Red Flag*, March, 1976, trans, in *Peking Review*, No. 10, March 7, 1975, pp. 5–10.

9. Ibid.

10. Ibid.

11. Ibid.

12. Ibid.

13. "On Exercising All-Round Dictatorship of the Bourgeoisie," *Red Flag*, April, 1975, trans, in *Peking Review* No. 14, April 14, 1975, pp. 5–11.

14. *China News Summary*, No. 557, March 5, 1975, p. 1.

15. Chang, *loc. cit.*

16. Ibid.

17. Ibid.

18. Ibid.

19. Ibid.

20. If anyone typified a "bourgeois" living style it was Chiang Ch'ing. Her biography reveals a life-style which can be termed jet-set Chinese-style, commuting as she did between Peking and her beautiful villa in Canton. In all fairness to her, however, she was the rule not the exception among the elite in China today. For her biography see Roxanne Witke, *Comrade Chiang Ch'ing* (Boston: Little, Brown and Company, 1977).

21. During the cultural revolution the children of the Party's ranking members formed their own Red Guard unit and distinguished themselves by wearing expensive silk armbands. Before the cultural revolution they attended special schools, dressed better, and generally enjoyed the privileges which went with their parents' rank. See Jean Daubier, *A History of the Chinese Cultural Revolution* (New York: Vintage Books, 1974), pp. 102–5.

22. "Let the Whole Party Mobilize for a Vast Effort to Develop Agriculture and Build Tachai-Type Counties Throughout the Country," (hereafter, First Tachai Conference) (Peking: Foreign Languages Press, 1975).

23. Ibid., p. 23.

24. *Peking Review*, No. 37, September 12, 1975.

25. Trans. *Peking Review* in No. 10, March 5, 1976, pp. 5–6.

26. *China News Summary,* No. 602, February 18, 1976, pp. 3–4.

27. *People's Daily,* December 17, 1976.

28. Text in *Foreign Broadcast Information Service: Daily Report,* June 1, 1976.

29. Ibid.

30. Trans. in *Foreign Broadcast Information Service: Daily Report,* July 30, 1976.

31. These figures were obtained by the *South China Morning Post* on January 5 and confirmed on January 7, 1976.

32. *Summary of World Broadcasts: Far East,* Nos. 5276 and 5286, August 3 and 14, 1976.

33. *South China Morning Post,* April 14, 1977.

34. Hong Kong also felt the effects of the drought. On June 1, 1977, mild water-rationing was introduced by the government.

35. *South China Morning Post,* April 16, 1977.

36. *South China Morning Post,* March 25, 1977.

37. *South China Morning Post,* March 22, 1977.

38. *South China Morning Post,* March 18, 1977.

39. *Summary of World Broadcasts: Far East,* Nos. 5335 and 5336, October 12, 13, 1976.

40. The decision to include the Military Commission, which organizationally is a major commission *under* the Central Committee may have been a stabilizing factor during the discussions. Its elevation to a level equal with the other three organs, however, found its precedent during the cultural revolution. On September 1, 1976, Hua delivered a speech in Peking on Chairman Mao's behalf in which he included the Military Commission alongside the other three organs (*Hsinhua News Bulletin,* Hong Kong: September 2, 1976).

41. *People's Daily,* December 17, 1976.

42. An-ch'ing is the sole surviving son of three sons by Mao and Yang K'ai-hui. Li Min was the fifth daughter born to Mao and Ho Tzu-chen. Li Min was raised by Chiang Ch'ing after Ho was committed to a mental institution (Witke, p. 160). Li Na is Mao's only daughter by Chiang Ch'ing. Li Min's and Li Na's fate after the arrest of Chiang Ch'ing is not known although speculation has it that both are also under arrest. Mao Yuan-chih and Mao Yuan-hsin are the sons of Mao Tse-min, Mao Tse-tung's brother who was killed by the Nationalists in 1943. Yuan-hsin, who referred to Chiang Ch'ing as "mother" (Witke, p. 160), was arrested on October 6. One relative whose name was left off was Wang Hai-jung, a young lady who often accompanied Mao to official State functions in her capacity as a vice-minister in the Foreign Ministry. She is reputedly Mao Tse-min's daughter, but an informant working with me claims that she is the granddaughter of Wang Chi-fan (d. July 13, 1972), Mao's first cousin (Wang Chi-fan's mother was Mao's maternal aunt) and Mao's teacher in Ch'angsha in the early 1900s. The informant, whose father was also

a professor, often visited Wang Chi-fan, but he never met Wang Hai-jung. Wang Hai-jung and Chiang Ch'ing were reportedly at odds with one another over the handling of the manuscript for Chiang Ch'ing's biography. According to the informant it was Wang who handed the transcript to Mao, who in turn was furious over its contents.

43. Quoted in Lucien Pye, *Mao Tse-tung: The Man in the Leader* (New York: Basic Books, 1976), p. 212.

44. Quoted in *Comrade Chiang Ch'ing on Literature and Art,* May 1968, n.p. This is a survey of Chiang Ch'ing's remarks and speeches on China's cultural life, a copy of which was obtained by Taiwan's intelligence sources. See, *Issues and Studies,* Vols. 10 and 11, Nos. 14 and 10, November, 1974 and October, 1975. Quote is in November, 1974 issue, p. 103. The authenticity of this source is supported by Witke, to whom portions of the source were read and who included this and other quotations in her biography on Chiang Ch'ing.

45. According to Witke (p. 224), from the time that they both moved into Chungnanhai, their official residence, they occupied "separate, but connecting" apartments, a practice most Americans have come to expect say from the first family, with of course, the exception of former President and Mrs. Gerald R. Ford.

46. *Ming Pao,* October 28, 1976. Between October 26 and November 1, *Ming Pao,* a Hong Kong newspaper, ran a seven-part series on the arrest of the gang of four based on a secret report which circulated in China sometime after their arrest. According to *Ming Pao,* a middle-ranking cadre from Kwang tung province personally heard it and relayed its contents to his son, who in turn told a friend, *Ming Pao's* source. After checking the source's information, background and motives (he hated the gang of four), *Ming Pao* published the series. I personally translated the entire series, and in cross-checking the contents with other reports, documents and speeches since released, the *Ming Pao* report is very consistent with what evidence the party has allegedly amassed against the four. Unknown to me at the time I was translating the series is that *Foreign Broadcast Information Service,* October 28, 29, November 1, 2 and 3, 1976, had already translated the entire report. The series is the Politburo report circulated in China after October 6 listing the crimes of the gang of four. My translation is used throughout, and hereafter, this series is identified as "Politburo Report."

47. Ibid.

48. *People's Daily,* September 16, 1976, trans. in *Hsinhua News Bulletin,* Sept. 16, 1976.

49. *People's Daily,* September 19, 1976, trans. in *Hsinhua News Bulletin,* September 19, 1976.

50. Ibid.

51. *People's Daily,* December 17, 1976.

52. Ibid.

53. Ibid.
54. Politburo Report.
55. See *China Record,* No. 112, December, 1976, p. 2.
56. Politburo Report.
57. *People's Daily,* December 17, 1976.
58. Witke, *Comrade Chiang Ch'ing,* pp. 40–41.
59. *People's Daily,* December 17, 1976.
60. Ibid.
61. Ibid.
62. Ibid.
63. Liang Hsiao is a homonym which sounds like "two schools." The characters themselves do not mean "two schools." The Liang Hsiao group was disbanded after the arrest of the four.
64. Wallposter seen in Peking in *Foreign Broadcast Information Service,* October 18, 1976.
65. Politburo Report.
66. Ibid.
67. Peking informant, who recalls walking the streets of Peking on October 6 and subsequent days, claims he learned of the arrests on October 10, from a friend who worked in the *People's Daily.* Informant confirmed what the foreign correspondents also reported: Peking was calm and peaceful during the period when the arrests occurred.
68. *Foreign Broadcast Information Service,* October 13, 1976.
69. Georges Biannic, French correspondent for France Agence Presse, *Foreign Broadcast Information Service,* October 14, 1976.
70. See footnote 46.

Bibliography

Belden, Jack. *China Shakes the World*. New York: Harper and Brothers, 1949.

Bertram, James M. *First Act in China: The Story of the Sian Mutiny*. New York: Viking Press, 1938.

Bianco, Lucien. *Origins of the Chinese Revolution, 1915–1949*. Stanford: Stanford University Press, 1971.

Boorman, Howard L. (ed.). *Biographical Dictionary of Republican China*. 4 vols. New York: Columbia University Press, 1967–1971.

Boyle, John Hunter. *China and Japan at War, 1937–1945* Stanford: Stanford University Press, 1972.

Brandt, Conrad. *Stalin's Failure in China*. Cambridge: Harvard University Press, 1958.

Brandt, Conrad, Benjamin Schwartz, and John K. Fairbank. *A Documentary History of Chinese Communism*. Cambridge: Harvard University Press, 1952.

Brinton, Crane. *The Anatomy of Revolution*. New York: Vantage Books, 1965.

Buck, John L. *Land Utilization in China*. New York: Paragon Book Reprint Corporation, 1965.

Bunker, Gerald. *The Peace Conspiracy: Wang Ching-wei and the China War, 1937–1941* Cambridge: Harvard University Press, 1972.

Chan, Wing-tsit, *A Source Book in Chinese Philosophy*. Princeton: Princeton University Press, 1963.

Chang, John K. *Industrial Development in Pre-Communist China*. Chicago: Aldine Publishing Co., 1969.

Chang Kuo-t'ao. *The Rise of the Chinese Communist Party, 1921–1938: Autobiography*, 2 vols. Vol. 1: 1921–1927; Vol. 2: 1928–1938. Lawrence: University Press of Kansas, 1971–72.

Chao Kuo-chun. *Agrarian Policy of the Chinese Communist Party, 1921–1959*. New Delhi: Asia Publishing Co., 1960.

273

Ch'en, Jerome. *Yuan Shih-k'ai: Brutus Assumes the Purple*. 1st ed. Stanford: Stanford University Press, 1961.

_____. *Mao and the Chinese Revolution*. New York: Oxford University Press, 1967. Paperback.

_____. "Defining Chinese Warlords and Their Factions," *Bulletin of the School of Oriental and African Studies,* vol. 31, no. 3 (1968), pp. 563–600.

_____. "Resolutions of the Tsunyi Conference," *The China Quarterly,* no. 40 (October–December, 1969), pp. 1–38.

_____. *Yuan Shih-k'ai*. 2nd ed. Stanford University Press, 1972.

Ch'en Kung-po. *The Communist Movement in China*. An essay written in 1924, edited with an introduction by C. Martin Wilbur. New York: Octagon Books, 1966.

Chesneaux, Jean. *The Chinese Labor Movement, 1919–1927*. Translated from the French by H. M. Wright. Stanford: Stanford University Press, 1968.

Chiang K'ai-shek. *The Collected Wartime Messages of Generalissimo Chiang K'ai-shek*. 2 vols. New York: John Day Co., 1946.

_____. *China's Destiny and Chinese Economic Theory*. Trans. Philip Jaffe. New York: Roy, 1947.

_____. *Soviet Russia in China*. New York: Farrar, Straus, and Cudahy, 1957.

Chiang Mayling Soong (Madame Chiang K'ai-shek). *Sian: A Coup d'Etat*. Shanghai: Kelly and Walsh, 1937.

Chien Po-tsan. *Collected Source Materials on the Reform Movement of 1898*. 4 vols. Shanghai: 1953.

Ch'ien Tuan-sheng. *The Government and Politics of China*. Cambridge: Harvard University Press, 1967.

China Handbook, 1937–1945 New York: MacMillan, 1947.

Chow Tse-tsung. *The May Fourth Movement: Intellectual Revolution in Modern China*. Cambridge: Harvard University Press, 1960. Paperback edition, Stanford University Press, 1967.

Clubb, O. Edmund. *Twentieth Century China*. New York: Columbia University Press, 1964. Paperback.

Compton, Boyd. *Mao's China: Party Reform Documents, 1942–1944*. Seattle: University of Washington Press, 1966. Paperback.

Curry, Roy Watson. *Woodrow Wilson and Far Eastern Policy, 1913–1921*. New York: Octagon Books, 1968.

Daubier, John Paton, Jr. *Dragon by the Tail*. New York: W. W. Norton and Co., 1972.

Dulles, Foster Rhea. *American Policy toward Communist China, 1949–1969*. New York: Thomas Y. Crowell Company, 1972.

Engle, Hua-ling Nieh and Paul Engle. *Poems of Mao Tse-tung*. New York: Dell Publishing Co., 1972.

Fairbank, John K. *The United States and China*. Cambridge: Harvard University Press, 1948.

————. "The People's Middle Kingdom," *Foreign Affairs*. (July 1966), pp. 574–86.

Fairbank, John K., Edwin O. Reischauer, and Albert M. Craig. *East Asia: The Modern Transformation*. Vol. 2. Boston: Houghton Mifflin Company, 1965.

Fifield, Russell H. *Woodrow Wilson and the Far East*. New York: Thomas Y. Crowell Co., 1952.

Fishel, Wesley R. *The End of Extraterritoriality in China*. Berkeley: University of California Press, 1952.

Franklin, Bruce (ed.). *The Essential Stalin: Major Theoretical Writings, 1905–1952*. New York: Anchor Books, 1972.

Gasster, Michael. *Chinese Intellectuals and the Revolution of 1911*. Seattle: University of Washington Press, 1969.

Gillin, Donald. *Warlord: Yen Hsi-shan in Shansi, 1911–1949*. Princeton: Princeton University Press, 1967.

Goldman, Merle, *Literary Dissent in Communist China*. Cambridge: Harvard University Press, 1967.

Griswold, A. Whitney. *The Far Eastern Policy of the United States*. New York: Harcourt, Brace and Co., 1938.

Guillermaz, Jacques. *A History of the Chinese Communist Party, 1921–1949*. New York: Random House, 1972.

Hamilton-Merritt, Jane. "A Case of Cavalier Neglect," *Saturday Review* (October 19, 1974), pp. 50–52.

Harrison, James P. *The Long March to Power*. New York: Praeger Publishers, 1972.

Hedin, Sven. *Chiang K'ai-shek: Marshall of China*. New York: John Day Co., 1940.

Ho Kan-chih. *A History of the Modern Chinese Revolution*. Peking: 1960.

Ho Ping-ti. *Studies on the Population of China, 1368–1953*. Cambridge: Harvard University Press, 1959.

Hohenberg, John. *Foreign Correspondence: The Great Reporters and Their Times*. New York: Columbia University Press, 1964.

Hou Chi-ming. *Foreign Investments and Economic Development in China, 1840–1937*. Cambridge: Harvard University Press, 1965.

Hsiao Kung-ch'uan. *Rural China: Imperial Control in the Nineteenth Century*. Seattle: University of Washington Press, 1960.

Hsiao San (Emile Hsiao). *Mao Tse-tung t'ung-chih ti ch'ing-shao-nien shih-tai* (Comrade Mao Tse-tung's Boyhood and Youth). Peking: Foreign Languages Press, 1949; Bombay: People's Publishing House, 1953.

Hsieh Pao-chao. *Government of China, 1644–1911*. London: Frank Cass and Co., 1966.

Hsiung, S. I. *The Life of Chiang K'ai-shek*. London: Peter Davies, 1948.

Hu Ch'iao-mu. *Thirty Years of the Communist Party of China*. Peking: 1954.

Huang Sung-k'ang. *Li Ta-chao and the Impact of Marxism on Modern Chinese Thinking*. The Hague: Mouton, 1965.

Johnson, H. Chalmers. *Peasant Nationalism and Communist Power*. Stanford: Stanford University Press, 1962.

————. *Revolutionary Change*. Boston: Little, Brown and Company, 1966.

Kahn, E. J. *The China Hands*. New York: Viking Press, 1975.

Karnow, Stanley. *Mao and China*. New York: Viking Press, 1972.

Langer, W. L. *The Diplomacy of Imperialism, 1890–1902*. 2 vols. New York: Knopf, 1935; reprint, 1950.

Lattimore, Owen. "China: The American Mystique," *The Listener* (October 1, 1964), pp. 491–94.

Legge, James. *The Chinese Classics*. Vol. 1. Oxford: Clarendon Press, 1893.

Levenson, Joseph. *Liang Ch'i-ch'ao and the Mind of Modern China*. Cambridge: Harvard University Press, 1965.

Levi, Werner. *Modern China's Foreign Policy*. Minneapolis: University of Minnesota Press, 1953.

Lewis, John Wilson. *Leadership in Communist China*. Ithaca: Cornell University Press, 1963.

Li Chien-nung. *The Political History of China, 1840–1928*. Trans. and ed. Ssu-yu Teng and Jeremy Ingalls. New York: D. Van Nostrand Co., 1956.

Li Jui. *Mao Tse-tung t'ung-chih ti ch'u-ch'i ke-ming huo-tung* (The Early Revolutionary Activities of Comrade Mao Tse-tung). Peking: China Youth Press, 1957.

Lieu, D. K. *China's Economic Stabilization and Reconstruction*. New Brunswick: Rutgers University Press, 1948.

Lindsay, Michael. *Notes on Educational Problems in Communist China, 1941–1947*. New York: Institute of Pacific Relations, 1950.

Linebarger, Paul M. A. *The China of Chiang K'ai-shek*. Boston: World Peace Foundation, 1943.

Liu. F. F. *A Military History of Modern China, 1924–1949*. Princeton: Princeton University Press, 1956.

Liu, Kwang-ching. *Americans and Chinese*. Cambridge: Harvard University Press, 1963.

Loh, Pichon P. Y. *The Kuomintang Debacle of 1949: Conquest or Collapse?* Boston: D. C. Heath and Co., 1965.

MacGregor-Hastie, Roy. *The Red Barbarians: The Life and Times of Mao Tse-tung*. London: T. V. Boardman and Co., 1961.

MacKinnon, Stephen R. "The Peiyang Army, Yuan Shih-k'ai, and the Origins of Modern Chinese Warlordism," *Journal of Asian Studies*, vol. 32, no. 3 (May 1973), pp. 405–23.

Mao Tse-tung. *Selected Works of Mao Tse-tung*. 4 vols. New York: International Publishers, 1954–56.

————. *The Chinese Revolution and the Chinese Communist Party*. Peking: Foreign Languages Press, 1954.

————. *Mao Tse-tung on Literature and Art*. Peking: Foreign Languages Press, 1967.

————. *Four Essays on Philosophy*. Peking: Foreign Languages Press,1968.

————. *The Poetry of Mao Tse-tung: Thirty-Seven Poems*. Peking: n.d.

McMurray, John V. A. *Treaties and Agreements With and Concerning China, 1894–1919*. Washington, D.C.: Carnegie Endowment for International Peace, 1921.

Meisner, Maurice. *Li Ta-chao and the Rise of Chinese Marxism*. Harvard: University Press, 1967.

Miller, Stuart C. *The Unwelcomed Immigrant: The American Image of the Chinese, 1785–1882*. Berkeley: University of California Press, 1969.

Morse, H. B. *The International Relations of the Chinese Empire*. 3 vols. London: Longmans, Green, 1910–1918.

————. *The Trade and Administration of China*. Rev. ed. Shanghai: Kelly and Walsh, 1913.

Mote, F. W. "China's Past in the Study of China Today," *The Journal of Asian Studies*, vol. 32, no. 1 (November 1972), pp. 107–20.

Nanthan, Andrew J. *A History of the China International Famine Relief Commission*. Harvard: East Asian Monographs. Cambridge: Harvard University Press, 1965.

Needham, Joseph. *Science and Civilization in China*. vol. 2: History of Scientific Thought. Cambridge: University Press, 1956.

New York Times, January 27, 1952.

Nixon, Richard M. *U. S. Foreign Policy for the 1970s: Building for*

Peace. A Report to the Congress by Richard Nixon, President of the United States, February 25, 1971. Washington, D.C.: U.S. Government Printing Office, n.d.

Paloczi-Horvath, George. *Mao Tse-tung: Emperor of the Blue Ants.* London: Secke and Warburg, 1962.

Payne, Robert, *Portrait of a Revolutionary: Mao Tse-tung.* Rev. ed. New York: Abelard-Schulmann, 1961.

————. *Chiang K'ai-shek.* New York: Weybright and Talley, 1969.

Peking Review.

Purcell, Victor. *The Boxer Uprising.* Cambridge: University Press, 1963.

Pye, Lucian W. *Warlord Politics.* New York: Praeger Publishers, 1971.

————. *Mao Tse-Tung: The Man in the Leader.* New York: Basic Books, 1976.

Reinsch, Paul S. *An American Diplomat in China.* New York: 1922.

Remer, C. F. *Foreign Investments in China.* New York: Howard Fertig, 1968.

Roy, M. N. *Revolution and Counter-Revolution in China.* Calcutta: Renaissance Publishers, 1946.

Rue, John. *Mao Tse-tung in Opposition, 1927–1935.* Stanford: Stanford University Press, 1966.

Schlesinger, Arthur M. *A Thousand Days.* Boston: Houghton-Mifflin Company, 1965.

Schram, Stuart. *Mao Tse-tung.* New York: Simon and Schuster, 1966.

————. *The Political Thought of Mao Tse-tung.* Rev. and enlarged ed. New York: Frederick A. Praeger, 1969 [1963].

Schwartz, Benjamin I. *Chinese Communism and the Rise of Mao.* New York: Harper and Row, 1967. Paperback.

Selden, Mark. *The Yenan Way in Revolutionary China.* Cambridge: Harvard University Press, 1971.

Selle, Earl Albert. *Donald of China.* New York: Harper and Brothers, 1948.

Service, John S. *The Amerasia Papers: Some Problems in the History of U.S.–China Relations.* Berkeley: Center for Chinese Studies, University of California, 1971.

Shao Chuan-leng and Norman D. Palmer. *Sun Yat-sen and Communism.* New York: Praeger Publishers, 1960.

Sharman, Lyon. *Sun Yat-sen: His Life and Meaning.* Hamden: Archon Books, 1965 [1934].

Sheridan, James E. *Chinese Warlord: The Career of Feng Yu-hsiang.* Stanford: Stanford University Press, 1966.

Siao Yu. *Mao Tse-tung and I Were Beggars.* New York: Syracuse University Press, 1959.

Smedley, Agnes. *The Great Road: The Life and Times of Chu Teh.* New York: Monthly Review Press, 1956.

Snow, Edgar. *Red Star over China.* New York: Random House, 1938.

_____. *The Battle for Asia.* New York: World Publishing Co., 1944.

_____. *The Other Side of the River: Red China Today.* New York: Random House, 1962.

Steele, A. T. *The American People and China.* New York: McGraw-Hill Company, 1966.

Stories of the Long March. Peking: Foreign Languages Press, 1958.

Stuart, John Leighton. *Fifty Years in China: Memoirs.* New York: Random House, 1954.

Sun Yat-sen. *San Min Chu I: The Three Principles of the People.* Taipei: China Publishing Co., n.d.

_____. *Fundamentals of National Reconstruction.* Taipei: China Cultural Service, 1953.

Tan, Chester C. *The Boxer Catastrophe.* New York: Columbia University Press, 1955.

Tang Tsou. *America's Failure in China, 1941–50.* Chicago: University of Chicago Press, 1963.

Taylor, George E. *The Struggle for North China.* New York: Institute of Pacific Relations, 1940.

Teng Ssu-yu and John K. Fairbank. *China's Response to the West: A Documentary Survey, 1893–1923.* Cambridge: Harvard University Press, 1961.

Tien Hung-mao. *Government and Politics in Kuomintang China, 1927–37.* Stanford: Stanford University Press, 1972.

Timperley, H. J. *Japanese Terror in China.* New York: New Modern Age Books, 1938.

Tong, Hollington K. *Chiang K'ai-shek: Soldier and Statesman.* 2 vols. London: Hurst and Blackett, 1938.

Tong, Hollington K. (ed.) *China: After Seven Years of War.* New York: MacMillan Co., 1945.

Townsend, James R. *Political Participation in Communist China.* Berkeley: University of California Press, 1967.

Trotsky, Leon. *Problems of the Chinese Revolution.* 2nd ed. New York: Paragon Book Gallery, 1962 [1932].

United States Department of State. *United States Relations with China* (The White Paper). Washington, D.C.: Government Printing Office, 1949.

Van Slyke, Lyman P. *Enemies and Friends: The United Front in*

Chinese Communist History. Stanford: Stanford University Press, 1967.

Volpicelli, Zenone. *The China–Japan War*. London: 1896.

Wang, Y. C. *Chinese Intellectuals and the West, 1872–1949*. Chapel Hill: University of North Carolina, 1966.

Wedemeyer, General Albert C. *Wedemeyer Reports*. New York: Henry Holt and Co., 1958.

White, T. H. and Annalee Jacoby. *Thunder Out of China*. New York: William Sloane Associates, 1946.

Whiting, Allen S. *Soviet Policies in China, 1917–1924*. Stanford: Stanford University Press, 1953.

Wilbur, C. Martin and Julie L. Y. How. *Documents on Communism, Nationalism, and Soviet Advisers in China, 1918–1927*. New York: Columbia University Press, 1956.

Wilson, Dick. *The Long March, 1935*. New York: Viking Press, 1971.

Witke, Roxanne. *Comrade Chiang Ch'ing*. Boston: Little, Brown and Company, 1977.

Woo, T. C. *The Kuomintang and the Future of the Chinese Revolution*. London: 1928.

Yu, George T. *Party Politics in Republican China: The Kuomintang, 1912–1924*. Berkeley: University of California Press, 1966.

Zagoria, Donald S. *The Sino–Soviet Dispute, 1956–1961*. Princeton: Princeton University Press, 1962.

Index